MEDIAEVAL SOURCES
IN TRANSLATION

19

GERSONIDES
THE WARS OF THE LORD
TREATISE THREE:
ON GOD'S KNOWLEDGE

A Translation and Commentary

by

NORBERT MAX SAMUELSON

PONTIFICAL INSTITUTE OF MEDIAEVAL STUDIES
TORONTO, ONTARIO, CANADA

1977

Canadian Cataloguing in Publication Data

Levi ben Gershon, 1288-1344.
The wars of the Lord, treatise three : on God's knowledge

(Mediaeval sources in translation; 19 ISSN 0316-0874)

Translation of Milhamot ha-Shem (romanized).
Bibliography: p.
Includes index.

ISBN 0-88844-268-8

1. God (Judaism) — Knowableness.
I. Samuelson, Norbert Max, 1936.
II. Pontifical Institute of Mediaeval Studies.
III. Title.
IV. Series.

BM610.L4713   296.3'11   C77-001048-2

PRINTED BY UNIVERSA PRESS, WETTEREN, BELGIUM

TABLE OF CONTENTS

PREFACE

It is the goal of this book to investigate through translation and commentary one aspect of Gersonides' total thought, namely, his position on God's knowledge. This aspect has been chosen because, in terms of the controversy it produced and the condemnation it aroused among the Jewish philosophers who followed Gersonides, from Crescas to Manassah ben Israel, Gersonides' discussion of God's knowledge is perhaps the most significant aspect of his thought with respect to the history of Jewish philosophy.

My commentary is contained in the Introduction and in the notes to the translation. The Introduction consists of the following: (ı) a brief discussion of the purpose of the book; (ıı) a brief picture of the life and writings of Gersonides and certain problems in his writings related to the text to be translated; (ııı) a characterization of the whole of *The Wars of the Lord*; (ıv) a presentation in the form of a summary of the arguments presented explicitly and implicitly in the text to be translated; (v) a statement of the central doctrines presented in this text and in the corresponding notes; (vı) a description of the main manuscripts used.

The presentation of (ııı) through (v) above of the Introduction is a summary of the material presented in the text and the notes to the text. Each topic in this presentation is given a title with a list of the applicable notes that discuss in detail the evidence for the claims that in this introductory summary are merely asserted. The reader is not expected to accept at face

value what is stated in the Introduction. Rather the purpose of
the Introduction is to orient the reader topically to the claims
that are made and it is to be hoped that these are satisfactorily
substantiated in the body of the text and textual notes. The
relevant notes are cited at the beginning of each topical
discussion in the Introduction in order to facilitate the reader in
his own investigation of the evidence for this author's conclusions about the thought of Gersonides.

The text translated is Treatise Three of *The Wars of the Lord*.
This book is divided into six chapters, which deal with the
following aspects of the discussion of God's knowledge: (1) a
statement of the views of Gersonides' predecessors on the
question of God's knowledge; (2) a statement of the arguments
used by Gersonides' predecessors to establish each of their views
as Gersonides found them in the statements of these thinkers or
in the logical implications of their words; (3) a critical
examination of the arguments of Maimonides ; (4) the completion of the discussion of God's knowledge of particulars as
considered on purely philosophic grounds (in this chapter Gersonides presents his own position and reexamines the arguments
of his predecessors in order to show that there is nothing in their
arguments to disprove Gersonides' own position); (5) a final
review of the entire discussion of God's knowledge in order to
show that Gersonides' position is adequate in every respect; (6)
a demonstration that what Gersonides presumably established
concerning God's knowledge on purely philosophic grounds is
also the view of the Torah.

Some notes discuss text corrections and additions as given in
the various manuscripts upon which the translation was based.
However the main concern in these notes is analysis and explanation of the meaning of the text. It should be emphasized

that what is explained is what Gersonides said and not what Gersonides said in the light of his predecessors and contemporaries. This is not to say that some of Gersonides' predecessors are not discussed. On the contrary the commentary contains extensive discussion of related doctrines of Aristotle, Ibn Rushd, and Maimonides. However in these cases the question is not what Aristotle, Ibn Rushd and Maimonides in fact said, but what Gersonides believed that they said. No question is raised within the scope of this book concerning the accuracy of Gersonides' exegetical conclusions. Where quotations are given from the writings of any thinkers other than Gersonides, the quotations are intended not to establish the views of their authors but either to explain some statement by Gersonides or to illustrate why Gersonides attributes to the author in question what in fact he does attribute to him. Nor is any attempt made to show all of the sources of Gersonides' thought. Other thinkers are discussed only to the extent that Gersonides refers to them. Whether or not Gersonides had sources other than the ones that he mentions is not questioned in this commentary. This is not to say that such historical questions are not important. Indeed there is much reason to question the accuracy of many of the doctrines that Gersonides attributes to others, particularly to Maimonides. Similarly it is very likely that Gersonides does not reveal all of his intellectual sources. Particularly with respect to Gersonides' doctrine of essences there is a definite possibility that he was greatly influenced by the writings of Thomas Aquinas and Duns Scotus. All that is said here is that the purpose of this commentary is primarily philosophic and not historic, and that there is enough material of philosophic interest to justify this limitation on the scope of the work.

There are many people to whom I am indebted for making this work possible. I specifically want to mention Norman Golb under whose direction at the Hebrew Union College-Jewish Institute of Religion this project initially was conceived, R. E. Allen, Henry Fischel, Milton Fisk and Kenneth Schmitz who encouraged me at Indiana University to pursue this project, and Shlomo Pines who gave me so freely of his time and thought in carrying out the initial research on this text at the Hebrew University. Also I wish to express my gratitude to the United States Department of Health, Education and Welfare who, through a Fulbright-Hayes N.D.E.A. research grant, made it possible for me to spend a full year in uninterrupted research on this study with Shlomo Pines in Jerusalem ; and to Dr. Francisco F. Levinson for his grant in aid of publication.

INTRODUCTION

I

THE PURPOSE OF THIS EDITION

Levi ben Gershom has been called "the greatest and most independent" of those men who devoted themselves to philosophic thought in the century and a half after the death of Maimonides.[1] Certainly as a highly technical and creative thinker, Gersonides ranks among the greatest figures in the history of Jewish philosophy. Yet as significant a figure as Gersonides is, little has been written on his contributions to Jewish thought.[2]

It is the goal of this book to investigate, through translation and commentary, one aspect of Gersonides' total thought, namely his position on God's knowledge. This aspect has been chosen because, in terms of the controversy it produced and the condemnation it aroused among the Jewish philosophers who followed Gersonides, from Crescas to Manasseh ben Israel, Ger-

---

[1] Isaac Broyde, "Levi ben Gershon," *Jewish Encyclopedia* (New York and London, 1904), 8: 28.

[2] An extensive bibliography of secondary sources on Gersonides is given by Menachem M. Kellner in "Gersonides, Providence, and the Rabbinic Tradition," *Journal of the American Academy of Religion*, 42 (1914): 673-685. Also see the bibliography given at the end of this book.

sonides' discussion of God's knowledge is perhaps the most significant aspect of his thought with respect to the history of Jewish philosophy.

II

THE LIFE AND WRITINGS OF GERSONIDES

Gersonides was born at Bagnols in 1288 into a family of renowned scholars and died April 20, 1344. Most of his life was spent in Orange and Avignon.

Although he lived in the Provence where there was less Jewish suffering than elsewhere in Christian Europe in the thirteenth and fourteenth centuries, Gersonides' own writings give evidence of the existence of Jewish persecution in his immediate world. For example he states in the preface to *The Wars of the Lord* that Jewish sufferings are "so intense that they render meditation impossible." We do not know how intense his suffering was, but we do know to some extent what influence this persecution had on Gersonides' writing. For example he states in the introduction to his commentary on Deuteronomy that he could not revise his commentary on the Pentateuch at Avignon because there was no copy of the Talmud there.

We also are aware as we go through Treatise Three of the *The Wars of the Lord* that Gersonides makes no reference to writings of Christian philosophers on the question of God's knowledge.[3] It is particularly surprising that there appear no references either

---

[3] Cf. Shlomo Pines, "Scholasticism after Thomas Aquinas and the Teachings of Hasdai Crescas and His Predecessors," *The Israel Academy of Sciences and Humanities, Proceedings*, 1 (1967), no. 10, 101 pp.

to Thomas Aquinas (1225-1274) or to Duns Scotus (1266-1308). Thomas Aquinas also attacks Maimonides on the question of equivocal terms as applied to divine attributes and his doctrine of essences closely parallels that of Gersonides. Similarly Gersonides' concern with knowledge of particulars and individuation closely parallels the specific concerns of Duns Scotus.

Gersonides wrote several major works in rabbinic, philosophic, mathematical and medical fields in addition to various *responsa,* two of which have been preserved. In addition to his *The Wars of the Lord* (which he began when he was less than thirty years old) Gersonides wrote commentaries on the Pentateuch, the Earlier Prophets, Proverbs, Job, Canticles, Ruth, Ecclesiastes, Esther, Daniel, Ezra, Nehemiah, and First and Second Chronicles, a treatise on direct syllogisms, algebra, and astronomy, super-commentaries on the *Middle Commentaries* and *Resumés* of Ibn Rushd and on the introduction to books 1, 3, 4 and 5 of Euclid, an astrological note on the seven constellations, and a remedy for the gout. In the rabbinic field Gersonides wrote a commentary on the thirteen hermeneutic rules of Ishmael ben Elisha and a commentary on the tractate *Berakot* of the Babylonian Talmud.[4]

As was true of all of the medieval Jewish philosophers, Gersonides in his philosophic writings was concerned with reconciling philosophy and Judaism. In this pursuit, he laid down the rule that "the Law cannot prevent us from considering to be true that which our reason urges us to believe."[5] It was his un-

---

[4] For a list of the published writings of Gersonides, see Bernhard Blumenkranz, *Auteurs juifs en France médiévale* (Toulouse, 1974), pp. 65-69.

[5] Levi ben Gershom, *Milḥamôt Haššēm* (Leipzig, 1866), p. 6. This point will be discussed below at length in section IV of this Introduction.

compromising adherence to this principle that led him to his particular conclusions on the question of God's omniscience in opposition to Maimonides, and that was responsible for the subsequent condemnations of his works by many Jewish scholars, such as Shem Tov Ibn Shem Tov, who changed the title of *Milḥāmôt Haśśēm* (The Wars of the Lord) to "*Milḥāmôt im Haśśēm*" (The Wars with the Lord).

III

THE WARS OF THE LORD

In *The Wars of the Lord* as a whole, of which our text is the third treatise, Gersonides deals only with those questions which Maimonides either resolved in direct opposition to Aristotelian principles or explained so vaguely that the student is left in the dark as to what was Maimonides' real opinion on the subject. These questions can be organized into six topics, each of which constitutes one of the six books of *The Wars of the Lord*. These six topics are the following: the Immortality of the Soul, Prophecy, God's Knowledge, Divine Providence, the Nature of the Celestial Spheres and the Eternity of Matter.

Gersonides' method in dealing with the question of God's knowledge, as in the other five sections of *The Wars of the Lord*, is as follows: Gersonides begins by presenting the various views of his predecessors on the given topic, gives a critical analysis of their views showing what in their arguments is valid and invalid, and then, on the basis of this investigation, presents his own view on the subject. He then proceeds to show that none of the arguments which he investigated raise any valid objections to his position, and concludes by showing the agreement between his position and that of the Torah, or religious authority.

IV

The Central Question:
God's Knowledge of Particulars

The central question of Treatise Three of *The Wars of the Lord* is whether or not God knows particulars and if He does, how He knows them. The question is discussed with respect to two sources of authority, philosophic and religious, which Gersonides carefully separates. In the first five chapters the question is discussed exclusively on the grounds of philosophic thought. In chapter six the question is reexamined from the evidence of religious sources.

Basically there are two answers to this question. One is the view of the sages of the Torah whose spokesman is Maimonides. Their view is that God in a single act knows the infinite number of particulars as particulars. The other view is that of Aristotle, who denies that God knows particulars. However this denial is subject to two different interpretations. In one interpretation God does not know particulars in any sense at all; God knows only Himself. In the second interpretation, which Gersonides judges to be the correct one, God knows the essences or universal natures that particulars exhibit, although He does not know the particulars as particulars.

Gersonides' own position then, the second, weaker interpretation of Aristotle's view, denies God's knowledge of particulars. However he notes arguments in support of all three positions and claims that each has certain aspects of plausibility. By this he means that in examining each of the arguments for each position some aspect of what is the true answer is revealed even if the arguments themselves are not valid. In some cases the premises are true and the inferences from these premises are correct, but the premises tell only part of the story that must be told. In these cases the conclusions reached are true but they are only partially true, i.e., the positions affirmed lack the needed context in which what is affirmed can be properly understood. In other cases the premises are true but the inferences from these premises are unjustified. Generally in such cases the derived conclusion is stronger than the premises justify. In such cases the truth to be gained from these arguments lies in affirming the proper weaker consequence. In still other cases the premises are false. The value of these arguments lies in their constituting the formation of a legitimate *reductio ad absurdum* argument. In other words all such arguments truly show that if the premises were true then certain false consequences would follow, which demonstrate that the premises themselves are false. By examining each of these arguments in the ways indicated above and by conjoining the derived insights, Gersonides arrives at his own position.

In Chapter One Gersonides briefly notes two arguments to support the stronger interpretation of Aristotle's denial of God's knowledge of particulars. The first is that if God knows particulars in any way then God's knowledge has different degrees of perfection, which is an inadmissible conclusion. The second is that if God knows particulars in any way then God's essence contains plurality, which also is an inadmissible conclusion. Gersonides does not discuss these arguments in detail. He simply notes that neither stated consequence is entailed by what the weaker claim asserts. If God knows particulars with respect to their universal nature or essence then it need not be the case that God's knowledge has different degrees of perfection or that God's essence is complex. As will be seen, in affirming that God knows particulars only with respect to their universal nature, no claim is made that the object of God's knowledge is anything other than God Himself, so that the simplicity of God is not denied. Similarly it is not claimed that God knows particulars as particulars. Rather He knows them in a unified way so that the objects of God's knowledge, and consequently God's knowledge itself, is not subject to varying degrees of perfection.

In Chapter Two Gersonides states the arguments supporting both the position of the sages of the Torah and the Aristotelian position. In support of the former affirmative position Gersonides states two arguments. These are examined for their aspects of plausibility in Chapter Three of the text. The second argument rests on the claim that there can be no analogy between God's knowledge and human knowledge. In the argument five ways are noted for how God's knowledge differs from human knowledge. In Chapter Five Gersonides examines these five ways. Both arguments and the five ways are taken from *The Guide of the Perplexed*.

In support of the latter, negative position, Gersonides states eight arguments. These are examined for their aspects of plausibility in Chapter Four. However after Chapter One Gersonides no longer refers to the two interpretations of the Aristotelian position. All eight arguments are presented simply as arguments in support of the denial of God's knowledge of particulars. Nonetheless two of the arguments, the stated third and fourth, are clearly noted as arguments which, if valid, would establish that God does not know particulars in any sense. Both arguments are judged to be spurious, which in Gersonides' terms means that while they have some aspect of plausibility the degree of truth that they contain is considerably less than the degree of truth of the other arguments considered. The one exception to this judgment is the eighth argument. This argument is noted by Gersonides to be the weakest of all the arguments considered. However it is properly in a different class from any of the other arguments because it is a new argument, i.e., it is an argument advanced by Gersonides' contemporaries rather than an argument of his philosophic and religious predecessors. Still, although Gersonides judges this to be the least plausible of the arguments, he uses more space discussing this argument than any other one.

Of all the arguments Gersonides judges the seventh to be the best and the one that led Aristotle to take the position that he did take. This argument, based on the problem of theodicy, dominates most of the discussion in Treatise Four of *The Wars of the Lord* and in Gersonides' commentary on the Book of Job.

For the sake of ease of identification with the text the arguments to be discussed will be identified by the number they are given by Gersonides which corresponds with the order of their appearance in the text; however, these arguments will not be discussed here in that order. Since arguments three and four are specifically arguments for the strong interpretation of the denial of God's knowledge of particulars, they will be presented first. Then we will discuss arguments one, two, and five through seven in their order of appearance as the arguments for the weaker interpretation. Then the eighth argument will be discussed. This will complete the discussion of the arguments of the philosophers against the claim that God knows particulars.

We shall then turn to Maimonides' two arguments affirming God's knowledge of particulars and we shall consider separately each of the five ways in which Maimonides claims in his second argument that God's knowledge and human knowledge differ. At this point Gersonides' own position can be stated and the discussion of the subject is concluded from the standpoint of philosophy. The final consideration will be how this conclusion is related to religious authority as Gersonides conceives it.

Gersonides' method was first to state all of the arguments, then his own position, and finally to examine what is and is not plausible in those arguments. We shall depart from his own method in that the analysis of the arguments will be stated initially with the arguments themselves.

It should be noted that this initial statement of Gersonides' discussion is superficial in that it summarizes only what Gersonides explicitly says. But what Gersonides says ultimately can be intelligible only if what Gersonides implies in this analysis is made explicit. Included in this class of implied doctrines are Gersonides' epistemology (divine and human), his understanding of what are essences, divine attributes, the Active Intellect, and particulars, as well as his understanding of logic. These will be discussed topically in the section following this summary.

Arguments for the strong denial of God's knowledge of particulars

The philosopher's third argument asserts the following. Knowledge is a perfection of a knowing agent insofar as he is a knowing agent. A cause of his knowledge is the object known in the sense that if the object did not in some way exist it could not be known. Hence it can be said that the object known, when it is known, perfects the knower. Since it is also the case that God is more excellent than anything else, it follows that if God knows particulars then what is excellent would be perfected by what is deficient. But the consequence is false. Therefore the antecedent must be false.

Gersonides' analysis of this argument turns on the range of its major premise. The major premise asserts that every knower is perfected by what it knows. Gersonides would admit this premise for every knower except God. God is an exception because God is the primary cause of the object known. Every existing entity has what Gersonides calls an intelligible ordering which it has received from God. This intelligible ordering both is what the thing is, i.e., its essence, so that it is what is properly known of the thing, and is the cause of the thing. As cause the intelligible ordering exists primarily in God and only secondarily in the thing. In knowing anything, what God knows is this intelligible ordering. But in knowing this God knows what properly and primarily exists in Himself. Hence God's knowledge cannot be said to be perfected by the thing known since the excellence of the particular known in this case derives from the knower, God. Thus if we limit the range of the major premise to exclude God as a knower then the premise can be asserted, but it does not follow that the excellent is perfected by the deficient, and if we do not so limit the range of the premise then it is false.

What this argument plausibly shows is the following : if God only knows the intelligible ordering of things[6] then what God ultimately knows is only Himself, since this intelligible ordering is on final analysis the essence of God. (Rather it is God, since God, unlike other beings, is His essence and nothing else.) But God cannot directly know particulars as such. If He did, it

---

[6] For a more detailed explanation of this term see Norbert Samuelson, "Gersonides' Account of God's Knowledge of Particulars," *Journal of the History of Philosophy*, 10 (1972): 399-416. Also see below, notes 13, 14, and 26 to the Translation.

would then follow that the excellent is perfected by the deficient. Thus God can only know them indirectly, not as particulars proper but only with respect to their essence, which is what they are.

* * *

The philosopher's fourth argument asserts the following. In the act of knowing the knower and the known are in some sense one. But particulars are many. Hence if God knows particulars then God must Himself be in some sense many. The consequence is false. Thus the antecedent also must be false, i.e., God does not know particulars.

Gersonides argues that the difficulty with this argument is the ambiguity of the claim that God knows particulars. As the word "knowing" is used here it can either mean sense perception or conceptually grasping. As perceived by the senses particulars are known as particulars. But such knowledge is imperfect. In such knowledge the thing is given to awareness without any discrimination between its essence, what it is, and its accidents, what is true of a thing but not what a thing is. To know particulars in this sense does entail complexity in the knower.

But particulars also may be conceptually grasped. In this sense, which Gersonides judges to be the primary sense of knowing, what is known is what the particular is. However it is the accidents of a thing that particularize it. Hence in this sense of knowing particulars are known with respect to their essence but not as particulars.[7]

---

[7] Ibid. As to whether or not Gersonides believes that there are individual essences, which he does not, see note 436 to the Translation, and section vi of this Introduction.

What is important with respect to this fourth argument is that in this sense knowledge of particulars need not involve complexity in a knower. In knowing individually different things which share a common essence what is known is a single thing, namely the essence. Hence the fourth argument is spurious. Either the major premise of the argument is false, for if God knows particulars in this latter sense then it need not follow that God is complex, or the conclusion of the argument is trivially true, for no one claims that God has sense perception.

What this argument plausibly shows is that what God knows is properly a single essence which is itself God. But this is not to say that God does not know particulars. Every particular is its essence. From our perspective even these essences are many. But they are so because we know them only by generalizing from their specific manifestations to the senses. However in God's case, since He knows them as their cause, no such sensation is necessary and thus no such differentiation is necessary. Therefore what we know as multiple essences can be said to be known by God in a single act. In other words this argument legitimately shows that what God knows, He knows in a single act, but once we distinguish the two ways in which particulars may be known, viz. with respect to their essences and as particulars, it does not follow that God does not know particulars.

The same analysis applies to what Gersonides states as a variation of this argument. Stated in this variant form the fourth argument reads as follows: some particulars are more perfect than others. Also the essence of a particular is more of a perfection of the thing than are its accidents. Hence if God knows particulars then God's essence is divisible into what is most deficient and most perfect with respect to both the many particulars that He knows and with respect to the essence and accidents of each particular. But there can be no such division in God. Hence God does not know particulars.

Here again the problem is what is meant by "knowing." If knowing is sense perceiving then the argument is trivially true. But if knowing is conceptually grasping the essences of these things, which ultimately are a single essence differentiated only because of the inadequacy of how we as opposed to God must know them, then it does not follow that by knowing particulars God's essence need be divisible into what is most deficient and most perfect.

Arguments for the weak denial of God's knowledge of particulars

The first argument of the philosophers is that everything that perceives particulars has a hylic faculty, but since God does not have a hylic faculty He cannot perceive them. Gersonides grants that God cannot have sense awareness of particulars, i.e., He cannot know particulars as particulars. But the argument does not demonstrate that God cannot know the intelligible ordering of particulars.

*
* *

The second argument may be summarized as follows. (1) Since in the act of knowing the knower and the known are in some sense one, and since every entity subject to time is also subject to motion and rest, it follows that (2) whatever knows entities subject to time is itself subject to motion and rest. (3) What is subject to time is subject to motion ; what is subject to motion is subject to change; something is subject to change if and only if it is a body. (4) From (3) it follows that what is subject to time is a body. (5) Only what is material, i.e., is a body, is particular. (6) It follows from (5) that all particulars are bodies. (7) From (4) and (6) it follows that all particulars are subject to time. (8) From (2) and (7) it follows that only what is subject to motion and rest can know temporal entities. (9) God is not subject to motion and rest. (10) Therefore from (8) and (9) it follows that God cannot know temporal entities.

Gersonides notes that this second argument, like its predecessor, legitimately shows that God cannot know particulars as particulars, since in this respect they are temporal. However with respect to their intelligible ordering they are not temporal, for essences are not subject to time. Therefore the argument does not negate the claim that God can know particulars with respect to their intelligible ordering.

*   *
*

In the fifth argument of the philosophers it is argued that knowledge by its very nature is an encompassing process which cannot apply to anything that is numerically infinite. In the proper sense of the term "knowing a thing" is knowing what the thing is. But to know what a thing is entails knowing what it is not, i.e., setting limits within which the thing known is characterized. But to set such limits on what is infinite, i.e., without limit, is a contradiction in terms. Now particulars as particulars are infinite in number, i.e., there is an infinite number of particulars which, insofar as they are particular, cannot be subsumed under any common essence. Therefore it is self-contradictory to claim that anything, including God, can know every particular as a particular.

In his analysis of this fifth argument Gersonides argues that the reason why particulars as particulars cannot be characterized through any single form is that what particularizes them are accidents. However with respect to the intelligible ordering of even an infinite number of particulars, this is not the case. No one can know every number because they are infinite in number. But every number can be known with respect to what it is, viz., a number. Such knowledge is finite, i.e., it consists in knowing a finite number of objects, even though the members of the class of what is known are numerically infinite. The same is true of particulars in general. Thus, this fifth argument establishes that since particulars as particulars are infinite in number they cannot be known, but this is not to say that they cannot be known with respect to their intelligible ordering.

*
* *

The sixth argument of the philosophers may be summarized as follows. (I) If God knows things which are subject to generation and corruption, then one of the following two states of affairs must be the case: either (A) God knows these things before they come to be, or (B) God knows these things only when they come to be.

(II) If (A) is the case one or the other of the following characterization must be true of God: either (1) God knows these things according to their nature as contingent. In other words given two particular states of affairs related in such a way that one can be true if and only if the other is not true (e.g., the fact that a sea-battle did take place at such and such a place and at such and such a time, and the fact that that particular sea-battle did not take place), God knows that either may happen, that the happening of one negates the possibility of the happening of the other, but that before either happens the happening of either is possible. What God does not know in this case is which event will take place before it does take place. Or

(2) of two states of affairs so related that one can occur if and only if the other does not, God knows which one will occur.

(III) If (1) is the case, then God's knowledge is related to what does not exist, for God would know things that do not as yet exist. But this cannot be. What does not exist is not anything, and what is nothing cannot be known.

Furthermore if (1) is the case, then God's knowledge is subject to change. Concerning any given particular state of affairs, b, which occurs at T_1, before T_1 God knows that b is a possible state of affairs, but after T_1 God must know that b is an actual state of affairs. Therefore God's knowledge undergoes change. But this cannot be. Therefore since two absurdities follow from asserting (1), it cannot be the case that God knows things according to their nature as contingent.

(IV) If (2) is the case, then it would follow that no state of affairs is contingent. If God knows every state of affairs and He knows eternally which will occur and which will not occur, then it is necessarily the case that these events will occur. Therefore if what we mean by calling a state of affairs contingent is that there is a real option between it occurring and not occurring, then there are no contingent states of affairs. But both philosophic thought and religious authority affirm that there is choice, and choice is possible only where there are contingent states of affairs. Therefore this consequence is inadmissible, from which it follows that (2) is inadmissible.

(V) Since both (1), from step (III), and (2), from step (IV), are inadmissible, (A), from step (II), is inadmissible.

(VI) But (B) also cannot be the case. If God knows these particulars only when they come to be, God's knowledge would be constantly in a state of flux, for every time that a new state of affairs would occur God would gain new knowledge. Furthermore since God, His essence and His knowledge are all one, it would follow that God is constantly subject to change. But these consequences are inadmissible. Therefore (B) is inadmissible.

(VII) Therefore since both (A), from step (V), and (B), from step (VI), are false, it follows, from step (I), that God cannot know things which are subject to generation and corruption.

In this sixth argument the denial of God's knowledge of things subject to generation and corruption rests on three inadmissible consequences of God having such knowledge. The first consequence is that God's knowledge is related to what does not exist — step (III). The second is that God's knowledge is constantly subject to change — steps (II) and (VI). The third is that nothing is contingent — step (IV). Gersonides argues that none of these consequences follow if what is claimed is that concerning things subject to generation and corruption God knows their intelligible orderings and that they are contingent with respect to choice. In this case God's knowledge neither is related to what does not exist nor is subject to change, for what He knows are eternally existent essences which exist in a unified way in God.

Similarly it does not follow that nothing is contingent. Events are contingent insofar as they are particular events. But in this respect God does not know them. Hence from God's knowing an event it does not follow that that event is not contingent. In knowing an event God knows its intelligible ordering and the fact that the event is contingent. What is entailed in knowing the intelligible ordering of an event can be expressed in a universal conditional judgment. Consider the case of a man drowning in a storm. What God knows may be stated in the following way: if on any given day certain conditions obtain then there will be a storm; if there is a storm and if some man chooses to be at sea on that day, then if certain other conditions obtain (e.g., the man is a poor swimmer, there is no one present to rescue him, etc.), that man will drown; a man can choose to be or not to be at sea on any given day. In knowing the first two parts of the statement God knows the nature of the storm and the drowning. What the last part of the statement expresses is God's knowledge that such an event is contingent with respect to choice. In other words God knows that if a certain man goes to sea on this day then he will drown, but he need not drown, because he need not go to sea; whether or not he drowns is contingent with respect to his choice.

* * *

The seventh and final argument of Gersonides' predecessors in philosophy applies the classic problem of theodicy to the question of the range of God's knowledge. Here it is argued that if God knows particulars then either God governs the world well or He does not. If the latter alternative is the case it is so either because God lacks the power to make the world any better than it is, or God is not interested. If God is not interested, this is so either because particulars are too lowly to be of interest to Him or because He is jealous. That the latter alternative, i.e., that God does not rule the world well, is false is shown by the data of biology which verify the excellence of the order that God has imposed upon the world. But experience also leads to the denial of the former alternative, i.e., that God governs the world well, for no one can make this affirmation who is aware of the constant specific evils which happen in this world. Therefore God cannot know particulars.

Gersonides notes that the first alternative consequence, viz., that God governs the world well, is ambiguous. If by "well" we mean that the world ruled by God is absolutely good, i.e., good without qualification, then this alternative must be rejected. What refutes it is our experience of particular events, many of which are undeniably evil. On the other hand what we may mean by "well" is not that this world of God is unqualifiedly good, but that it is the best possible world. Against the weaker thesis the specific data of our senses are not conclusive. For example from the illustration given above in the sixth argument there is no question that it is bad that the man drowned and in the best world things such as this would not happen. But, on the other hand, the event happened because that event was an instantiation of a number of laws of nature, e.g., laws of meteorology (so that when certain conditions obtain storms occur) and laws of biology (so that when certain conditions obtain a man can no longer maintain his normal life functions). And there is nothing in this specific event to deny that these laws themselves are good, since these laws are what make life possible. That these laws are good is what we learn from the natural sciences. Hence what experience teaches us is that the world is not absolutely good, but that this world is the best of possible worlds. Concrete experiences confirm the first part of the statement, and the universal laws by which individual events are determined with respect to human choice confirm the latter part.

In consequence of this analysis Gersonides again asserts what he concluded in his analysis of each of the preceding six arguments, namely that if we distinguish the two senses of what it means to know particulars, then we can see how this argument is and is not plausible. If by knowing particulars we mean that God knows particulars as particulars, then this argument undeniably shows that God does not know them. For if God knows them then God knows specific evils, so that it cannot be said that God governs well. But if He does not govern well then this is so either from ignorance, which denies God's perfection, or from indifference, which denies God's goodness. However if by knowing particulars we mean that God knows them with respect to their intelligible ordering, then what God both knows and governs is undeniably good and there is no dilemma. Therefore God does not know particulars as particulars, but He knows them with respect to their intelligible ordering as contingent.

The arguments of Gersonides' contemporaries

The eighth argument reads as follows. Magnitude is by definition what is divisible. Therefore the number of parts into which magnitude may be divided is infinite, since every given magnitude by definition must be capable of further division. Now if God has perfect knowledge of magnitude He must know all of the parts into which magnitude is divisible. But it is not possible to know what is infinite in number. Therefore God cannot have such knowledge. But God can know some particulars if and only if He knows all particulars. Therefore God cannot know particulars.

Gersonides notes that the acceptance of this argument has led some of his contemporaries to reject the thesis that magnitude is infinitely divisible. They argue that God has perfect knowledge of magnitude, but this would not be possible if the parts of magnitude were numerically infinite; therefore this number must be finite, which is to say that magnitude is ultimately composed of indivisible parts.

Gersonides comments that the eighth argument, which he judges to be spurious, appears to be valid only because of the ambiguity of the term "all" in saying that God must know all of the parts of magnitude. The term "all" can be used distributively or collectively. In the major premise of the argument, viz., if God knows magnitude, then God must know all of its parts; if the term "all" is used collectively, the major premise is true. Insofar as all of the parts of magnitude are magnitude Gods knows them. But in this sense the minor premise, viz., that God must know each instance of magnitude, does not follow. In principle I can know all that there is to know about magnitude as magnitude without knowing each instance of it, as in principle I can know all that there is to know about rational numbers even though I cannot know each rational number. Either the term "all" is to be understood collectively, in which case the major premise is true but the minor premise is false, or the term is to be understood distributively, in which case the minor premise follows from the major premise but the major premise is false, i.e., it is not the case that if God knows magnitude then He must know every instance of magnitude. In other words to know magnitude is to know the nature of intelligible ordering of magnitude and not to know particular magnitudes. The eighth argument fails because it confuses these two senses of knowing magnitude.

Gersonides applies the insight gained from his analysis of this eighth argument to a parallel problem raised by Aristotle in his *On Generation and Corruption* (1.2, 316a15ff.). Aristotle raises the following paradox in support of the position of the Atomists. Let us assume that every division of which a given magnitude is capable is carried out. Such an assumption can be admitted since something is possible only if it is logically possible that it be actualized even if in fact it is never actualized. After such a total division has in fact occurred what remains is either itself magnitude or points or nothing. It cannot be nothing, for from nothing cannot come something. Neither can it be points, for magnitude cannot consist of what is not itself magnitude. Therefore the ultimate parts are magnitude. In other words there are individual magnitudes or atoms from which all other magnitudes are constituted.

Ibn Rushd's solution to this paradox is to deny the admissibility of the initial assumption. It is not possible to divide a magnitude completely in all respects at the infinite number of points at which division is possible. What is the case is not that magnitude is divisible simultaneously at each of these points, but that there are an infinite number of points at which division may occur. However these points are so related that the occurrence of actual division at certain points excludes the possibility of division at certain other points, so that two specific points are related in such a way that division at one is possible if and only if division does not occur at the other. For example it is possible for a given man to know all of the sciences, but he cannot know them all simultaneously. He must learn them one at a time. And if the total number of sciences were infinite, then there would be no specific time at which he would know them all even though it is possible to know many of them. Similarly all of the points at which a given magnitude may be divided cannot simultaneously be divisible. This would be possible only if the points met. But since magnitude is continuous, this is not the case.

However Gersonides rejects Ibn Rushd's doctrine that simultaneous division at each point of a given magnitude is not possible. To say that actual division at a given point excludes the possibility of actual division at an adjacent point is tantamount to saying that something has a potentiality but does not really have it. A potentiality which is not really a potentiality is no potentiality at all.

However even if we grant Ibn Rushd this point,[8] Ibn Rushd has not solved the paradox. If magnitude is divisible at an infinite number of points, then between any two points there is an infinite number of additional points. Now on Ibn Rushd's solution division cannot occur simultaneously at two immediately adjacent points. But since there is an infinite number of points between any two points, no two points can be immediately adjacent. In other words Ibn Rushd's judgment of the conditions under which simultaneous division is not possible is intelligible only if there are immediately adjacent points, which is possible only if there are ultimate indivisible magnitudes. But this means that Ibn Rushd must assume the very thing which he sought to deny.

Gersonides' solution to Aristotle's paradox is the following. It is a mistake to grant the possibility of infinite division. What can be admitted is endless division, i.e., continuous division of a magnitude which is without end. But there can be no actual state in which unending division is ended. In other words in noting Aristotle's statement of the paradox the reader must not forget what actual infinite division is, namely, unending division. Thus with respect to God's knowledge God knows that given any part

---

[8] At least on the basis of Gersonides' argument alone, it seems that we must. In his refutation Gersonides commits the same confusion of the two senses of the term "all" for which he condemns this eighth argument. Ibn Rushd may respond to Gersonides' criticism and say that a given magnitude may be divided at any of its points, which is what it means to say that it is potentially divisible at all of them, but it may not be divided at every point, which is what it means to say that it is not really capable of division at all of them.

of a continuum it is capable of further division, but God does not know what cannot be, namely an actual, complete, infinite division.

Gersonides' main point in this case is that anything completed of necessity is numerically finite, as anything numerically infinite of necessity is incomplete. This point is true in dividing magnitude as it also is true in augmenting rational numbers. It might be argued that if God knows number perfectly then He must know every number, from which it would seem to follow that there must be an ultimate inaugmentible number that God knows. But as infinite division refers to an unending process rather than some actual or potential state, so does infinite augmentation refer to a process rather than a given number of states. In general this is true of all statements of the capacity of a thing. If I say that b is p-ible, what I mean is that b has a nature or intelligible ordering such that b participates in a certain kind of process. But to say that b is p-ible does not assert that n instances of this given process reside potentially in b. Thus to say that rational numbers are infinitely augmentible is to say that any rational number can be augmented; it is not to say that there is an actual infinite number of rational numbers. All actual numbers are finite, and no number can be augmented to what is not a number.

Maimonides' arguments for the affirmation of God's knowledge of particulars

Maimonides presents two arguments in *The Guide of the Perplexed* to support the claim that God knows particulars as particulars. The first argument is that no imperfection can be ascribed to God; ignorance is an imperfection; it then follows that no ignorance can be ascribed to God; therefore it cannot be said that God does not know particulars even as particulars.

Those philosophers who used the seventh argument discussed above saw the force of that argument rest on the disjunction that either God does not know particulars or God does not govern them perfectly. They then judged the latter consequence to be more reprehensible than the former, so they affirmed God's perfect rule and denied His knowledge of particulars. Against this choice Maimonides argues that on the contrary it can be denied that God governs particulars perfectly without denying God's perfection, but, as he stated in his first argument above, no knowledge can be denied to God.

That it can be said that God does not govern particulars perfectly without denying God's perfection is explained as follows. While the rule of the world of particulars is not perfect, it is as perfect as is possible. The empirically self-evident presence of evil in this world can be accounted for either by the imperfection of the ruler, as the philosophers in the seventh argument assume, or by the imperfection of the ruled subjects. In other words on this latter interpretation it can be said that God in His perfection imposes the best possible order, given the imperfection of the objects on which this order is imposed. In this way we ascribe no imperfection to God by saying that He does not rule perfectly. But to ascribe some ignorance to God, as the philosophers do, is inescapably to attribute an imperfection to God.

Gersonides' objection to this argument is that just as it is not an imperfection of God that His rule of this world is not perfect, so it is not an imperfection of God that His knowledge of the things in this world is not perfect. As the former imperfection is due to the imperfection of the ruled object rather than the ruling subject, so is the ignorance due to the imperfection of the known object rather than the knowing subject. More accurately not every apparent imperfection is really an imperfection. For example to say that God cannot move is not to say that God is imperfect; rather this denial is a consequence of His perfection, i.e. all motion is towards an end, but a perfect being has no end other than itself as it is, so that a perfect being can have no motion. As with motion so too with knowledge of particulars as particulars. To have such knowledge would be to have a hylic faculty, but a perfect being is not material, so that a perfect being cannot know particulars as particulars. In most instances when we say that a subject is not subject to a certain predicate p, the unstated assumption is that that subject is the sort of thing which may or may not be p. But this is not the case here. By saying that certain predicates such as motion and knowledge of particulars cannot be attributed to God, we do not mean that their contraries are predicable. Rather what we are saying is that both the predicate in question and its contrary cannot be attributed to the subject in question. A turkey may be fat or thin, but the color red is neither. Thus to say that red is not fat does not mean that red is thin; it means that such characterizations have no application to red. It is not false that red is thin; it is unintelligible. Similarly God neither knows nor is ignorant of particulars as particulars; rather both claims are unintelligible.

* * *

This objection should not be strange to Maimonides, for the claim that predicates as they are normally affirmed in human contexts constitute category mistakes when affirmed of God, is the main point of Maimonides' second argument. Here Maimonides argues as follows. It is granted that God knows in a single act a single object, which if it were known by us would require an infinite number of acts with an infinite number of essences as the objects of knowledge. Thus there is no analogy between God's knowledge and our knowledge. Similarly in the case of God, since His essence and His existence are one, and it is granted that no analogy holds between God's existence and our existence, again it is clear that there is no analogy between God's knowledge and our knowledge. But all of the arguments of the philosophers which deny that God knows particulars as particulars presuppose some analogy. What they prove is that if God's knowledge is anything like ours, then God could not know particulars. But the antecedent is false. Hence philosophic thought can in no way settle the question. In such cases the dictates of religious authority are to be followed, and what our religious authority teaches in this case is that God knows particulars as particulars.

Briefly Gersonides' judgment on this argument is that it plausibly shows that predicates affirmed of God and man are not univocal in meaning, but Maimonides overstates his case in claiming that such predicates are in no way analogous. From his overstatement he develops his doctrine of the absolute equivocation of divine attributes without which his dismissal of the arguments of the philosophers could not stand. Gersonides argues that properly divine predicates are to be understood as *pros hen* equivocals, in which case the arguments of the philosophers would have the degree of plausibility that Gersonides claims that they have. This conclusion results from Gersonides' analysis of this second argument in Chapter Three. There Gersonides raises four objections to this argument as well as two ways in which the argument is plausible. The position summarized in the preceding paragraph is Gersonides' reconciliation of the noted objections to and the granted plausibility of this argument.

Gersonides' analysis of Maimonides' second argument

Gersonides' first objection is the following. (1) All human knowledge originates with the senses. We first gain sense perceptions of given things from which we subsequently abstract an essence or intelligible ordering which generalizes what is common in the various manifestations of the perceived object. (2) As such our knowledge of the essence of a thing is an effect of that thing. However God knows the thing as its cause, for it is the essence of God which is the source of the essence of the thing known. (3) Hence it follows that knowledge as predicated of God is not the same as knowledge predicated of man. (4) But this is not to say that the term as applied to both is absolutely equivocal. The similarity is not simply nominal or verbal. There is a greater connection than the irrelevancy that it happens to be the case that the same term is used to express totally different meanings. The meanings are different, but not totally so. (5) Rather it is the case that knowledge as applied to God is perfect knowledge and as such constitutes the prime instance or meaning of the term, whereas human knowledge, which is less perfect, is a derivative use of the term. Such a relationship is called "*pros hen* equivocation."

What a man in Indiana means when he says of some box that it weighs one pound is that somewhere in the office of standards and measures in Washington, D.C. is a bar which is one pound, i.e. which sets the standard by which all pound weights are determined, and this box with respect to weight approximates the weight of that bar in Washington. This box is not exactly one pound. Properly, i.e. in a primary sense, only the bar in Washington is. Rather it is one pound derivatively by reference to the one pound bar. To be sure the expression "is one pound" as applied to both is equivocal, but it is not absolutely equivocal. It is a *pros hen* equivocal, i.e., a term which refers primarily to one instance from which it derives secondary applications. Logically this is the situation with any term predicated of God and of anything else. Terms such as "existent," "one," "entity," etc. refer primarily to God and derivatively to anything else. Thus when we say that God knows and man knows we are asserting that what applies perfectly and properly to God applies secondarily and derivatively to man.[9]

(6) Therefore while we must grant that God's knowledge is different from ours, since the term "knowledge" applies to God in a primary and perfect sense, the term can have no implications of what is inferior to human knowledge when it is predicated of God. (7) But the arguments of the philosophers, particularly the sixth and seventh, have shown that if God knows particulars as particulars, then God's knowledge is more like human error or opinion or confusion than it is like human knowledge. If God knows particulars as particulars, then concerning things that do not as yet exist God must either believe that they exist when they do not, or believe that they will exist when they need not, both of which are instances of error, or He thinks that they will exist but is not sure, which is opinion, or

[9] The difference and similarity of these two uses of a term can be alternately expressed as follows: the bar in Washington, D.C. is identical with the pound. The box in Indiana is like that bar which is the pound. God is identical with the knower. We know insofar as we are like the knower with respect to knowing. Given any property P, applied to God, God = the-P, whereas something other than God, b, is like the-P with respect to P.

He does not know whether or not they will exist, which is confusion. But human error, opinion and confusion are all inferior to human knowledge.

* * *

Gersonides' second objection is the following. (1) Since all of man's concepts have their origins in sense experience, any of man's intelligible concepts which do not refer directly to objects in the sense world are inferred from such data. For example the reason why we say that God has conceptual knowledge at all is that we assume that God is an intellect and in the range of human experience conceptual knowledge perfects the intellect. (2) But if statements about God and statements about anything else within the range of human experience are absolutely equivocal, then inferences from the human situation to the divine are not legitimate. For example while it is true that man is rational and it is also true that elephants have sensation, it makes no sense to say that man is rational because elephants have sensation. The state of knowledge of elephants does not enable us to make any statement about a purported comparable state in man, since with respect to knowledge elephants and men are not comparable. (3) All statements are either univocal in meaning or equivocal, and if they are equivocal, they are either absolutely equivocal or *pros hen* equivocal. No statement about God can be univocal, from step (1), but neither can it be absolutely equivocal, from step (2). Hence statements about God, including statements about His knowledge, must be *pros hen* equivocals. (4) Furthermore, since God and His knowledge are one, and in some sense every knower and his knowledge are one, it follows that God's knowledge would be related to our knowledge as God's essence is related to the essence of our acquired intellect. Since the relation of these two essences is *pros hen* equivocal, so the relation of these two instances of knowing is *pros hen* equivocal. (5) As *pros hen* equivocals, predicates refer primarily to God in a perfect sense and secondarily or derivatively to anything else in a less perfect sense. Hence, concerning statements about God's knowledge, that knowledge must be more perfect than our knowledge. Therefore God's knowledge is clearer and more precise than our knowledge. But on the basis of the arguments of the philosophers if God knows particulars as particulars, then God's knowledge would be inferior to ours, since His knowledge would be comparable to what we call error or opinion or confusion.

* * *

Gersonides' third objection is the following. Let f be any predicate. Let g be any predicate other than f. Let R stand for the logical relations which hold between statements in which f is predicated and statements in which g is predicated. Let $R(f,g)$ stand for the assertion of those logical relations. Let f' be any predicate stated of God which nominally or verbally is the same as f. Let g' be a predicate stated of God which nominally or verbally is the same as g. Now, a statement of the form $R(f',g')$ is possible only by inference from a statement of the form $R(f,g)$. But if divine predicates and all other predicates are absolutely equivocal, then it is not possible to make any statement of the form $R(f',g')$. For example because everything that has motion has a body and God does not have a body, we say that God is motionless. But this conclusion follows only if the entailment relations between body and motion in this world also apply to the body and motion predicated of God. But if the latter terms with reference to God are absolutely equivocal with the former terms, then no such inference can be made.

Furthermore, given any predicate f predicated of God, f must have a single meaning in both the statement "God is f" and the statement "God is not f." Otherwise the conjunction of the two would not be self-contradictory. For example, it is logically admissible to say that "a wall is bolor" where we mean by this that the wall is a body, and that "a wall is not bolor" where we mean by this that the wall is black or white but not colored. However, while such a conjunction is not self-contradictory, the use of the one term, "bolor," in these instances is sufficiently confusing to render its use unintelligible. Minimally we must demand that in its use the conjunction of its affirmation and negation with respect to a single subject is judged to be false. This requirement for the use of predicates would also have to apply to divine predicates. But if divine predicates are absolutely equivocal with respect to all other predicates, not even this minimal rule can be imposed on the use of the former. For example, we may say that "God is not good" where we mean by this that "good" as it applies to man has no application to God, and we may also say that "God is good" where we mean by this that God is in no sense bad.

It might be replied that Maimonides does propose rules of usage for divine predicates. In the case of any predicate f if the affirmation of f is a perfection in human cases then God is f follows, and if the affirmation of f is not a perfection in human cases then God is not f follows. But Gersonides argues that this suggested rule of procedure is not legitimate. It confuses terms with the meaning of the terms. No term is a human perfection. Rather it is what the term refers to that does or does not perfect the subject. Thus, on Maimonides' scheme, if we say that the term, "knowledge" by definition is what is otherwise the definition of corporeality, and that the term "corporeality" is by definition what is otherwise the definition of knowledge, we may legitimately say that God is corporeal and unknowing.

Therefore, if divine predicates are absolutely equivocal, there are no rules for their use, which is to say that they have no intelligible use. But neither can divine predicates be univocal terms. Hence they must be *pros hen* equivocal, with the same consequences for statements about God's knowledge already stated in the first two objections.

* *

Gersonides' final objection is the following. As the sixth and seventh arguments of the philosophers show, if God knows in the way that He knows, then God's knowledge is both changing and unchanging in the same respect. On one hand God's knowledge is unchanging, since God cannot be subject to change. On the other hand, since God knows particulars as particulars, His knowledge must be subject to change if in fact it is knowledge. But if this is so, then the law of non-contradiction has no application to statements about God. But even to Maimonides this consequence is inadmissible. For example, he explicitly states that it is false to say that "God is ignorant" in spite of the fact that his analysis of such statements cannot justify his negative judgment.

* *

At this point in the argument Gersonides makes the following accusation: Maimonides is not merely guilty of conceptual error, his whole discussion of divine predicates is intellectually dishonest. Maimonides believed that religious authority demands that we affirm God's knowledge of particulars as particulars and he also was aware that philosophically such an affirmation is unjustified. Therefore, he created this devious device of his theory of divine predication in order to hide or discredit what he saw to be the dictates of philosophic thought. His motivation was not to discover the truth. Rather he sought to pervert the truth on behalf of what he thought to be the demands of the Torah. (That he was even mistaken in this judgment about religious authority is Gersonides' concern in the sixth and final chapter of the book.)

However, in spite of his dishonesty, Maimonides' two arguments are not without certain aspects of plausibility. Maimonides has legitimately shown that since God is a necessary being and everything else is a contingent being, it follows that there is no genus common to God and anything else. Secondly, in every other case of predication the affirmation of a predicate to a subject entails complexity in that subject, but this cannot be the case with predicates legitimately predicated of God if we are not to deny God's simplicity. Thus, for both these reasons any account of divine predication, if it is to be adequate, must neither presuppose a common genus ranging over God and anything else nor propose a method of predication which entails complexity in God as the subject.

As Gersonides' objections to Maimonides' second argument have already indicated, Gersonides maintains that both these features can be accounted for if we posit that divine predicates are *pros hen* rather than absolutely equivocal. Concerning the first aspect of plausibility of Maimonides' second argument, with terms that are *pros hen* equivocal the primary instance of the term is necessarily in a different genus than all of the things to which the term in question derivatively applies. For example the term "existent" applies primarily to substance and derivatively to accidents, and both exist; no claim need be made that both substance and accidents belong to a single genus.

Concerning the second aspect of plausibility, it need not be assumed that positive attribution to God entails complexity in God. Gersonides distinguishes between statements in which the subject is a "subject of existence" and statements in which the subject is only a "subject of the statement." In statements of the former kind the subject is the real essence or intelligible ordering of what is described. Statements about such subjects are what Aristotle called "real definitions." They exhibit the reality of the subject, so that the predicate expression must correspond to what is in reality structurally true of the subject. In these cases and in these cases alone does it follow that if the predicate is other than the subject (i.e. if what is being said is not simply a statement of the form "A is A"), then the subject must be complex. In other words in such cases to say that "b is C" says that b consists of C and something other than C, namely B, so that b is a complex entity. But this is not the case where the subject is merely the subject of the statement. For example in speaking about a specific hue which is in reality a simple thing, I can say that "this is a red color" without meaning that this hue is a complex entity consisting of at least two properties, color and red. Furthermore, concerning that same hue, I may say that "this is a color intermediate between black and white, leaning more towards black than white." In this statement I have not asserted that this hue is a complex entity in which reside three entities (black, white and color) which stand in two three-termed relations ("... intermediate between ... and ..." and "... leaning more towards ... than"). In these cases the subject is not the existent; rather it is the term which refers to the existent. What is described is not what in fact exists. Rather what is said is how a given term can be used with reference to a given existent.

This distinction also applies to statements of facts in which the subject does not materially exist, as is the case with all statements about the intelligences, sice they are non-material forms. Thus the statement that "*b* is that intelligence which conceives of *y* nomos by which the movements of *z* sphere are ordered" does not say that *b* is a complex entity composed of intelligence, nomos *y*, and sphere *z* joined together by the three-termed relation, "... conceiving of ... to order ...."

Thus there is nothing in Maimonides' second argument to necessitate the conclusion that God knows particulars as particulars. Rather what his argument shows is that "knowledge," predicated of God and of man, is a *pros hen* equivocal rather than a univocal term. Furthermore not only is this true of the term, "knowledge," but it is equally true of all other divine predicates. Gersonides illustrates this generalization with the terms "entity," "existent," and "one," and he notes that the same analysis can be applied to the terms "intellect," "living," "comprehending," "benevolent," "powerful," "willing," and "doing." Furthermore in all of these cases the term "God" is to be understood as the subject of the statement rather than as the subject of existence, since each and all of these predicates designate a single thing, namely God Himself.

Five illustrations of the difference between God's knowledge and ours

Maimonides gave five illustrations of why there is no analogy between God's knowledge and our knowledge in order to support his contention that the term "knowledge" is absolutely equivocal with respect to God and to us. Although Maimonides' arguments do not support this claim, perhaps his examples do. Hence in chapter five Gersonides examines the illustrations in independence of Maimonides' arguments for them.

The central point in Gersonides' analysis of these five illustrations is that the examples are valid only if we posit that God knows particulars as particulars. In other words if we assume that God knows particulars as particulars then God's knowledge certainly is different from ours. But the examples do not prove that God's knowledge is different, for if we posit that God knows particulars with respect to their intelligible ordering and not as particulars then in all five cases God's knowledge is analogous to our own. What the examples do show plausibly is that if God knew particulars as particulars, then God's knowledge would be so radically different from our own in these respects that there could be no analogy between God's knowledge and our knowledge. But it has been seen already that such a consequence is inadmissible. Hence, since Maimonides' five illustrations depend on the assumption that God knows particulars as particulars, these illustrations constitute a *reductio ad absurdum* argument that while God can know particulars with respect to their intelligible ordering, He cannot know them as particulars.

* * *

Maimonides' first illustration is that God's "knowledge while being one, corresponds to many known things belonging to various species." In other words God knows in absolute simplicity and unity an infinite number of things which lack any natural unity. In our case we can know a multiplicity of things in a single act only insofar as they share a common essence, for in knowing that essence we know the things that have that essence. Thus we know all rational numbers when we know the definition of number even though it is impossible to know each individual number. But there is no essence common to every particular. Hence it is impossible for us to know all particulars, and if God should have such knowledge then God's knowledge and our knowledge in this respect would be radically different.

The reason why there can be no essence common to all particulars is the following. The unity of a thing lies in its final cause. With respect to the essence of any particular, we may speak of a hierarchy of essences so related that in principle it is possible to know all of these essences. But our concern is with knowledge of particulars as particulars. As such the only way we might conceive of knowing all particulars would be if some particulars as particulars served as the end or final cause for other particulars. But if this were the case, then either particulars are so related that each is the end for the other (i.e., *a* is the end of *b*, which is the end of *c*, which is ..., which is the end of *a*) or there is some particular which is its own end. The former situation would not enable us to perceive particulars in unity, with the consequence that knowledge of all of them would be impossible for us, and the latter situation is inadmissible, since no particular can be its own final cause. Therefore, particulars as particulars lack natural unity without which they cannot be known in simplicity and oneness. Therefore in this respect God's knowledge, since God is purported to know particulars as particulars in absolute simplicity and oneness, is radically different from ours.

Gersonides notes that if we say that God knows the intelligible ordering of all particulars in a single act then there is no fundamental difference between God's knowledge and ours, for we too know in a single act the intelligible ordering of any number of different particulars which are naturally unified. In such cases the different objects are so related that the intelligible ordering of some is the form and perfection of the intelligible ordering of others, which is why they are knowable both by God and by us in a single act of cognition. Hence God's knowledge differs from ours in this respect only if God knows particulars as particulars. Otherwise the sole difference in this respect between our knowledge and God's is that what we know through multiple essences in multiple acts God knows through a single essence (namely, the essence of God) in a single act of cognition. But this difference is accountable within the structure of *pros hen* equivocation, as has been explained above. Thus no appeal to absolute equivocation is justified in this instance.

* * *

Maimonides' second illustration is that God's knowledge "may have as its object something that does not exist." In other words if we assume that God knows particulars as particulars then God will have knowledge of things which do not yet exist or already have ceased to exist. Hence God's knowledge is connected with the non-existent as its object. But this is conceivable for us, since knowledge and its object are one, so that if the known does not exist, neither can the knowledge.

Gersonides raises and dismisses two objections to this illustration. The first objection is that we also know objects that do not exist. Our knowledge of numbers is an example of this, for clearly we know them, but they have no real existence outside of the soul. Gersonides replies that in knowing entities such as numbers we do not know something that does not exist. The numbers that we know refer to forms which exist outside of our intellect in the Active Intellect, so that numbers do have an existence outside of our souls. Gersonides then notes that the same is true of the intelligible ordering of all particulars, past, present or future, i.e. these essences all eternally exist in the Active Intellect, even though the particulars as particulars which exemplify this ordering have no such immortality.

The second objection is an attempt to defend what Maimonides here is claiming on the grounds that God knows particulars as their cause, whereas our knowledge arises as an effect of the existence of the particulars. Gersonides replies that from this legitimate difference between our knowledge and God's knowledge it only follows that what God knows is the intelligible ordering of particulars, but it does not follow that He knows particulars as particulars. But if this is the intent of Maimonides' illustration, then Maimonides has misled us by saying that God's knowledge is connected with non-existence, for the intelligible ordering of particulars is itself eternal. But this intepretation is not correct. Maimonides intended to say that God knows particulars as particulars from which it would follow that His knowledge is connected with non-existence. But he did not intend, as this second objection implies, to tell us how God knows these things. Indeed no such explanation can be given.

Gersonides' own comment on this illustration is that if God knows the intelligible ordering of particulars rather than particulars as such, as his response to the first objection to this illustration indicated, then it does not follow that God's knowledge is connected with non-existence. Hence, given Gersonides' position, the truth of the illustration must be denied. Neither God's knowledge nor our knowledge is connected with what does not exist. In both cases the object of knowledge is the intelligible ordering eternally present without change in the Active Intellect which exists in a unified way in God.

* *

Maimonides' third illustration is that God's knowledge "may have as its object something that is infinite." In other words if God knows every particular as a particular and He knows them in a single act of knowledge, then, since the number of particulars is infinite, God knows something that is numerically infinite. But this would be inconceivable to us. By definition knowledge is a limiting, encompassing process. Hence to say that we could know what is infinite would amount to saying that we can limit what is without limit.

Gersonides considers two objections to this third case. Both objections assert that we also can know what is numerically infinite. The first objection appeals to our knowledge of essences to which correspond a class of particulars. For example in knowing the essence *man* we know an infinite number of men. Against this objection Gersonides points out that Maimonides is asserting that God knows all particulars as particulars, in which respect they are infinite, and not merely with respect to their intelligible ordering, in which respect they are numerically finite. Certainly in the latter respect God's knowledge does not differ from ours, but in the former respect it necessarily does.

The second objection appeals to the example of our knowledge of continuous quantities and numbers, both of which are numerically infinite. The former are infinitely divisible and the latter are infinitely augmentable. Again Gersonides responds that the cited cases are inappropriate, since the respect in which we know both magnitude and number is their intelligible ordering rather than as particulars, and, in the respect in which they are known, magnitudes and numbers are respectively one. In other words we know that number is such that if anything is a number it is augmentable, which is to know a single thing, and we know that magnitude is such that if anything is a magnitude it is divisible, which again is a single thing, but we do not know each magnitude and each number. However it is this latter kind of knowledge rather than the former to which Maimonides appeals in order to assert the purported difference between our knowledge and God's knowledge.

Once more Gersonides notes that the asserted difference follows only on the assumption that God knows particulars as particulars. However if God knows particulars only with respect to their intelligible ordering, then neither man nor God knows what is numerically infinite.

*
* *

The fourth illustration[10] is that God's knowledge "does not bring about the actualization of one of two possibilities even though" God "knows perfectly how one of them will come about." In other words given two states of affairs so related that one will be realized if and only if the other is not, both remain possibilities even though God knows which one of them will be realized. However this situation is inconceivable from a human perspective. Given such a situation, one of the following alternatives would have to be true: either (1) God knows that a given state of affairs, b, is a possible state of affairs and He believes that b will come to be, but He cannot know this, or (2) God believes that not only is it possible for b to come about, but in fact b will come about, even though this is only a possibility, or (3) God knows that b is a possibility but He has no idea whether or not it will come to be.

In the language of man the first case is an instance of opinion, for God believes that b will come to be without

---

[10] As presented by Maimonides in *The Guide of the Perplexed*, this is the fifth illustration.

knowing. The second case is an instance of error, for God believes that He knows that something will be actual when there is no way to know this. At best under the pretense of knowledge God will have made a lucky guess. The third case is an instance of confusion. Therefore what we call "knowledge" with respect to God turns out to be analogous to human opinion or error or perplexity rather than to human knowledge. As such the term "knowledge" as applied to God certainly is absolutely equivocal with the term, "knowledge" as applied to man.

Gersonides does not raise the third situation stated above as a serious interpretation of Maimonides' meaning in asserting this illustration. However he argues that this situation is definitely a possibility if what Maimonides here asserts to be the case concerning God's knowledge is in fact the case. This is particularly so concerning particulars as particulars where the number of alternative mediate causes needed to actualize a given contingent event is itself infinite. In general the more conditions that are specified and known about a given thing, the more defined the thing is, and the more defined the thing is, the less contingency there is in determining whether or not the thing in question will be realized, since the realization of these mediate conditions constitutes the necessary conditions for the realization of that thing. But in the case of all particulars, the number of mediating conditions is infinite.

This time Gersonides accepts Maimonides' characterization of how God knows, but he adds that this situation also is found in the case of human knowledge. In other words there are instances where man too knows which one of a set of contingencies will be realized even though the members of that set remain contingent. In this case Gersonides appeals to the experiences of dreaming, having visions and prophecy, especially to the dreams of

Pharoah interpreted by Joseph and the dreams of Nebuchad-nezzar interpreted by Daniel. However, in such cases what is known is the intelligible ordering of the state of affairs, from which respect the events are necessary. Such knowledge does not negate the contingency of the event with respect to human choice. What the knower discovers in his dream, vision or prophecy is that if such and such happens then such and such necessarily will follow, but whether or not the antecedent is true depends on human choice. Thus Pharoah learns that if he does not take certain measures then the people of Egypt will die of starvation seven years later, but they need not die of starvation, since Pharoah is free to take the required measures. Thus even though events as particular events are contingent, with regard to their intelligible ordering they are determined. Hence, given that God knows the intelligible ordering of particulars rather than particulars as particulars, man as well as God can know future events without in any way denying either the contingency of those events or the credibility of the knowledge.

* * *

The final illustration[11] is that God's knowledge "undergoes no changes in its apprehension of things produced in time. And yet it might seem that the knowledge that a thing will exist is not identical with the knowledge that it already exists; for there is in the latter case a certain surplus, namely, the fact that what had been in potentia became actual." In other words that God knows things which undergo change in time does not involve any change in God's knowledge.

---

[11] As presented by Maimonides in *The Guide of the Perplexed*, this is the fourth illustration.

Such a case would be inconceivable for us for two reasons. One, to know that "b will be" is not identical with knowing that "b is," since the former asserts that b is a possible rather than an actual state of affairs, and the latter asserts that b is actual rather than possible. But if Maimonides is correct in this case, God knows both that "b will be" and "b is" as a single eternal judgment. Two, we could only understand a situation such as this as an instance of either change in knowledge or human error, but not as an instance of unchanging knowledge. Consider two states of affairs, b and c, so related that b is the case if and only if c is not the case. Assume a given time, t_1, before which b is the case and after which c occurs. Now one of the following two conditions must be true of God's knowledge: either God continues to believe that b is the case after t_1, in which case God is mistaken, or God knows that c is now the case instead of b, in which case His knowledge will have undergone change. But in no case can we understand what it means to call this an instance of unchanging knowledge.

Gersonides notes that Maimonides must assert that God's knowledge cannot undergo change, since God Himself cannot change and God and His knowledge are one. Furthermore anyone who asserts that God knows particulars as particulars must grant this final illustration. Maimonides realized this, and for this reason he proposed that the term "knowledge" is absolutely equivocal with respect to God and man. Maimonides might have avoided this situation by asserting that by God knowing that b will occur where b may occur if and only if c does not occur, it is not possible for c to occur. But the consequence of this option would be to deny that events are really contingent, and if no event is contingent then there is no human choice. But such a price to preserve God's knowledge of particulars as particulars was too high for Maimonides to pay, since the affirmation of the reality of human choice also is a fundamental dictate of religious authority.

However Gersonides again notes, as he has in his analysis of the previous four illustrations, that if we posit that God knows particulars with respect to their intelligible ordering rather than as particulars, then God's knowledge of objects which undergo generation and corruption is not categorically different from our knowledge. The particular as a particular is first possible and then actual, but the intelligible ordering of the particular always is actual in the Active Intellect. Hence both God and man can know these essences without that knowledge undergoing change when the particulars which exemplify these essences come or cease to be.

* * *

In general what Gersonides' analysis of these five illustrations has shown is the following. If God knows particulars as particulars, then "knowledge" with respect to God and man is absolutely equivocal. But the term "knowledge" is *pros hen* equivocal if God knows particulars with respect to their intelligible ordering rather than as particulars. Thus, in the light of chapter four and Gersonides' analysis of what is entailed in claiming that divine predicates are absolutely equivocal rather than *pros hen* equivocal, it follows that God knows particulars with respect to their intelligible ordering, but not as particulars.

Gersonides' arguments for God's knowledge of particulars

What has been stated above completes Gersonides' consideration of Maimonides' case for asserting that God knows particulars. However, in addition to Maimonides' two arguments and five illustrations, Gersonides presents three arguments of his own to demonstrate the plausibility of the claim that God knows particulars.

Gersonides' first argument is the following. An artifact is something created intentionally by a craftsman. Thus the existence of any artifact presupposes the existence of a conscious being who knows the artifact he has or will make. Now every substance and accident in our sublunar world is an artifact of which God is the craftsman. Therefore God must know every substance and accident in our world.

Gersonides' second argument is the following. (Step 1) Since God is absolutely simple and one, God and everything that is true of God necessarily are one. Thus there is no distinction between God's existence and God's essence. Furthermore, since knowledge and its object are one, it also follows that God's knowledge of His essence, God's essence, and God's existence are one. Therefore there can be no difference between the level of perfection of God's knowledge of His essence and the level of existence of God's essence. In other words if we assume two scales by which the level or degree of perfection is measured, one scale measuring knowledge and the other existence, where these two scales are isomorphic, the determined level of perfection of God's knowledge of His essence must agree with (i.e. occupy the same place in the two scales as) the determined level of the existence of God's essence. Now God's essence has perfect existence. Therefore God's knowledge of His essence also must be perfect.

(Step 2) Every existent substance and accident emanates from God's essence, so that among those propositions true of God's essence is a set of propositions which state that an infinite number of substances and accidents derive their existence from God's essence. Now if God does not know particulars then God cannot know those propositions which express the causal connection between His essence and the particulars which emanate from His essence. Thus there would be facts about God's essence which are unknown to God. But if this were so, then God's knowledge of His essence would be less perfect than the essence itself. But this cannot be the case (from Step 1). Hence God must know every existent substance and accident which emanates from His essence. In other words God must know particulars.

Gersonides' third argument is the following. God is the cause, the form, and the end of all separate intelligences. As such every cognition found in these intelligences must be found in God. Now, since the Active Intellect is the tool by which God created our sublunar world, the Active Intellect knows everything in this world subject to generation and corruption. Therefore, since the Active Intellect must know these particulars, God must know them.

Concerning all three arguments, Gersonides reasons that they plausibly show that God must know particulars, but this does not entail that He knows them as particulars. Rather, all that necessarily follows is that God knows particulars with respect to their intelligible ordering. For example the first argument contends that the relationship of God and the particulars in this world is analogous to the relationship of a craftsman and his artifacts, and just as the craftsman must know his artifacts, so God must know particulars. But the craftsman need not know the particulars in every detail. What he must have is a design or a blueprint by which his workmen can build what is to be built. Thus the individual workers on a given house must be familiar with the specific parts of the planned house with which they must work, (e.g., the lumber, the bricks, the mortar, etc.), but the architect only requires general knowledge of these materials. Rather the architect's knowledge is of the plan of the house by which he constructs the blueprint from which the workers carry out their tasks. Now to satisfy the conditions for a blueprint with respect to the particulars existent in this world, the Active Intellect, and therefore God, must know these things generally, i.e., with respect to their intelligible ordering, but not specifically as particulars.

Thus there is nothing in these three arguments to refute Gersonides' determined position. On final analysis they, like the arguments of the philosophers and Maimonides, are plausible arguments only insofar as they demonstrate that God knows particulars with respect to their intelligible ordering. It is in this respect that they are defined. God also knows that there is a respect in which particulars are not defined, and it is in this respect that they are particulars and contingent. But, whereas God knows that particulars are particulars, He does not know them as particulars. In other words, while God knows what particulars are and how particulars are, He cannot know that any specific particulars are.

* * *

In chapter four Gersonides presents his position directly. There he notes not only that his position reconciles what is plausible in all of the arguments considered but that it provides a key by which other problems can be solved. He discusses three, viz., the problem of human choice and determinism, the determination of the nature of divine providence, and the nature of prophecy. As Maimonides had explained, the prophet is a man whose intellect, through the man's attainment of a high degree of intellectual and moral excellence, has been united with the

Active Intellect. While the prophet is in this state of unity with the Active Intellect he sees the world as the Active Intellect does. Such perception is not sense perception. In such a state the particulars of the world are not seen as particular, for this is possible only through the senses. Rather what is grasped are the essences of the particulars, which are conceptual or intelligible rather than material entities. In knowing the essence of a thing, the prophet and the Active Intellect alike know what is necessarily and universally true of the thing. In this way the future of a thing is both known and determined. But this is not to say that the future occurrence of a specific event known by prophet and Active Intellect alike is determined. Rather, while that event is determined generally it is contingent with respect to human choice concretely. For example the prophet Jeremiah knows the essence of Israel, the essence of Babylonia, and what is universally and necessarily true in warfare. This knowledge can be expressed in a proposition of the following form: the nature of war is such that if any nation of which F is true should go to war with any other nation of which G is true, then F will be destroyed by G. Now because Jeremiah is a man and has both senses and imagination, he knows that Judah is the nation of which F is true and that Babylonia is the nation of which G is true. Hence Jeremiah can say to King Zedekiah that it is necessarily the case that if Judah goes to war with Babylonia, Judah will be destroyed. But this does not mean that it is determined that Judah will in fact be destroyed. This particular fact is contingent with respect to human choice. In other words Zedekiah has the option of going or not going to war with Babylonia. What is known is what will be the consequence of his choice. But his choice itself is not determined. Hence the destruction of Judah is not determined.

It is in this way that all human events are both determined and free. It is also in this way that divine providence is to be understood with respect to man. God has given to all of His creatures ways of protecting themselves from danger. What these ways are vary from species to species. For example one kind of animal has a keen sense of smell which enables it to detect other animals from which it instinctively flees. This instinct to flee is itself a tool of divine providence given by God to this creature. But man has no such instinct. Instead he has a far better survival device. It is his intellect. Because an animal has a special sense rather than a special intellect, it cannot adequately distinguish safe from dangerous situations. Thus a deer sensing any man flees. But a man through his intellect can know the universal conditions by which a situation is or is not dangerous, and through the power of judgment can determine when flight is or is not necessary. Thus, whereas a certain animal always will fear the sea, a man can distinguish between when it would be safe and not be safe to take a sea voyage. In this way God favors man above all other creatures in the sublunar world.

It might be argued that although the source of Jeremiah's knowledge in the example given above is the Active Intellect, his knowledge is in one respect superior to that of the Active Intellect and consequently it is superior to God's knowledge. Knowing that if any nation of which F is true goes to war with any other nation of which G is true, by means of his senses and imagination Jeremiah can instantiate the F-expression with Judah and the G-expression with Babylonia. But lacking both senses and imagination, neither God nor the Active Intellect can do this. In other words Jeremiah's knowledge is superior to that of the Active Intellect and God because Jeremiah alone can know that if Judah battles Babylonia, then Judah will be destroyed.

Gersonides' reponse to this objection is the following. Because what makes a particular a particular is its matter, no essence or form can be a particular. However, the more specified the characteristics of a thing are, the more individuated is that to which the characterization refers. Hence, while no conjunction of predicates can express a particular as a particular, it is possible to refer uniquely to an individual. Therefore, let "*the-F*" stand for that which is *F* where *F* is expressed through a set of statements which in fact apply to a single entity, and let "*the-G*" stand for that which is *G* where *G* is expressed through a set of statements which in fact apply to a single entity. This *F* and this *G* theoretically could refer to more than one entity, but in fact they do not. For example my social security number expresses a series of universal relations which in fact refers only to me, but in principle could refer to more than one individual. Now God and the Active Intellect know that if *the-F* battles *the-G* then *the-F* will be destroyed. In addition to this Jeremiah knows that *the-F* is Judah and *the-G* is Babylonia. But what is the difference between *the-F* and Judah on one hand, and *the-G* and Babylonia on the other? *The-F* is what Judah is. What Judah is other than *the-F* consists in accidents. The same is true of the difference between *the-G* and Babylonia. Hence God and the Active Intellect both know what Judah and Babylonia are. What they do not know are accidents of each, which is not what either is. Therefore Gersonides argues that the so-called deficiency in God, namely, that He cannot instantiate what He knows generally, is no deficiency at all, for to know a thing as other than it is is properly error and not knowledge. The proper knowledge of a thing is to know its essence, i.e., what it is. To know the essence exclusively is perfect knowledge, for it is not to confuse in any way what the thing is with what it is not. Thus

Jeremiah's additional knowledge is either trivial or it is error. In the former case Jeremiah does not confuse the respective essences of Babylonia and Judah, so that what he knows is reducible to the triviality, A is A. In the latter case he fails to distinguish the essence of these two nations from their respective material principles, in which case his identity statement is not trivial, but it contains an aspect of error, for Babylonia and Judah are in part identified with what they are not, namely, their accidents. Hence the inability of God and the Active Intellect to make the additional judgments that Jeremiah can make is a precondition of the superiority of the knowledge of the former over the latter.

Arguments from religious authority

So ends Gersonides' discussion of the question of God's knowledge of particulars with respect to philosophic thought. From this point of view, Gersonides concludes, there is no question that God knows that particulars are contingent with respect to human choice and God knows particulars with respect to their intelligible ordering, but God does not know particulars as particulars. Now Gersonides turns in the final chapter of Treatise Three to reconsider this question with respect to the Torah. Maimonides believed that this authority demands that God know particulars as particulars. But Gersonides argues that this is not the case. He presents five arguments specifically against Maimonides in support of the position which was determined with respect to philosophic thought. Two of the arguments, the second and the fifth, are appeals to religious authorities which support Gersonides' position. The second argument consists in an analysis of specific biblical texts. The fifth argument appeals to Abraham Ibn Ezra's commentaries on the Bible in support of Gersonides' position.

Gersonides' fourth argument rests on Maimonides' expressed method for interpreting biblical texts. Both Maimonides and Gersonides are committed to the thesis that there can be no conflict between religious and philosophic authority. All apparent contradictions can be only apparent, for both are sources of truth and there can be only one truth. Thus Maimonides had argued that where there is an apparent conflict, and there is no question of the correctness of the conclusion arrived at by philosophic thought, the Torah can no longer be taken in its literal sense, but must be reinterpreted to agree with the conclusions reached by means of philosophic thought. Now, Gersonides argues, even if the literal sense of the Torah was that God knows particulars as particulars, by Maimonides' own recommended methods of procedure it would not follow that God knows them in this respect. Since philosophic thought dictates that God knows particulars only with respect to their intelligible ordering (the conclusion of Chapters One through Five), we must reinterpret the biblical references. But, as arguments two and five establish, there is no need to do this, since our religious authority in its literal meaning claims no more than the proposition that God knows particulars with respect to their intelligible ordering.

Gersonides' first and third arguments from religious authority constitute what might be called a transcendental deduction. Here Gersonides argues that his determination of what it is that God knows must be accepted on the basis of religious authority because this interpretation and only this interpretation agrees with other equally basic tenets of the Torah.

In the first argument Gersonides reflects on two apparently contradictory tenets, namely that contingents exist, and that God makes known future contingent events through his prophets. The former tenet must be granted, for otherwise the very legitimacy of the commandments would be called into question. If no event is contingent, then it is not intelligible to speak of man being commanded. But the latter tenet also must be granted, even though this tenet cannot entail the consequence that the prediction by a prophet that a given event will occur entails that it must occur. As we have seen already in the discussion of prophecy above, Gersonides argues that these two tenets are reconcilable only if we posit that in one respect contingents are ordered and in another respect they are not. Once this is posited we can affirm that in the respect in which they are ordered, which is the respect in which they are their intelligible ordering, they are known by the prophet and determined by God, but that in another respect they are neither known nor determined, which is the respect in which they are properly particulars.

In the third argument Gersonides reflects on two different apparently contradictory tenets, namely, that God's will is not subject to change and that God repents of some things. Both claims are supported by direct biblical texts. The former is a necessary condition of God's being perfect. But the latter also necessarily must be affirmed, for otherwise religious concepts such as prayer, repentance and forgiveness would not be intelligible. Again Gersonides argues that these two tenets can be reconciled only if we posit what we have so far concluded. There is a difference between knowing particulars with respect to their intelligible ordering and as particulars. God knows them only in the former sense. In this sense and this sense alone do we say properly that God's will is not subject to change. But in the latter sense God does not know particulars. Thus it is in this latter sense that God is said to repent. This does not means literally that He repents. Literally God never changes in any way. Rather we are to understand such statements in the following way: the prophet Jonah told Nineveh that if it did not change its ways then it would be destroyed. It changed its ways. Therefore it was not destroyed. This is what it means to say that God repented of His decision to destroy Nineveh. But this change was a change in Nineveh insofar as the events of Nineveh are particular and subject to change; it involved no real change in the will of God.

Thus Gersonides concludes from religious authority as well as from philosophic authority that God does not know particulars as particulars. Rather, concerning every particular God knows its intelligible ordering, from which He further knows that it is a particular and as such that it is contingent.

V

SOME ASPECTS OF GERSONIDES' PHILOSOPHIC VIEWS

In Treatise One and Two of *The Wars of the Lord* Gersonides presents his views on the nature of the Active Intellect, man's acquired intellect, and prophecy. These discussions are presupposed in his presentation of his views on God's knowledge of particulars in Treatise Three. However these are not the only concepts presupposed. In this section we will make explicit a number of these views which are central to Gersonides' analysis of God's knowledge of particulars.

Epistemology[12]

Gersonides' theory of knowledge contains two parts, how we know and what we know. Actually the two are interrelated in

---

[12] The following discussion is a summary of the textual analysis presented in textual notes 25, 26, 28, 38, 68, 105, 107, 125, 130, 138, 150, 163-166, 178, 218, 283, 348, 352, 456, 457, and 560.

such a way that one both entails and clarifies the understanding of the other. Hence the decision as to which to present first is arbitrary. We shall begin with the question: how do we know? The discussion that immediately follows this one concerning the Active Intellect is part of the answer to this question. In the subsequent discussion concerning essences we shall turn to the related question of what we know.

All knowledge that is human knowledge begins with sensation. Man is equipped with two kinds of senses, external and internal. His external senses are touch, taste, smell, hearing and sight. With these senses he receives multiple impressions from material objects external to him in his world. These impressions are all distinct. As received they lack any order. It is the internal senses which impose this order. These are the common sense, estimation, memory, and recollection, together with various kinds of imagination. Through these internal senses the diverse impressions are unified, interrelated and generalized so as to form an image of the object or objects in question.

Both sets of senses are powers of the soul. According to Gersonides the soul is a single thing which contains various powers or capacities. In common with animals and plants, man's soul has a nutritive and generative power. In common with animals, man's soul has what he calls an animative capacity. Subsumed under this power are the capacities for voluntary motion, imagination and perception. It is to this capacity of the soul that the functions of the internal and external senses belong.

To man alone of the creatures in this material world is given an additional power of the soul, which Gersonides calls the human capacity, *kôaḥ 'enôsi' yùt*. It is exclusively with respect to this power that man's soul is called an intellect. Its function is to know. What it does is form concepts by which the individual objects of the material world are known "in a universal way."

What is called the "material intellect" is the capacity of the soul to receive the universal forms of material things; it is not itself a separate entity within the soul. Where this capacity is actualized, the soul possesses actual concepts. These concepts are the formal or essential aspect prescinded from the material images which were generalized from the sense data. They constitute what is called the "acquired intellect." The material intellect is a cause of these concepts only in the sense that if a thing is not capable of a certain realization, then it cannot achieve that realization, i.e. it cannot have conceptual knowledge. The material intellect simply names the soul's capability to have this knowledge. The actual causes are the images formed through the senses and the Active Intellect. In other words the sense images are the matter from which the Active Intellect brings about actual conceptual knowledge in the human soul which has the capacity to receive such knowledge.

The Active Intellect[13]

The Active Intellect is not itself part of man's soul. It is the lowest of ten separate intelligences which emanated from God. Each intelligence is a simple form through which the intelligence endlessly performs a single act through which it governs its associated sphere. The sphere of the Active Intellect is the moon. The world that it governs and orders is our material, sublunar world.

Although the Active Intellect has only one activity, which consists in knowing its own essence, the consequences of that

---

[13] The following discussion is a summary of the textual analysis presented in textual notes 26, 127, 129, 130, 337, 342, 347, 352, 372, 375, 560, and 602.

single action in the sublunar world are many. Thus since we are aware of the Active Intellect through the consequences of its activity in our world, its act may be spoken of in the plural. How a single act can be thought of as many can be illustrated in the following way. Consider a train passsing through a field. The train is doing a single thing, namely moving in a direct path along the tracks. But, as a result of that single action, many other things may happen. For example a cow may happen across the track at the moment that the train is passing, with the result that the cow is killed by the train. Hence we can speak of the train performing two actions, moving through a field and killing a cow. But in fact both actions are only a single act on the part of the train. The secondary act, namely the killing of the cow, is a consequence of the train's single, primary act in relation to a decision of the cow, namely to cross the railroad tracks at the precise time that it did. In this way the multiple apparent actions of the Active Intellect are to be understood. They result from the single action of the Active Intellect in relation to distinct acts by the inhabitants of the sublunar world.

For Gersonides' purposes these consequent or secondary actions of the Active Intellect are divided into two classes. One, the Active Intellect gives order and intelligence to the material world. Two, the Active Intellect actualizes conceptual knowledge in human souls which have the necessary preconditions for such knowledge. In both cases what the Active Intellect does is know itself, i.e., its essence. In the Active Intellect this essence is a single form. But in the sublunar world of matter this single essence manifests itself as multiple essences. It is these essences, or rather, this essence diversified or disunified in matter, that is the order and the intelligibility of the entities of our world. Hence these essences are at one and the same time the order in the world and the object of knowledge.

Essences[14]

Two radically different worlds — the translunar world of separate intelligences and forms, and the sublunar world of sense particulars and matter — are bridged by essence.[15] The term essence expresses order (*seder*)[16] and law (*nimùs*). In other

[14] The following discussion is a summary of the textual analysis presented in notes 12-15, 26, 38, 40, 53, 72, 107, 127, 130, 153, 178, 204, 283, 285, 346, 352, 371, 436, 446, 457, 507, 542, 547, and 581.

[15] The term essence in Hebrew is *'esem*. Its root meaning is the Greek *ousia*, and, as Gersonides uses the term, the meaning of *ousia* as Aristotle uses the term is preserved. However, as we shall see, the term takes on many other connotations as well.

[16] The system of transliteration of Hebrew into English letters to be used in this text is that given in *The Catholic Biblical Quarterly*, which is the following:

'	=	א	BÂ	=	בָה	BĀH	=	בָֿה
B	=	ב	BÔ	=	בוֹ	BĒH	=	בֶה
G	=	ג	BÜ	=	בוּ	BĀ'	=	בָֿא
D	=	ד	BÊ	=	בֵי	BEH	=	בֶּֿה
H	=	ה	BÈ	=	בֵּי			
W	=	ו	BÎ	=	בִי			
Z	=	ז	BĀ	=	בָ			
Ḥ	=	ח	BŌ	=	בֹ			
Ṭ	=	ט	BÜ	=	בֻ			
Y	=	י	BĒ	=	בֵּ			
K	=	כ	BĪ	=	בִּ			
L	=	ל	BA	=	בַ			
M	=	מ	BO	=	בָ			
N	=	נ	BU	=	בֻּ			
S	=	ס	BE	=	בֶּ			
'	=	ע	BI	=	בִּ			
P	=	פ	BĂ	=	בֲ			
Ṣ	=	צ	BŎ	=	בֳ			
Q	=	ק	BE	=	בֱ			
R	=	ר	Bᵉ	=	בְּ			
Ś	=	שׂ						
Š	=	שׁ						
T	=	ת						

words the essence of a thing is that which is the order in a thing and that in the thing which is subject to law. As such it is what Gersonides calls the "limit" (*taklit*) of the thing. As limit essence has the multiple meanings associated with the Greek term *peras*. At one and the same time essence in this primary sense is form (*eidos* or *morphe* in Greek), end (*telos*) and final cause or substance (*ousia*). As the end of a thing it also is the good and the perfection of that thing. As substance it is that which determines the potencies of a thing. In other words all statements about the capacities or dispositions of a thing follow from statements of the essence of a thing. It is this aspect of the primary sense of essence, namely as that from which the capacities of a thing are consequent, that explains the association of essence with law.

"Essence" is used in a primary and a secondary sense. In the primary sense of the term, essence is an entity. It is the model by which God creates, orders and governs the world. It is a single thing which is identical with the Active Intellect. Essence in its primary sense is a single thing which is the object of knowledge of the Active Intellect. But the Active Intellect is itself a single, simple form, and as form it is indistinguishable from what it knows, which is essence. Hence in the primary sense of the term, what was said above about the Active Intellect is also true of essence. The difference between the two terms, "Active Intellect" and "primary essence" is that while both refer to a single, simple entity, the former term expresses that entity as knowing subject and the latter term expresses that entity as known object.

In the secondary sense of the term, essence refers to classes of things, i.e., it is an expression of genus and species, and the term designates universals. These two aspects of the secondary sense of the term are not distinguished. In stating a given essence, what is named is a universal, but at the same time that universal defines or designates a class of things. Thus the term "chair" both names a universal or concept in the intellect or mind of the speaker and collectively designates a class of things.

The term "essence" in its different senses is to be understood as *pros hen* equivocal. In the primary sense of the word essence is said to exist in "complete reality." But such existence is existence in the mind of the Active Intellect. It is a kind of existence distinct from both mental and material existence. These latter kinds of existence are appropriate to essence, but only to essence in its secondary sense. Where essence has mental existence it is a universal. Where essence has material existence it is a particular thing.

In the light of this understanding of the term "essence," we may fill out our earlier discussion of epistemology in the following way. Essence manifests itself in matter as multiple, diverse, particular entities. Through our sense experience of these entities we construct images from which the Active Intellect actualizes concepts in our soul or mind. These concepts are universals, i.e., essences which exist in our mind. In possessing these universals we have the only thing that can properly be called knowledge.

But the universals are not what we know. They are only the tools by which we know. In some sense what we know is the essence that is the Active Intellect itself. Real or primary essence, which is a single thing, is not directly known to us. Rather we conceive it indirectly through our multiple universals. Our universals are related to primary essence, the relation being that of *pros hen* equivocals. But they differ from primary essence in mode of existence. Whereas universals are multiple and have mental existence, primary essence is a single thing which exists "in complete reality," i.e., in or as the Active Intellect.

In a second sense what we know by possessing universals are particulars. But we do not know them as particulars. Rather we know them in a universal way. In Gersonides' terms, we know them with respect to their intelligible ordering. Insofar as any particular is intelligible or ordered, it possesses an essence. These essences of particulars are the primary essence of the Active Intellect. These essences are similar to the primary essence in the way that copies are similar to their model. Thus the essences of the particulars and the primary essence are related as *pros hen* equivocals. And they also differ from the primary essence in mode of existence. Whereas the essences of things are multiple and have material existence, primary essence is again a single thing which exists in complete reality.

From a divine or absolute point of view, there is only one thing, namely essence. This essence is the Active Intellect. Yet in existence, mental in the case of universals and material in the case of particulars, this single thing is many. However, once again, all of these different things, universals and particulars, insofar as they are anything are ultimately a single thing, namely the Active Intellect itself. Hence in this way knower and known in the sublunar world are joined together, as is the sublunar world itself, with the translunar world. Essence links the former pair; the Active Intellect links the latter; and on final analysis essence is the Active Intellect.

Individuals and particulars[17]

The above analysis of knowledge would seem to lead to the conclusion that God only knows Himself. What the Active In-

[17] The following discussion is a summary of the textual analysis presented in notes 26, 31, 130, 135, 177, 178, 286, 288, 294, 399, and 436.

tellect knows is its essence, which it knows as a single thing, which in turn is identical with itself, and if this is the case with the Active Intellect, how much the more so must this be the case with God. But Gersonides does not accept this conclusion. At the beginning of Treatise Three Gersonides distinguished two interpretations of Aristotle's position concerning God's knowledge of particulars. The first was that God only knows Himself. But Gersonides judged this to be an erroneous interpretation and a false position. The truth is that God knows individuals, but He knows them in a universal way. Gersonides' analysis of the knowing situation is that it is not universals that are known. Otherwise there would be no alternative but to deny God's knowledge of anything other than Himself. However universals are only the tools of knowledge. What is known is something that is, in the terminology of both Aristotle and Ibn Rushd, accidentally individual and essentially universal. What this means and how Gersonides can claim that God does have the kind of knowledge that Gersonides insists He has, rests on a distinction between what is individual ('iši or y^ehidi in Hebrew) and what is particular (p^erāṭi in Hebrew).

An individual is that which is capable of unique reference. Thus something is known as an individual insofar as that thing is subject to unique reference. Now, all particulars are individuals, but not all individuals are particulars. God and the intelligences are all individual, but none of them are particular. The necessary and sufficient condition for being a particular is having matter. Thus a particular is a material or an embodied individual.

Gersonides claims that God knows particulars as individuals, but He does not know them as particulars. That He does not know particulars is clear. A particular as a particular is material, and there can be no conceptual knowledge of the material. Properly, the material cannot be known at all. Rather, entities which possess senses may have sense acquaintance with particulars. But, again, this is not knowledge.

As we have seen, we know a thing only to the extent that we have concepts which refer to that thing. But concepts are universals which refer to essences and there are no individual essences, i.e., any given essence determines a class to which in principle more than one single entity may belong. However, while it is true that essentially no universal can express a single entity, it may be the case that accidentally the known essence determines a class with only one actual member. This contention may be explained in the following way: the more that is known of a given individual, the more specified that individual is. For example, if I say that Socrates is a philosopher, I have excluded some individuals from this classification, but there are still any number of individuals who fit the description. Once I add that Socrates is Greek, the number of actual candidates for being Socrates is further narrowed, but still there remain many possible candidates. But as each specification is added to the description the list of candidates is narrowed so that by stating that Socrates is an ancient Greek philosopher who lived in Athens, had a snub-nose, and drank hemlock, only one actual candidate remains. It is important to note that there is no essential reason why this description can fit only the single entity, Socrates. The description of Socrates and the particular Socrates are not identical. The description could be satisfactory in this sense only if the matter of Socrates as such could be specified. But this is impossible. Rather it only happens to be the case that there was one and only one individual to whom this description applies. This is what Gersonides means by saying that the object known, namely, the essence, is essentially universal and accidentally individual. Hence, God knows individuals. But He knows them only accidentally. What God knows is a single essence, but this divine essence is expressible in an infinite number of universal, conditional sets, the conjunction of which happens to apply to each and every existent individual.

Our knowledge of individuals is to be understood in a similar way. What we know is a number of essences through which particulars may be singled out for reference. Thus, concerning any existent individual, whether or not we are acquainted with it, we may know it as individual. Thus, I am acquainted from television with President Johnson and to some extent I know him, but I also know Socrates, although I am in no sense acquainted with him. In knowing both individuals I possess a number of universals which refer to a number of essences in such a relation that the combination happens to apply only to single entities. What differentiates God's knowledge from ours in this case is that what we know through multiple essences God knows through a single essence, and whereas the essences that we know in principle can be expressed through a finite number of universal, conditional propositions, the essence that God knows would require for expression an infinite conjunction of these kinds of propositions.

On the basis of this characterization of epistemology and Gersonides' distinction between individuals and particulars, a number of features of Gersonides' understanding of logic can be stated.

Logic[18]

Gersonides is committed to a reference theory of meaning. In other words, for Gersonides, if a term has meaning it refers to some object and that object is the meaning of the term. From this commitment arises a number of problems of logic of which Gersonides is aware and discusses. Specifically these problems revolve around the understanding of references to non-existent objects, general terms, definitions, and modal statements. At the center of Gersonides' answers is his doctrine of essences. However that is not to say that his solution to these problems of logic follows from his position on essences. It might even be the case that his position with respect to essences is a consequence of his solution to these problems of logic. All that properly can be said is that the two discussions are intimately connected in such a way that one entails the other.

*   *
  *

If the meaning (*kiwûn* in Hebrew) of a term is the object to which that term refers (*môreh* in Hebrew), how are we to understand references to mathematical objects on the one hand and non-existent particulars on the other? In both cases there are no existent objects of reference to be what such terms mean. Gersonides' solution to this problem is to reject this last statement, i.e., Gersonides maintains that they do refer to existent objects. There are three ways in which an entity may exist. It may exist materially, in which case the entity is a particular. It may exist

---

[18] The following discussion is a summary of the textual analysis presented in textual notes 3, 10, 20, 22, 26, 42-49, 76, 89, 91, 92, 125, 130, 149, 150, 153, 157, 159-162, 166, 178, 182, 186, 208, 212-214, 270, 283, 285, 293, 301, 316, 322, 352, 358, 457, 476, 507, 542, and 582.

mentally, in which case the entity is a universal or a concept in the mind of the knower. Or it may be an essence, in which case it exists in complete reality. To exist in complete reality is to exist in the Active Intellect. Such existence is distinct from both mental and material existence.

What generates the above problem is the failure to distinguish this third kind of existence. Clearly mathematical objects and non-existent particulars do not have material existence. Recognizing this, if the only other mode of existence is mental, it would follow that these entities exist only in the mind of men. But if this were so, there could be no objective statements about such entities. Yet, in fact there are. Such statements are statements about essences which exist eternally in complete reality in the Active Intellect.

* * *

A similar problem and a similar solution arises concerning general terms. Such terms do not refer to particulars. Yet, only particulars exist materially. Thus, if they refer to universals, since universals exist only in the mind, no general term could have objective reference. Yet in fact general judgments or judgments involving general terms are objective. Again the solution is that general terms refer to essences. They are not class expressions, but neither are they statements about universals. Rather they are expressions which, by means of universals in the mind, refer to essences, which are objective. In other words the objects of reference in this case are external to the mind of the speaker; they exist in complete reality in the Active Intellect.

This is not to say that general terms are not related to class expressions. An essence determines a class of entities of which that essence is what they are. In referring to the essence the speaker refers to the entities in this class with respect to what they are. Thus statements about an essence can be translated into statements about a class of entities. For example the statement "man is mortal" is primarily a statement about the essence, 'man.' But secondarily it is a statement to the effect that if anything is a man then it is mortal. In such cases the members of the class are referred to collectively rather than distributively. This judgment is a consequence of Gersonides' assumption that statements about an infinite number of things as infinite are unintelligible, and classes such as 'man' have an infinite number of members.

* * *

How we may speak about what is numerically infinite is answered as a corollary to the above discussion of references to classes of entities. The essence of a thing, being what a thing is, is the prime cause of a thing. What "cause" means in this case can be expressed in the following way: if something happens to a particular entity, that event could befall that entity only because the entity is the kind of entity that it is. If wood burns under the same circumstances in which iron does not, this is only because wood is the kind of thing that it is and iron is the kind of thing that it is. Thus one way of stating what wood is includes the statement that if certain circumstances obtain then wood will burn, which is what it means to say that wood is combustible. Similarly one way of stating what iron is includes the statement that iron is not combustible. In other words statements about essences entail statements about the dispositional properties of what has the essence. But what dispositional properties state are processes to which an entity may be subject

which are infinite in number. In other words if I say that wood
is inflammable, I am saying that every time something that is
wood is subject to certain circumstances then it will burn, and
the number of such possible instances are infinite. But the
statement "wood is inflammable" is not a statement about an
infinite number of entities with certain properties. Rather it is a
statement about a process to which anything that is wood will be
subject, and that the occurrence of instances of this process is
endless. However the statement is about the process itself and
not about the instances of that process.

* *
*

In a similar way Gersonides approaches the question of what
are definitions. Predicates are either accidents, in which case
they state something about a subject, or they are essential, in
which case they state what a subject is. Definitions always involve the latter kind of predicates. Now all definitions are identity or equivalence statements, so that in saying "*a* is *b*" I am
asserting that *a* and *b* are identical or equivalent. Given this
characterization, it follows that there are two kinds of
definitions. The first kind are called "nominal." In such cases I
simply explain how a word is used. For example the sentence,
"men are *homo sapiens*" tells us that the terms on both sides of
the equation have the same meaning and reference. Such
statements are tautologies which give us no information about
the world. Yet there are other definitions to which this characterization does not apply. In statements such as "man is a
rational animal" we presumably know something about the
world that we did not otherwise know. Such statements are
called "real definitions." They are to be regarded as statements
about the essence of things and not about terms. Thus the state-

ment "man is a rational animal" is a statement about the essence, 'man,' and not about the term, "man."

Real definitions also are characterized as disguised causal statements. Since an essence is the cause of the existence of those things which have that essence, to state an essence is to give a formula which exhibits the cause of a thing's existence. The statement of the essence is a disguised causal statement because, as we already noted, such a statement can be expressed in a secondary sense in terms of the dispositional properties of the things which embody that essence.

The distinction between these two kinds of definitions may be summarized as follows. The former kind, which deal primarily with the use of words, are reducible to the form, "*a* is *a*." But this is not so with the latter kind, which deal primarily with designating essences. Their form is "*a* is *b*." However, by such a statement we may understand the definition to state that *b* is the cause of something becoming *a*.

From this discussion of definitions it follows that while everything that exists in the sublunar world is a particular and everything that characterizes a particular is a universal, a definition is neither. For example, in the statement "a unicorn is a single-horned horse" we are not discussing, in the primary sense of the statement, all unicorns. In other words, the statement "a unicorn is ..." is not identical with the statement "if anything is a unicorn, then ...," although the latter is entailed by the former. But neither are we discussing something which is a unicorn. If that were the case it would be false to say "a unicorn is ...," since there are no unicorns. Rather "a unicorn" refers to the essence, unicorn, which exists in complete reality, i.e., eternally in the Active Intellect.

It also follows from this characterization that terms as defined and as used with reference to things are *pros hen* equivocal. Thus, the "unicorn" of the definition and the "unicorn" in "given anything if it is a unicorn then ..." are *pros hen* equivocal.

* * *

Gersonides employs three modal expressions, which are possibility, impossibility and necessity. This set of terms is applied in two different ways. It is applied to propositions, and it also is applied to things. A proposition is necessary if and only if there is no doubt that the proposition is true. A proposition is impossible if and only if there is no doubt that it is false. A proposition is possible if there is such doubt. What it means to say that there is no doubt that the proposition in question is true is that the contrary state of affairs cannot obtain. Thus the criterion is objective and not subjective. In other words to say that a proposition is necessary, impossible or possible is to say something about the nature of the reported state of affairs and it is not a statement about the mental state of the person or persons uttering this statement. In other words the use of these modal expressions with regard to propositions is secondary with respect to their use with regard to things.

As applied to things, these modal terms express how something exists. Something is possible if the cause of its existence is other than itself. A corollary of this definition is that everything possible, if and when it exists, has material existence. Conversely something is necessary if the cause of its existence is itself and not something other than itself. Two corollaries of this definition are that a necessary being is identical with its essence and that no necessary being is material. Something is impossible or a chimera if the cause of its not existing is itself. Such things do not exist in any way, i.e., there is no essence of a chimera which exists in the Active Intellect.

The logical and ontological status of possible entities that do not exist presented a problem for Gersonides and his Aristotelian contemporaries. The question was not so much with possible entities which will exist in the future, but with possibles or contingents which will never come to be. The problem is how to account for entities being possible while at the same time never being realized. In other words how can something that will never be realized be possible?

The question is closely tied to Gersonides' understanding of Aristotle's problem of the status of propositions about future contingents. As expressed by Aristotle, the problem was stated in the following way. Consider a sea-battle that either will or will not take place tomorrow. The compound proposition "a sea-battle will occur tomorrow or a sea-battle will not occur tomorrow" is necessarily true. Now all propositions are either true or false, and the truth value of compound propositions is a function of the truth value of the simple propositions of which they are composed. But this would seem to mean that the truth value of the component simple propositions is determined, so that the proposition "a sea-battle will occur tomorrow" is now, before the event, determined to be true or false. But if this were so, the occurrence of the sea-battle would be determined to take place or not to take place, in which case it would be a necessary and not a possible state-of-affairs.

Ibn Sina solved this problem by distinguishing two senses of necessity. Something is necessary in itself if it is determined by itself, and something is necessary in virtue of a cause if it is determined by some cause other than itself. Ibn Sina maintained that only God is necessary in the primary sense of the term, i.e., in itself, but that everything else also is necessary, but they are necessary in the secondary sense of necessity, i.e., in virtue of a cause. However, such a solution would not be acceptable to either Aristotle or Gersonides for whom being possible meant really being subject to choice.

Aristotle's solution to the problem is that statements about future contingents are either true or false, but their truth value is not determinate before the event. The truth value of the proposition, "a sea-battle will or will not occur tomorrow" follows from the range of possible truth values of the component simple propositions rather than from the actual truth values of the components. In other words, the proposition "a sea-battle will occur tomorrow" where the sea-battle does not occur, has no truth-value before the event, and after the designated time that the event will have occurred if it would have occurred, the proposition is false. However what makes Aristotle's solution problematic for Gersonides is the introduction of the consideration of God's knowledge. If Aristotle is right, then the truth-value of this proposition changes, i.e., at one time it has no determinate value and at another time it has one. But if God is to know this proposition, then God's knowledge would have to be subject to change, which is not possible.

Gersonides' solution is to deny that God knows at any time a proposition such as this. God knows the essence or nature of sea battles and similarly God knows the essence and nature of the participants who may or may not enter into this sea-battle. In this way He knows the sea-battle, i.e., with respect to its intelligible ordering. But God does not know the sea-battle as a particular sea-battle. Hence, in this way the objection to Aristotle's solution of the problem is removed.

By implication Gersonides also distinguishes two senses of

the term "necessity" as it modifies propositions. In one sense a proposition is necessary if the contrary of the state of affairs that it expresses cannot be possible. Let us call such necessity "logical necessity." But this necessity is to be distinguished from another sense of necessity where a proposition is necessary if the contrary of the state of affairs expressed can be possible, but cannot be actual. Let us call this kind of necessity "natural necessity." The distinction is meant primarily to account for situations such as the following: it is necessarily the case that if Israel goes to war against Babylonia, then Israel will be destroyed. The necessity is a consequence of the essence of Israel, the essence of Babylonia, and the essence of war. But this is no logical necessity.[19] It is something different, inexplicable within the framework of material implication. This kind of necessity is natural necessity. The essence of a thing is the cause of a thing becoming in a certain way. As caused by its essence, that thing necessarily is what it is. But this is not simply a verbal necessity. Statements of essences, as we already have noted, are not tautologies. Rather they are causal statements giving real knowledge.

* * *

The underlying logic of Gersonides' discussion of God's knowledge differs from modern logic of material implication in yet another way. For Gersonides most propositions are not simply either true or false; rather they admit of degrees of truth.

---

[19] For example, we cannot reduce the statement "it is necessarily the case that if Israel goes to war with Babylonia, then Israel will be destroyed" to the statement "Israel will be destroyed if and only if Israel goes to war with Babylonia," for the truth may be that Israel will not go into this war and Israel will be destroyed anyway.

Superficially it might seem that the difference is only verbal. At one level what Gersonides seems to mean by saying that arguments contain aspects of plausibility is the following: with some arguments the premises are true but the conclusion is false. Where we would say in this instance that the argument is invalid, Gersonides would say that insofar as the argument contains true premises it is in some respect true.

However most of the cases that Gersonides has in mind are not of this sort. Primarily Gersonides is thinking of cases where the premises are true and the conclusion is ambiguous, so that on one reading the conclusion is true and on another reading it is false. Here again the difference would seem to be verbal. Whereas we would say that the argument in its present ambiguous form is invalid, Gersonides would say that insofar as the ambiguity is expressible in a true and clear proposition, the argument contains an aspect of plausibility or truth.

But the difference is even more radical. We would say that only arguments and propositions which are univocal in meaning can be considered to have truth values and concerning such propositions they are either true or false. But by this criterion, given Gersonides' theory of knowledge, no proposition conceived by man purporting to yield knowledge could be considered true or false, for all human conceptions of the world are to some extent ambiguous. This can be explained in the following way: As we have seen already, to know a thing is to know its essence. But only God who is the cause of the thing has an adequate conception of the essence of anything. Since our knowledge of a thing arises as a consequent of the effects of the thing upon our senses, our conception of the essence is necessarily limited. It is in some sense like the real essence that only God knows, but the likeness is only a likeness. As we have noted already, the relation of the essences that we know to the essence that God knows is that of *pros hen* equivocation. Thus only the essence that God knows, as the primary instance of that essence, is unqualifiedly true. All other essences that we know are also true, but not absolutely. They are subject to degrees of truth.

Gersonides' doctrine of degrees of truth can be explained in terms of picturing. The essence that God knows is the original. It is unqualified reality. Every essence that we know, as is also the case with everything in the material world, is an image or a likeness of that original, and as pictures vary in degree of accuracy in copying or imaging the original, so do things and concepts vary in degree of accuracy. With respect to the variation of entities, we speak of degrees of reality. Thus the intelligences have a greater degree of reality than do material things, since they, as likenesses of the divine, are closer to or more like the divine than are the entities of the sublunar world. Similarly, with respect to the variation of concepts, we speak of degrees of truth. Thus all concepts can be organized in principle into a hierarchy of concepts varying in degree of truth as they more or less closely approximate the single essence which is God.

VI

Postscript to the Discussion

What is the relationship between God (the essence in complete reality), universals (essence whose existence is mental) and particulars (essence whose existence is material)? They are all one thing, viz. essence, but they are essence *pros hen* equivocally. In saying this Gersonides is not confusing the general nature of *pros hen* equivocation with the specific relation that holds between these three instances of essence. Gersonides assumes, as did his Aristotelian predecessors, that things named and not names are equivocal in the primary sense of the term. A name is equivocal because the things that it names are equivocal and the way in which the term is applied equivocally to multiple things is the sign of the way in which the things named themselves are equivocal. Thus by telling us that these three instances of essence are *pros hen* equivocal Gersonides is expressing what he contends is the relationship between these three instances of essence and not merely three applications of the term, "essence."

In general when a name applies to one thing in a primary sense and the sense of the application of that same name to other things is different from but made with reference to the one original thing, those things are *pros hen* equivocal. In this way a knife and a scissors are called "medical" because they refer to the "medical"-in-the-primary-sense-of-the-word activities of the physician. Now it is clear how the knife and the scissors are related to the physician so that all three can be called "medical" *pros hen* equivocally. They are tools for the physician in performing his art. In saying that they are "medical" we refer through them to medicine, the art of the physician, and express a relationship between the knife, the scissors and the physician, viz. we assert that the former two are tools by which the latter performs his art. But it is not clear how universals and particulars are related to God so that all three can be called "essence" *pros hen* equivocally. Gersonides does not tell us, but this answer needs qualification.

Gersonides does not tell us because it is not his problem. He is not presenting a total system. Both Gersonides and his readers are informed and believing "Aristotelians." Gersonides comes not to replace this system. Rather he seeks to solve certain problems that arise within the system. The source of the problems is Maimonides' *Guide*. Gersonides limits his discussion only to the problems discussed that arise in the *Guide*. He does not provide an analysis of *pros hen* equivocation in this context because he does not consider this form of equivocation to be problematic and he can assume that his readers are familiar with *pros hen* equivocation from Aristotle's discussion in the *Metaphysics* of *ousia* as equivocal in this sense. Thus Gersonides simply tells us that all of the attributes of God including the attribute of knowledge are related to our attributes in the same way that we and God are *ousia*.

At the same time, while no account of the relationship in question is given, Gersonides does give us a "hint" in his account of how we are to understand the relationship between God's knowing and our knowing as *pros hen* equivocal. This is his use of the architect analogy for God's creation of the world. Consider a building. The way by which we who encounter this building know the building is different from how the architect knows it. We walk around and through the building seeing it and feeling it. Each view from each new perspective gives us a picture of a different aspect of this building on the basis of which we construct an image of the building itself independent of any of the particular perspectives from which we are viewing the building. Our picture of the building is derived from the building itself. But the case is entirely different with the architect. He has conceived a model or a blueprint which is for him the building that he wants to build. From this blueprint he constructs the building itself. In his case the building is an effect of the conception whereas in our case the conception is an effect of the building. As our picturing of the building is more or less like the building, the building is more or less like the architect's conception of the building. Now we might be inclined to say in this case that the primary application of the term "building" is the material structure and both the architect's blueprint and our picture are called "building" in a derivative sense, but as Gersonides intends the analogy the primary instance of "building" is the conception or plan of the architect.

However, once we move from the discussion of the knower and the known with respect to knowledge to the related discussion of the knower and the known with respect to existence, Gersonides' explanation becomes less clear. On the architect analogy the building, the architect's plan for the building, and our conception of the building are numerically distinct entities. Are the essence in matter, the essence in complete reality, and the universal numerically distinct? Clearly Gersonides would answer in the affirmative for he neither denies the real existence of particulars, nor the real existence of the intellects which have universals, nor the real existence of God. Yet are they not also a single thing? Again clearly Gersonides would have to answer in the affirmative since God knows every individual with respect to its essence as a single essence. But how can both affirmations be made?

The problem may be stated more precisely in the following way: the essence of a particular is not something predicated of that particular; it is what that particular is. The same is true of the essence which is a universal and the essence that God knows. This leads Gersonides to assert an identity between the essence of a particular and that particular. Furthermore we can generalize this statement and assert an identity between the essence that is material and each and every particular. Similarly we can assert an identity between the essence that is mental and each and every universal as well as between the essence that is in complete reality and God. Finally we can assert an identity between all three essences. Thus an infinite number of seemingly distinct particulars and a great number of seemingly distinct universals and God are all identified as one through the identification of a thing with its essence. Now there is no objection to identifying God and His essence. In any case this identification is a consequence of God's unity. Nor need it be objectionable to say that a universal is identical with its essence, even though we might say that this is a strange way to speak about a universal. A universal being non-material simply is what it is. But surely no particular is identical with its essence. Such an analysis overlooks that the particular is material. Furthermore if essence in mind is every universal then every universal is identical, and since essence in matter is every particular then every particular is identical. Clearly Gersonides cannot plausibly make either assertion, let alone affirm the ultimate identity of God and the world.

The answer and the problem lie in the ambiguity of Gersonides' use of the term "numerical unity." Aristotle tells us that things are one in number when they have the same matter. In this sense universals, material objects, and God are not one. Yet what Gersonides seems to mean when he asserts that things are numerically one is the sense in which Aristotle says that diverse things are one when there is a single essence which determines them to constitute the same numerical unit of measure. In this sense two things a and b are said to be one when there is a single predicate F which is essentially true of both a and b. In this sense universals, material objects and God are one in that they are ultimately a single essence, God. In other words particulars and their essence are one with respect to essence, universals and their essence are one with respect to essence, God and His essence are one with respect to essence, and the essence spoken of in each of these statements is the same essence.

The way in which these different things are both distinct and yet one may be illustrated in the following way. Imagine a single object reflected through ten thousand mirrors related in such a way that mirror 1 reflects the original, mirror 2 reflects the reflection in mirror 1, ..., mirror 10,000 reflects the reflection in mirror 9,999. Imagine further that each mirror has its own unique built-in distortion which alters the reflection that it is reflecting. Finally imagine an infinite number of additional mirrors each with its own peculiar distortions reflecting the reflection in mirror 10,000. This metaphor was used widely by the rabbis to explain in what way man knows God. Therefore it is likely that Gersonides was familiar with the image. In the metaphor the single object is God, mirror 10,000 is the Active Intellect, and we are the infinite number of additional mirrors mirroring mirror 10,000. Each reflection is distinct from the original in species and in genus. Also each reflection is distinct in number where what it means to be numerically one is to have the same matter. (Each mirror is a different mirror.) Yet what each mirror is is a mirror that reflects a given reflection. In the metaphor the reflection is the essence of the thing and the mirror itself is the matter. Insofar as the reflections of the mirror are the mirror, all of the mirrors can be said to be one in the sense of numerical unity where there is an essence, viz. the original object God, which determines them to constitute a same numerical unit of measure. In other words in each mirror what one sees is not properly speaking a copy of the original in the same way that a picture is a copy of its model. Rather it is the original. Only it is that original distorted through the limitations of the mirror itself. Thus concerning any reflection we can say that it is the original reflected. Similarly each individual is God reflected through matter in the case of particulars and through intellect in the case of universals.

* *
*

I think that this is the most satisfactory interpretation that can be given of what Gersonides means when he says that God knows particulars with respect to their essence and that God does so in knowing a single essence. It is the best that Gersonides can do to preserve both the claim that God knows particulars and the claim that God can have only a single object of knowledge. Can it not be objected that the price that Gersonides has paid for his solution is to deny the reality of everything other than God? Not in the light of his doctrine of degrees of reality. It is true that God alone exists in complete reality, but for Gersonides this is not the only way in which things exist. Everything else also exists, but its degree of existence is less than the degree of God's existence. Again consider the mirror metaphor. The reflection of an object is real and in a certain sense is distinct from the reflected object. But it exists as a reflection of that object and not as something in itself. In this sense what it means to say that the degree of existence of the reflection is less than the degree of existence of the reflected object is the following. (1) The existence of the former is causally dependent upon the existence of the latter and this relationship is not reciprocal. By asserting that the reflection is "causally dependent" upon the reflected object what is meant is that the former is present only if the latter is present. (2) The former exists in order to be a reflection of the latter. As such it is more or less like that for which it exists, and this relationship is not reciprocal. To the extent that the reflection is unlike the reflected object the degree of the existence of the former is less than the degree of existence of the latter.

It might be objected that while the reflection is less like the reflected object than is the reflected object like itself that does not mean that the reflection has less existence than does the reflected object. But remember that on the basis of this metaphor what distinguishes the reflection from the reflected object is the mirror itself and on the basis of this analogy the mirror is matter or the way in which the single reflected essence exists. The essence independent of its mode of existence is not subject to variant degrees of perfection. The variation arises only with respect to the different modes or ways of existence.

However there is another level at which Gersonides cannot escape criticism. While on Gersonides' account God can know an individual with respect to what an individual is, I cannot see how God can know one individual as distinct from another individual given that God can know only a single essence. In knowing the essence of numbers I may know what each number is, but what sense does it make to say that I know any number if I cannot distinguish *1* from *2* from *3* etc.? I would see them as distinct only if each had a distinct essence. At times this seems to be a correct inference when Gersonides speaks of knowledge of the essence being sufficient to identify an individual. On the mirroring analogy in knowing the nature of the distinct distortion of each mirror one can know how the reflection in each mirror is unique without the implication that what is reflected in each mirror is unique. But then God must not only know the original reflected. Also He must know the mirror, and God cannot know this since the mirror itself according to the analogy is matter. We might make the move that Crescas subsequently makes to posit a material form. But this move only puts off the problem and does not solve it. Again we must explain how God can know in a single act of knowing each distinct mirror irrespective of what it reflects.

There seems to be one other alternative open to Gersonides. He might argue that for both God and us there is no knowledge of the individual. The only proper object of knowledge is God. There are times when Gersonides seems to be saying this when he emphasizes that the universals which we attain from acquaintance with material objects are the tools by which we know essences. In other words the only real candidates for objects of knowledge are essences and essences ultimately are God. By following this path Gersonides seems to reconcile successfully what he sought to reconcile. But he pays a great price for his success since most of the kinds of things of which we *prima facie* would claim to be instances of knowledge are no longer instances of knowledge, viz. knowing that certain predicates, whether they be essential or accidental, are predicated of material objects. Thus from the fact that I see a red table it is true that the table is red but for Gersonides it could not be said that I *know* that the table is red. This seems to be the implication of Gersonides' claim that for God not to know particulars attributes no imperfection to God. In other words God is not lacking in not knowing propositions about particulars since truly affirmed propositions about particulars would not be for Gersonides instances of knowledge.

VII

THE TEXT

The library of the Hebrew Union College-Jewish Institute of Religion in Cincinnati, Ohio possesses two first editions of *The Wars of the Lord* published in 1560 in Riva di Trento.[20] One of these copies contains manuscript notes written in an Italian hand in the seventeenth or eighteenth century. These notes for the most part are variant readings from an evidently better manuscript than the one upon which the editio princeps is based. All variations are apparently recorded in these notes, and on the basis of them it is possible to conclude that the author must have had before him one of the best manuscripts in existence. The readings are better than any manuscript readings given by Kellermann in his German translation of *The Wars of the Lord*,[21] with the exception of those taken from the Oxford manuscript to which our manuscript notes are closest. Furthermore of the one hundred fifty-three text corrections listed by Touati, ninety-six of them are included among these readings and of Touati's remaining fifty-seven text corrections only twelve of them in any significant sense affect the meaning of the passages in question.

These manuscript notes extend over the whole of the book. These glosses, together with the textual corrections suggested by Touati on the basis of his examination of eight other

---

[20] [Levi ben Gershon], מלחמות השם [Milḥamot ha-Shem], (Riva di Trento, 1560).

[21] [Levi ben Gershon], מלחמות השם [Milḥamot ha-Shem], (Leipzig, 1866).

manuscripts,[22] have been incorporated into the Hebrew text that served as the basis for the English translation presented here. I have indicated the pagination of both the Leipzig and the Riva di Trento editions in the text of the translation. The pagination of the Leipzig edition is included in parentheses in the body of the text itself, while the pagination of the editio princeps is given in the margins.

In my translation I have attempted to be as literal as is possible without losing the text's meaning, leaving my commentary on the text for the footnotes.

Manuscript variations from the Leipzig edition used in this translation

Arabic numerals refer to pages in the Leipzig edition.

( ) encloses letters or words omitted from the Leipzig edition.

< > encloses letters or words added to the Leipzig edition.

120· ‹והוא נחלק לששה פרקים› || זכר ‹הרב› המורה ‹בזה› || נאות (מאד) מכל הפנים· || (אם יודע) או ידע … (אם) ‹או› לא ידעם· || נבאר (בו) הצד אשר ‹בו› יפול (בו) האמת (בבטולו) (הנמשכים אחריו בזה לשתי דעות)· || לא ידע (מ)אלו הדברים ||

121 אבל (הוא) לא ידע || אבל (התחדש מה שהיה יודע מקומם שיתחדש על) ‹כפי› מה || כבר יחשב (לו שיהיו) ‹שיהיו לו› פנים ‹רבים› מה הראות·

122 בלתי (יודע) ‹משיג› אלו הדברים הפרטיים· || אי אפשר (להשיג) ‹שישיג› הדברים הזמניים· || שישיג (הענינים) הזמניים· || נחבר (לו) ‹אל› זאת

---

[22] Levi ben Gerson, *Les guerres du seigneur, livres 3 et 4*, transl. Charles Touati (Paris: Mouton, 1968), pp. 31-36.

התולדה הקדמה אחת ‹יודע› (יודע) ‹ידוע› בה· ‖ תהייב (ב)‹שלא תפול› ‖ שאם
הונח ‹העניין כן› ‖ באלו ‹הדברים› המתחדשים ‖

123   בענינים (האפשריים) ‹המתחדשים› ‖ (ועתה) ‹ואחר היותם› הוסר ‹ששתי
החלוקות האחרונות מאלו› האפשרות· ‖ החלוקות ‹האחרונות› מאלו
החלוקות (האחרונות) ‖ מהחכמ(ות)‹ה› ‖ (והמבואר) ‹וזה מבואר› ממה
שאמר

124   הפלוסופים ‹או› מכח (משיג) ‹יודע› בלתי ‹יודע› אלו העניינים הפרטים· (וזה)
‹והיא› שאם ‹היה· ‖ המתדבק ‹הוא› מתחלק ‖ הנה יהי(ה)‹ו› בכמה ‖ וזה
בטל (כל) ‹ר״ל· שיהיו בכמה המתדבק ‹כמה ‖ שהוא› יודע ‹כל הדברים›
לא ‖ יודע ‹דבר מ› אלו ‖ טוב ‹י›ברח מן (הטוב) ‹הרע› (ונפל) ‹ויפול›
ביותר ‖ שכבר (יראה) ‹יקרה· ‖

125   ידיע (אמיתית) שלימה ‖ כל מה ש(נ)‹י›תחדש בו ‖ הטביעו‹בו› ואנחנו ‖
כל ‹אלו› הדברים המתחדשים ‖ כי (מי) שלא יראה ‹ב›הרבה ‖
מ(מי)‹שיראה·

12.   הוא ‹מבואר ראוי שהוא› (ש)‹יונח ‖ החמשה (אם) ‹אשר› הם ‹אשר ‖ אפשר
שימצא› בידיעתנו ‖ אבאר לך ‹זה› בזכרי ‖ הרבים ‹ה›ידועים
מתאחדים· ‖ והוא ‹מבואר› שאי ‖ הרבוי ‹הבלתי› מתאחד

12.   שהם ‹עתה› נעדרים ‖ הפלוני ‹ויעדרו בזמן הפלוני· הנה ‖ המקרה
ה‹נעדר ‖ הידוע› ‹בו› בלתי נמצאת· ‖ שאם הי(ת)‹ה› הידיעה ‖ שיהיה
הידוע(ה) אשר ‖ בנפשו (כי) ‹אשר› הוא ‖ שיקיים בה(ם) הרב ‖ פרטים
(עהוא ירצה) ‹שכבר ידמה מהטעונה› עתהיה

12.   לא רצה (לנו) לבאר ‹לנו› מזאת ‖ ז״ל (יעויין שם) ‹בזה העניין שם›·
הוא ‹בו בלתי ‖ הידוע (מחויב) ‹מגיע› אבל

12.   שיחשב ש(י)רצה אותו· ‖ האפשר ‹הנה› הוא ‹מה שהשבנו שיגיע›
הנה ‖ טעות (ו)‹לא› להמחשבה גם כן מקבלת ‖ על ‹דרך› ייחוד ‖
מבואר (ב)‹מ›לשונו ‖ יותר רבי(ם) המספר ‖

1:     שנה ‹דרך משל› חלקים ‖ שלמקר(י)‹ה› האחרון ‖ שיגיעו יהי(ה)‹ו› ‖
העניין (נמצא ש)‹יתבאר שאי ‖ גם כן ‹כבר› מחויב ‖ שהתחדש (היא) ‹הוא›
(סכלות) ‹חסרון› יותר (וחסרון) ‖ ימנע ‹העניין ‹העניין› מחלוקה: ‖

1:     כבר (יראה) ‹יקרה› בהרבה ‖ ומי ‹שיחשוב› שכבר ‖ ובלתי מתחדש‹ת›כמו
‖ כאלו השתדל(ו)‹נו›

1   בזאת (הידיעה) ‹החקירה› הוא ‖ יתברך (או) ‹אל שיהיה ‖ או ‹אם›

יהיה || הנה ⟨זה⟩ ממה || זה⟩ עליהם ⟨הוא ⟨הוא⟩ באחור || הוא⟩ מנהגם ⟨רצוני⟩ שהם ||
ועצמותו ⟨הוא לו מעצמו וממנו ישפע מציאות כל נמצא ואחדותו ועצמותו·
ומה || השמות (הנקראים) ⟨הנאמרים⟩

133   שהיא ⟨ממה שהוא⟩ שלמות || מזולתה· (ו)במה שהוא⟩ בפועל· ⟨נאמר
שהוא⟩ ⟨חייבנו בשם· יתברך ⟨שהוא⟩ || לנו ממ(ה) ⟨נו⟩ || אחד ל⟨מ⟩שכ⟨י⟩ל
ולמתדבק || כמו (שקדם) ⟨שהתבאר במה שקדם⟩ ·

134   הנמצאים ⟨לנו⟩· כשנשללם ⟨לפי ⟨סבל⟩ מחשבתנו⟩ [Touati text reads
« אצל מחשבתנו »] || חייבנום ⟨לו⟩· או || יהיה ⟨ב⟩כאן || בשוללות
⟨מ⟩השם || ונחייב ⟨לו⟩ הידיעה || שלמות ⟨לנו⟩· וזה

135   בזאת (הדברים) ⟨הידיעה⟩ אלו || שבארנו ⟨מ⟩מה שהשרישו || ר''ל (מפני ש)
⟨שכמו⟩ זאת ⟨כ⟩ רב (מאד) אמר || מהדברים ⟨הנאמרים ⟨בנבריאו || יתואר
(ב)⟨ה⟩שם ⟨ב⟩איזה תאר· שיהיה ⟨הנה⟩ || העניין ⟨בזה⟩ מי

136   גלגל הש(כל) ⟨מש⟩ ⟨דרך משל⟩ || אין שם ⟨ה⟩שכל נושא || אותם (זה) ⟨שם⟩
השכל || שיסכימו קצת⟨ם⟩לקצת || כל ⟨שאר⟩ הדברים (השאר) בתאר ||
ו(כל)שאר ⟨כל⟩ הנמצאים || ועומד מזולת(ם)⟨ו⟩·

137   מה שמו (מה אומר אליהם)· || ורוצה ⟨ועושה⟩ ושהוא || רוחק ⟨כוונת ⟨אלו
נאמרים ⟨בו⟩ בזולתו || שיהיה ⟨ה⟩מחלוקת || מפני ש(הוא) ⟨יהיה⟩ מבואר
|| כי מ⟨ה⟩שפע ||

138   העניינים ⟨הפרטיים·⟩ כלם || כל ⟨שאר⟩ הנמצאות || הוא מ⟨בואר שי⟩ חייב
⟨מזה⟩ שיהיה || כמו ש(ראוי) ⟨יחויב⟩ למי ⟨בו⟩ הם || מסודרים || שם
אות(ם)⟨ה⟩· באדם

139   הוא ⟨אשר⟩· יגיע (ל)⟨ב⟩חקו· || חסרון (ל)⟨ב⟩חקו· || כמו ⟨שצוה⟩ צדקיה || נבאר ⟨ש⟩אלו
הטענות || הדברים ⟨איך⟩ לא קיום || אלא (ב)⟨שידע הסדורים || מקבל
רצו(נ)⟨י⟩⟨ה⟩פועל || גדול ו⟨לזה⟩ לא יצטרך || שהוא ⟨זה ה⟩פרטי· || החומר
רצו(נ)⟨י⟩ הצורה

140   בנפשו יתנועע⟨ו⟩ תכף מהציור ההוא (אל) ⟨כלי הקול⟩ באלו⟩ התנועות ||
בדרך שיב(ו)⟨ט⟩א(ו) באות ⟨ו⟩ יודע ⟨כל⟩ אלו הדברים להרחיק ממנו ⟨חסרון
הסכלות

141   פרטיים ⟨ורמוז עליהם וזה מבואר בנפשו⟩· – || שהם ⟨בו⟩ כוללים ולא
מה שהם בו || אשר הקנה ⟨ל⟩אלו || בכאן לא (ב)⟨מה שהם ⟨בו⟩ משותפים
(בו) || ולא (ב)⟨מה שהם || כי היא (לא) ⟨אינה⟩ תהיה || מתחלק (ע)⟨א⟩ל
היותר חסר ו(ע)⟨א⟩ל היותר

142 שהנחנוהו‹מ›ה ידיעה ל‹ה›שם יתברך באלו ה‹צדד›‹דבר›ים· || אבל הם ‹מופפר› ‹מוקף› ים בהכרח || בטבעם מהאפשר‹ות›· || אשר הם ‹בו› מסודרים

143 הצד אשר ‹ל›‹אלו || וזה ‹ה›‹הפך מה ‹ה› יודע ‹כל› אלו || השם יתברך ‹ל›‹ב›אלו החלקים· || בזאת ‹החלוקה› ‹ה›ידיעה חסרה· – || אשר לו ‹בה› ‹ב›‹חלק· הנה ‹לא› || ישאר ‹בחלק› אפשרות ‹טעות ‹ו›‹לא ידיעה· || ‹ו›‹אולם מה || מורכב ‹ל›‹מ›חלקים בלתי || אשר היא אפשר‹ו›‹י›ת לכמ‹ות›‹ה› בשלמות· ‹וזה ‹ה› החלקים ‹אשר אפשר› שיחלק

144 דברים ‹בלתי› מקלים || יחשב ‹שיחויב› מזה || הספק ‹ב›‹כמו ההתר || ההתר ‹ה›‹הוא || אפשר הוא ‹ה›החלק בכח· לא ‹ה›‹החלק || בכללות‹ו› בכח || בגשם גשם שה‹ו›‹י›א מקבלת ‹ה›החלק || מקבלות ‹ה›‹החלק || הדבר ‹ה›‹נפרד || הגודל על ‹ה›‹נקודת שאי אפשר שיפול ה‹נ›‹ה›‹חלק על ‹הנקודה אשר תלוה אליה· וכבר היה אפשר זה בה קודם שיפול ההחלק על ה‹נקודה אחרת· כמו ש‹ה›‹היה ‹ל› עליה ‹ה›‹החלק·

145 נפל עליה ‹ה›החלק בראשונה· נתבטל ‹ה›‹אפשרות ‹ב›‹ה›‹החלק ‹כ›‹ב›‹אשר ‹פגשת הנקודה› || שנחלקהו ב‹חלוקת› נקודה || מבוארי· ‹וזה› כי || ימנה ‹ה›החלק על ‹י› שיעור מו‹ק›‹ג›‹בל לא || אפשר ‹יקרה מהנחתו בטל· והנה יבאר שכבר הונח בזה המאמר נמצא מה שלא היה אפשר· וזה || אל מה ש‹א›י‹ אפשר שיחלק· || כפי מה ש‹ו›‹י›א בטבעה || תכלית ‹ה›‹ל›‹חלוקה אשר

14 נמצא ‹בהם› בפעל || מפני ש‹שני› אלו || מהם ‹במספר› בלתי בעלי תכלית ‹במספר›· || ‹וזה ‹מבואר› ‹בתכלית› ‹הבטול· || אל שני ‹ה›חלקים· || אל שני ‹ה›חלקים·

14 כלה ע‹ד›‹ל› שיהיה || בבאורנו לספר‹י› ‹השמע› ‹הטבע›· || ימצאו ‹יחד› בכח || השם יתברך ‹אלו› הדברים ‹האלו› ‹כלם›· || בשלמות ‹על› ‹ש›‹מה שהתבאר‹ל›‹נו || והוא ‹ב›‹כ›שנשכיל || יתברך ‹ל›‹ב›אלו הדברים || הוא ‹מבואר› שלא יחויב

14 אשר הם בו ‹מפורדים› ‹מסודרים› ‹וישארו || לבא ‹עלינו› ונקח || הידיעה ‹ההיא› בו· || הנה ה‹י›‹ו›‹א ‹א›‹ג›‹ם כן דבר || על פי שיגיע ‹מקביל›‹מה

14 ידיעתו בהתחדש ‹המתחדש מ‹אל הדברים· || ידיעה בו· ‹וזה מבואר מאוד למעיין בזה הספר·› || בואם· באמר‹ם› ‹ו› || כי || מסודרים· ו‹הוא›

יודע שהם ‖ יצר (לב) יחד ⟨לב⟩ בני ⟨לב⟩ ‖ לא שת(כ)⟨ת⟩לה ידיעתו ‖ תורתנו
היא ש⟨רצון⟩ השם

150 מה שהנחנו אות(ו)⟨ה⟩ ‖ לפי מה ⟨ש⟩ אשר התבאר⟨ו⟩מצד ‖ בשלא תהר(ו)ס
בזה ‖ רבים ממנ(ו)⟨ה⟩ ‖ בספרו ‖ בפרק (ה)⟨עשרים ‖ שכבר נט(ו)⟨ה⟩ קצת ‖
העיון ⟨לאמר⟩ שהידיעה ‖ חלק על ⟨דרך כל ולא על⟩ דרך חלק·

TREATISE THREE OF
THE WARS OF THE LORD :
ON GOD'S KNOWLEDGE

TREATISE THREE

ON GOD'S KNOWLEDGE OF THINGS, MAY HE BE BLESSED

(*120**) It is divided into three chapters. — In chapter one we shall mention the views of our predecessors on this question. — In chapter two we shall mention the arguments used by our predecessors to establish each one of their views as we find them in the statements of these thinkers or in the logical implications of their words. — In chapter three we shall investigate whether or not the arguments of The Master The Guide, may his memory be blessed,[1] logically suffice. — In chapter four we shall complete the discussion of how God, may He be blessed, knows things as considered from the speculative point of view, and we shall make clear that nothing in the arguments of our predecessors disproves what is evident to us concerning this knowledge. — In chapter five it will be made completely clear that what is evident to us concerning this knowledge is adequate in every respect. — In chapter six it will be explained that our conclusion from Philosophic Thought concerning this knowledge is the same as the view of our Torah.[2]

---

* Marginal numbers give the pagination of the 1560 Riva di Trento editio princeps, italic numbers in parentheses within the text give the pagination of the Leipzig 1866 edition. See section VII of the Introduction.

[1] Or "the master of the *Guide*." Moses Ben Maimon (Maimonides, 1135-1204) was the author of *Môreh Nᵉbôkîm, The Guide of the Perplexed.*

[2] As Gersonides uses the word throughout this book, "Torah" means more than the Pentateuch or even the whole of Scripture. The word is used loosely to designate all of the tradition of Rabbinic Judaism, including the philosophical speculation of rabbis such as Maimonides. In fact many illustrations given by Gersonides of what he here calls "the view of our Torah" are taken from statements of Maimonides in *The Guide of the Perplexed.*

CHAPTER ONE

In Which We Shall Mention the Arguments Used by Our Predecessors on This Question

It is proper that we should investigate whether or not God, may He be blessed, knows contingent[3] particulars which exist in this world,[4] and if He knows them, in what way He knows them. Since the philosophers[5] and the sages who are the masters of the Torah are divided in this subject, it is proper that we examine

[3] *Ha'epṣāriyim* in the Hebrew. Its contraries are "impossibility" and "necessity." All three terms are to be understood as modal properties of a subject which characterize the way in which the subject exists rather than as modifiers of a proposition asserting the existence or non-existence of the subject. For example, the statement, "God is necessary and man is contingent" is a qualitative statement about man and God asserting the different ways in which man and God exist. This statement logically entails "Necessarily God exists and it happens to be the case that man exists" but these two statements are not equivalent. In fact the latter statement is ambiguous in a way that the former statement is not. Since "contingent" and "necessary" express ways of existing, the word "existence" has a different meaning when "God" is the subject of the sentence than it does when "man" is the subject of the sentence.

[4] *Bᵉka'n* in the Hebrew. Although in some contexts the term simply refers to existence as such, as Isaac Husik has pointed out ("Studies in Gersonides," *Jewish Quarterly Review*, N.S., 7 (1916-1917), 580), in this context, as in most places throughout this work, the meaning is existence in only the sublunar world, which necessarily is contingent existence. In other words, all sublunar particulars are contingent and all contingent particulars exist in the sublunar world.

[5] I.e., the Greek philosophers.

first their views.[6] What we find to be correct we shall take from them, and we shall make clear with what we do not find to be

[6] Throughout the whole of *The Wars of the Lord* Gersonides constantly explains and justifies the order of the subjects that he is discussing. In this introduction to this work he presents a lengthy explanation of the logical and pedagogic principles which guided his giving this work the order that it has. At the end of this explanation he warns the reader,

It is proper for you the investigator, if you want to grasp the truth of this book, that your investigation should follow our ordering, because if you do not follow this practice, you will be confused greatly on most of this book's subjects and that confusion will be from what is not hidden from your grasping the hidden and secret things of this book (i.e., the confusion will not be caused by any hidden or secret doctrines).... Therefore it is clear that it is not proper that anyone who investigates our words should change anything included in this book, neither in its order nor in its explanations, because perhaps he will lose our meaning.

(p. 10, Leipzig edition)

It is not difficult to explain why Gersonides is so concerned to make his order perfectly clear and why he fears that readers will doubt that the stated order is the correct one or even the order that the author himself had intended.

In his introduction to *The Guide of the Perplexed* Maimonides gives seven causes to account for contradictory or contrary statements in a book. The seventh, which he tells us will apply to *The Guide* itself, is the following:

In speaking about very obscure matters it is necessary to conceal some parts and to disclose others. Sometimes in the case of certain dicta this necessity requires that the discussion proceed on the basis of a certain premise, whereas in another place necessity requires that the discussion proceed on the basis of another premise contradicting the first one. In such cases the vulgar must in no way be aware of the contradiction; the author accordingly uses some device to conceal it by all means.

(English translation of *The Guide* by Shlomo Pines
(Chicago: University of Chicago Press, 1963) p. 18.)

In the middle of his discussion of the order of *The Wars of the Lord*

correct the way in which what follows from it concerning these
two views is true.

We say that on this subject there are two views of our predecessors whose words we find to be worthy of investigation.[7]
The first is the view of the Philosopher[8] and his followers, and
the second is the view of the great sages of our Torah. The
Philosopher had believed that God, may He be blessed, did not
know particulars. His followers are divided into two views on
this issue. The one group thinks that the view of Aristotle was
that God, may He be blessed, does not know either the universals or the particulars which exist in this world. The reason is
that if He knows either the universals or the particulars there

---

Gersonides angrily argues against the thesis, which he attributes to
Maimonides, that there are doctrines demanded by reason which contradict the
tenets of Judaism which therefore must not openly be discussed. Gersonides
denies that there are any such doctrines and throughout this work he re-
peatedly accuses Maimonides of intellectual dishonesty, i.e., that Maimonides
mistakenly thought that certain rational consequences would be contrary to the
Torah, so he restrained himself at least publicly from drawing these conclusions. (This motif particularly applies to Maimonides' discussion of
creation *ex nihilo* — discussed in Treatise Six of this book — and, as we shall
see, to Maimonides' account of God's knowledge and his theory of divine attributes.)

Gersonides wanted to be clear that no such motif is present in his own
discussions. Hence he continuously emphasizes that the order of *The Wars of
the Lord* is the correct one. He has nothing to hide and so there is no reason
to pervert the order of the text.

[7] The Hebrew Union College-Jewish Institute of Religion copy of the first
edition published in Riva di Trento which contains manuscript notes written in
an Italian hand in the seventeenth or eighteenth century, which henceforth will
be referred to as "(MS)", introduces this paragraph with דעת מסלקי
ידיעתו ית' מן המרטים ומן הבללים

[8] I.e., Aristotle.

would be plurality in His knowledge, and[9] there would be here plurality in His essence. In general His essence would be divided into what is more perfect and what is less perfect, as is the case with things that have a definition. This is because part of what is in a definition possesses a greater degree of perfection than its other part.[10]

The second group[11] thinks that the view of the Philosopher was that God, may He be blessed, knows those things which exist in this world insofar as they possess a universal nature, (121) i.e. essences,[12] (but He does) not (know) them insofar as

[9] The second clause is a necessary consequence of the first clause since, because of God's unity, there is no difference between the essence and the knowledge of God.

[10] A definition consists of a genus and a specific difference. The perfection of any genus is in its species. Hence in anything that has a definition there is a distinct part (the genus) which is less perfect than another part (the difference).

This comment by Gersonides is meant only to explain why things that have a definition are divided into what is most perfect and what is most imperfect. This is not the reason why there would be such a division in God's essence. Since that which God knows, if He knows such things, varies in degree of perfection and since God's knowledge and His essence are the same. God's essence would contain a plurality the parts of which vary in degree of perfection. However, the relations of these parts need not be that of genus-species.

[11] (MS) introduces this paragraph with סילוקה מן הפרטים

[12] All He knows of them is their essence, i.e., genus and species. The word 'eṣem is the Hebrew equivalent of the Greek term ousia. It is used in three contexts. There is individual essence, 'eṣem 'iši, secondary essence, 'eṣem šēni, and universal essence, 'eṣem kᵉlālī, the latter two uses referring to the same thing, viz. genera and species. Cf. Harry Wolfson, Crescas' Critique of Aristotle (Cambridge, Mass., 1929), p. 699. In this context it is clear that only the sense of universal essence is intended.

As this view is stated here it is not very clear. Gersonides needs to tell us more about this universal essence that God knows. However, as we shall see,

they are particular, i.e. contingents. In this way there is no plurality in His essence, because He only knows Himself and in His knowledge of Himself He knows everything which exists insofar as it possesses a universal nature. The reason for this is that He is the nomos, the order and the arrangement[13] of existing beings. Yet He does not know particulars. Therefore they possess a lack of order from this aspect, although they do possess order and arrangement from the aspect by which He knows them.[14] It will be clear from what we say in the fifth

the view summarized here is the view of Gersonides and the subsequent discussion will make this position clearer.

[13] The terms *nimūs*, *seder*, and *yôṣer* are used here and throughout the book as synonymns. *Seder* basically means "to order or arrange." *Yôṣer* basically means "to go straight." As applied to elements the term expresses a state of equilibrium, which may be the basis for its association with *seder*. *Yôṣer* also means "to be pleasing or agreeable" which links it and *seder* to *nimūs*. *Nimūs* expresses good or right manners while at the same time meaning "law." A combination of these various senses of the three terms in question gives some initial understanding of what it is that God knows. He knows that which is the order or arrangement of the things themselves which at the same time is the perfection or natural virtue of those things. The term is both descriptive and valuative at the same time.

The object of God's knowledge, that by which the particular things are ordered for their perfection, is that in them which is their respective universal essences. This connection between essences and the ordering of things is quite clear in this passage. However, the nature of this ordering and what exactly are these essences is still not clear. As we said above the subsequent discussion of this position will shed some light on the problem.

[14] The universal essences are one since knowledge of them does not entail any plurality in God. Yet they are components of each particular thing. Insofar as a thing is ordered at all it is in some sense composed of these essences. These essences do not exhaust what the particular is, but what is other than the essences totally lacks order. The obvious answer to our problem at this

treatise of this book, God willing, that this latter view was the view of the Philosopher.[15]

The great sages[16] of our Torah, such as the exalted philosopher the Master The Guide, may his memory be blessed,[17] and other great sages of our Torah who agree with his view, believed that God, may He be blessed, knows all of these contingent particulars as particulars. They say that God, may He be blessed, knows by a single act of knowing all these things which are infinite.[18]

It is clear that this is the view of the Master The Guide, may his memory be blessed, because he stated in Part 3, chapter 20 of his honorable book *The Guide of the Perplexed* the following:[19]

---

point is that the essences are the forms of things, so that God knows everything of a thing except its matter, the other component of particulars which in itself is orderless. However, there are still difficulties. It is clear now that the essences are forms and the unknown-to-God additional element in things is matter. But it still is not clear what for Gersonides constitutes a form.

[15] As we shall see subsequently, the discussion of Divine Providence sheds considerable light on what it means to know the ordering of a thing. However it also complicates our picture of what Gersonides means by universal essences if in some sense these essences are the forms of things. What results is a view distinctly characteristic of Gersonides and not at all the view of Aristotle.

[16] (MS) introduces this paragraph with דעת חכמים בהנחת ידיעתו ית' באלו הפרטים בצד אשר הם בו פרטיים

[17] I.e., Maimonides.

[18] I.e., infinite in number.

[19] With the exception of one phrase, (MS) agrees completely with the Hebrew translation of *The Guide* by Samuel Ibn Tibbon. The one variant reading substitutes the word בכמי for על and adds the word עליו to the phrase that reads in the Ibn Tibbon translation as follows: בכמי מה שהוא נמצא (Pt. 3, Chap. 20, pp. 29-30. (Berlin, 1925; reprinted Jerusalem, 1960)).

Similarly we say that He knows all things subject to change
before they come to be. He constantly knows them, and therefore
He in no way acquires new knowledge. This is because in
knowing that a given person is now non-existent, but will come
into existence at a given time, will continue to exist for a given
period of time, and then will cease to exist, His knowledge is not
increased when that person comes into existence in accordance
with God's foreknowledge. Nothing new came about that was not
known to Him before. Rather something took place that was
known previously exactly as it would take place. It necessarily
follows from this belief that God's knowledge extends to things
not in existence, including what is infinite. We believe this and we
say that His knowledge may extend to what does not exist whose
existence God foresees and is able to affect.[20]

_____

[20] The passage continues, "But that which never exists is completely non-
existent with reference to His knowledge. His knowledge does not extend to it,
as our knowledge does not extend to what is for us non-existent." To say that
God knows everything could include in addition to what does exist chimeras
and non-existent contingent beings. If God knows chimeras then the following
difficulty would arise: God knows something both round and square at the
same time. But it can be objected that there is and can be no such thing, so
that what God knows is false. To avoid this difficulty Maimonides here
chooses to exclude such propositions from the infinite list of divine truths.
Other solutions were available to him. For example, what God knows is not
"there is something both round and square at the same time," which is false,
but "if anything is a round square then it is both round and square at the same
time," which is true.

We can distinguish two kinds of non-existent contingent beings. There are
those things that do not as yet exist but will exist. There is no question for
Maimonides that God knows these. But there also are things that do not as yet
exist and will never exist although they may exist. It is not clear from
Maimonides' statement if God's knowledge includes these or not.

The answer that Maimonides would be expected to give following Aristotle
is that the class of contingent things which never exist is a null class. To be

Thus says Maimonides.[21] It is clear from this that he believed that God, may He be blessed, knows contingent particulars as particulars.

----

contingent is to have the possibility of existing. But a possibility never realized is not a possibility. However, this Aristotelian answer is not without difficulties of its own. Consider the proposition, "A sea-battle will occur tomorrow and a sea-battle will not occur tomorrow." Presumably both alternatives are possible; yet once one occurs the other ceases to be possible. Assume that the sea-battle will occur. Does God know the non-existent fact "the sea-battle will not occur tomorrow"? If He does then He knows something vain, i.e., something that will never happen, with the consequence that the original problem that Maimonides sought to avoid recurs, namely, that God knows false propositions. On the other hand, if He does not know this non-existent fact then it must appear to God that the fact "A sea-battle will occur tomorrow" will be necessary and not merely possible since we would judge any proposition with no conceivable contrary to be necessary. In this way arises the problem of future contingents which, as we shall see, is at the center of Gersonides' discussion of God's knowledge.

[21] Literally, "so far is his speech."

CHAPTER TWO

W<small>E</small> S<small>HALL</small> M<small>ENTION</small> <small>THE</small> A<small>RGUMENTS</small> U<small>SED</small> <small>BY</small> O<small>UR</small> P<small>RE</small>-<small>DECESSORS</small> <small>TO</small> E<small>STABLISH</small> E<small>ACH</small> O<small>NE</small> <small>OF</small> T<small>HEIR</small> V<small>IEWS</small> A<small>S</small> W<small>E</small> F<small>IND</small> T<small>HEM</small> <small>IN</small> <small>THE</small> U<small>TTERANCES</small> <small>OF</small> T<small>HESE</small> T<small>HINKERS</small> <small>OR</small> <small>IN</small> <small>THE</small> L<small>OGICAL</small> I<small>MPLICATIONS</small> <small>OF</small> T<small>HEIR</small> W<small>ORDS</small>.

Having mentioned the views of our predecessors on this question, it is proper that we investigate which of those views is correct, and because of this it is proper that we should investigate the arguments of our predecessors which establish each one of their views as well as those views which negate them.

We say first of all that what the Philosopher thought — that God, may He be blessed, is without knowledge of these contingent particulars — is thought to have many aspects of plausibility.[22]

---

[22] Each argument given is valid and its conclusion is true, but the truth of the conclusion is only a partial truth. Gersonides here presents arguments to support the Aristotelian position. Afterwards he will present arguments to support the position of Maimonides. Although these two positions are contrary one to the other, both sets of arguments are valid "as far as they go." Gersonides will then present his own position which does not deny the validity and the truth of the previous stated arguments but incorporates them into his own position. In this way the arguments presented to support the partial insights of Gersonides' predecessors become arguments to support what Gersonides judges to be his complete and adequate statement.

Gersonides uses this method throughout *The Wars of the Lord*. It is reminiscent of the intuitive method that Aristotle describes in Book I of the *Ethica Nicomachea*. What is of interest in this is that what Aristotle distinguished as two different kinds of argument, discursive (*dianoia*) and intuitive (*noesis*), each with its own sphere of application, has collapsed in Ger-

(*122*) One[23] of them[24] is that the particular is perceived only
by a hylic faculty such as the senses, the imagination, and other
such faculties,[25] whereas God, may He be blessed, as is clear
from His essence, does not possess a hylic faculty. Therefore it
necessarily follows that God, may He be blessed, is without perception of these particulars. The syllogism is structured as
follows: God, may He be blessed, has no hylic faculty;
everything that perceives a particular has a hylic faculty;[26]

---

sonides' hands into a single form of argument universally applicable to all
spheres of philosophic interest.

[23] (MS) introduces this paragraph with מבי הראות לשתי
דעות הפלוסופים.

[24] I.e., of the aspects of plausibility.

[25] Namely, common sense, estimation, memory and recollection which,
together with various kinds of imagination constitute the internal senses. The
external sense are touch, taste, smell, hearing, and sight. This argument
presupposes the epistemology and psychology that Gersonides presents in
Treatise One of the *Wars of the Lord*. For variantly termed but equivalent lists
of the internal senses and the different kinds of imagination see H. A. Wolfson, "Maimonides on the Internal Senses," *Jewish Quarterly Review*, N.S. 25
(1937), 441-468.

[26] The epistemology presupposed here is that of Aristotle seen through the
eyes of the Greek commentators Themistius and Alexander of Aphrodisias and
the Moslem commentators Al-Farabi, Ibn Sina, and Ibn Rushd, incorporating
Gersonides' own "improvements" on the understanding of Aristotle's position.
The primary source is Ibn Rushd's short commentary on *De Anima* joined
with Gersonides' critique of the conceptions of passive, active, and acquired
intellects in Treatise One. The consequent understanding of what is involved
in human knowledge may be summarized as follows.

Every natural being has matter and a form, which expressed as the nature of
the thing causes the motion of the entity in question as well as the accidents
which are its intrinsic determinations. The matter is in itself unintelligible
although it is that which individuates the thing. The form is that which determines the essence which in turn is the nature of the entity. Generally "soul" is

therefore it follows that God, may He be blessed, is without perception of the particular.

---

the name given to the form of every living thing. The soul is that capacity of a
thing through which it originates different operations. Corresponding to each
distinct type of operation is what is called a "power," "faculty," *kôaḥ*. The
different powers of the soul are nutritive and generative, *simʿḥiyût*, common to
plants and animals, the powers of perception, imagination and voluntary
motion, *ḥiyûniyût*, common to animals but not to plants, and the aptitude to
know intelligible form, *'enôsiyût*, common only to human souls, *nepeš
ho'odom*. The faculty corresponding to this "human" aptitude is called "intelligence" or "intellect," *śēkel*.

The process of knowing consists in a series of successive abstractions from
the object known. In each step more and more of the matter is prescinded until
finally in intellection, the final stage, the remaining matter in the phantasm
(the object as it is imagined) is prescinded and what remains now is the concept itself, residing in the intellect. The term, "knowledge" is reserved exclusively for the possession of such concepts.

What the word "concept" means is not clear. The above picture holds true
for all of the philosophers in the medieval Moslem-Jewish pro-Aristotelian
tradition, but the agreement is possible only because the above picture is intentionally vague, particularly about the meaning of such terms as "concept" and
"intellect." The relation of these latter two terms is such that variations in the
use of one produces variation in the understanding of the other. The medieval
Moslem-Jewish philosophers concentrated on the meaning of the term, "intellect." The word, "intellect" was applied to what was called "Material Intellect," "Acquired Intellect," and "Active Intellect." The respective positions
on what these three kinds of intellect are, are discussed at length by Gersonides, as we said above, in Treatise One. The details need not concern us
here. All that is important for the present are Gersonides' conclusions.

According to Gersonides the Material Intellect is, as Alexander of
Aphrodisias claimed, a capacity of the soul to receive the universal forms of
material things. It is not itself a distinct substance as Themistius had argued.
As a capacity it is found in the sensible soul with its imaginative faculty. This
capacity is actualized by the Active Intellect. The Active Intellect is not part of
man, as Themistius had argued, but neither is it identical with God, as

The second way[27] is that particulars are temporal, i.e. their existence is at a specific time. Therefore, that of which neither

---

Alexander of Aphrodisias had claimed. In agreement with Ibn Sina it is the intelligence who governs everything sublunar. As such the Active Intellect has two functions. One, it endows all sublunar nature with intelligence and purpose. Two, it enables the rational power in man to rise from a *tabula rasa*. What results from this actualization is the Acquired Intellect, which consists solely in the concepts consequent upon the activity of the Active Intellect upon the phantasms of the imagination through the sensible soul's capacity for intellection or conceptualization.

Among the many problems that Gersonides claims that his position solves, for our purposes the following is the most important. After presenting his position on the nature of the Active Intellect, Gersonides says the following:

And it is proper that it should not be hidden from us that from what was here explained all of the doubts are solved / which moved our predecessors either to deny that there is knowledge or to posit universal forms existing outside of the soul, each of which (i.e., each alternative) is false, as is explained in the *Metaphysics*. The reason for this is that they believed that these concepts have no existence outside of the soul, since what exists outside of the soul are individuals which continuously change and also perish, and clearly concerning the content of knowledge it is proper, if there is knowledge in this world, that it and its object exist, as is explained on the topic of true knowledge in the *Analytics*. They judged because of this that there is no knowledge in this world. But others of them saw clearly that it is impossible to deny knowledge, because our existence is established and there is that which persists through time in some manner, i.e., the general ordering of these things, and it necessarily follows because of this that these universals of which there is knowledge must exist as essences outside of the soul. But many falsehoods necessarily follow for them from which there is no escape, as is made clear in the *Metaphysics*. But when the matter is posited as it was explained here concerning the Active Intellect, knowledge has as its object something existent remaining in its essence outside of the intellect. It is the ordering which is in the soul of the Active Intellect, and universals

motion nor rest is predicated cannot possibly perceive temporal
entities.[28] But neither motion nor rest are predicated of God,

---

are something accidental to it from the side of our abstracting what exists
of sensible individuals outside of the soul. Just as the ordering in the soul
of the craftsman is found in every one of the vessels which in some manner are created from it, so this ordering is found in every individual
created from that ordering. It is clear that none of the falsities which
necessarily follow from positing universals which exist outside of the soul
follow from this position.

(*The Wars of the Lord*, pp. 46-47, Leipzig edition.)

Especially concerning knowledge of the sublunar world, everything that is
real is particular. But particulars cannot be known. Knowledge consists in conceiving of universals, but universals have no existence outside of the mind.
Hence, either universals exist independently of the mind or there is no such
thing as knowledge since what is known cannot exist. Gersonides' solution to
this dilemma is that the object of knowledge is neither the external particular
nor the universal; it is the essence.

But what exactly are essences? It still is not clear completely, but we can say
the following about them. Essences are what the Active Intellect knows and
they are that by which the sublunar world is governed. Seen collectively they
are the same things that Gersonides otherwise calls *siddūr*, the ordering of
things. Gersonides does not explicitly tell us what this means, but he does
provide us with a picture by which we can understand what they are. This is
the analogy of the craftsman and his artifacts. The craftsman is the Active Intellect and the artifacts are the contingent particulars. The craftsman has a
model in his mind. From this model he creates things. Let us say that the
model is the model of a chair and with this one model he creates many chairs.
The chairs are all different. What differentiates them is their material from
which the craftsman has formed his chair. But they are all his chairs as well,
i.e., applications of the determining model. This model is one, which is to say
that the fact that all these chairs are recognizable as the same kind of chair is
that they all have the same model. Such models are essences. They and not
universals are the real objects of knowledge.

This doctrine of essences is a radical break from the epistemology of

may He be blessed,[29] from which it necessarily follows that God, may He be blessed, is without perception of particulars.

Aristotle. Gersonides' immediate source is Ibn Rushd. In reply to Al-Ghazali in the *Tahafut al-Falasifah* who has used the Aristotelian claim that concepts, the objects of knowledge, exist only in the mind to refute what he lists as the fourth argument of the philosophers for the eternity of the world, Ibn Rushd says the following:

> This argument is sophistical because possibility is a universal which has individuals outside the mind like all the other universals, and knowledge is not knowledge of the universal concept, but it is a knowledge of individuals in a universal way which the mind attains in the case of the individuals, when it abstracts from them one common nature which is distributed among the different matters. The nature, therefore, of the universal is not identical with the nature of the things of which it is a universal.
>
> ... The universal, however, is not the object of knowledge; on the contrary through it the things become known, although it exists potentially in the nature of the things known; otherwise its apprehension of the individuals, in so far as they are universals, would be false. This apprehension indeed would be false if the nature of the object known were essentially individual, not accidentally individual, whereas the opposite is the case: it is accidentally individual, essentially universal.
>
> (*Tahafut al-Tahafut*, ed. and transl. Simon van den Bergh (London: M. Luzac, 1954), p. 65)

Universals are not themselves the objects of knowledge; they are merely the tools by which the real existent individual is known. But it is not the individual as a particular that is known. What accounts for the particularity of the thing is its matter. In knowing, the matter of the object is prescinded. Hence what remains is not particular. In Ibn Rushd's words, what is known is "accidentally individual and essentially universal." However, Ibn Rushd's terminology at this point is confusing. Clearly for Aristotle (see *Meta.* B.10) the universal only has mental existence. Hence just as what is known cannot be the particulars, Ibn Rushd's own argument clearly shows that it is not the universal either. A different term than universal is needed for the real existent

21b   The syllogism is structured/as follows. Neither motion nor
         rest is predicated of God, may He be blessed. Nothing of which

---

object of knowledge which only accidentally (i.e., through association with
matter) is particular, which expresses the purported fact that we do not know
universals but we know "individuals in a universal way." Gersonides uses the
terms *'esem* and *seder*. The former is applied to the function of the Active Intellect in affecting human knowledge. The latter is applied to the function of
the Active Intellect in governing the sublunar world. But the referent of both
terms is the same.

Aristotle also used the expression "knowing individuals in a universal way"
(see *Meta.Z*.10, 1036a8), but this phrase does not denote for Aristotle
something other than universals. For Ibn Rushd and Gersonides it clearly
does. However, what is the relationship between universals and essences is not
spelled out by either. On Gersonides' theory of concepts, see "Levi ben Gersons Theorie des Begriffs," by Isaac Julius Guttmann in *Festschrift zum 75
Jahrigen Bestehung des Jud. Theol. Seminars* (Breslau, 1929), 2: 131-149;
reprinted as "Torat Hamûšag Sel Ralbag," in Guttmann, *Dat Umada*
(Jerusalem, 1966).

[27] I.e., the second aspect of plausibility.

[28] Maimonides sets down twenty-six propositions as basic premises of
Aristotelian physics and metaphysics (*The Guide*, Book 2, Introduction).
Upon these premises Maimonides constructs his demonstrations of the
existence and unity of God. Excluding the twenty-sixth (which asserts that the
universe is eternal, which Maimonides himself claims cannot be demonstrated
and that Aristotle did not maintain that it could be demonstrated [*The Guide*,
2.13-14]), this list was commonly accepted by the Jewish philosophers who
followed Maimonides as a correct listing of the fundamental principles of
Aristotelian science. That "nothing of which neither motion nor rest is
predicated can possibly perceive temporal entities" follows from two doctrines,
viz. the Aristotelian doctrine of the unity of subject and object in knowledge
and the conception of time as a predicate of motion. The latter dogma is proposition fifteen in Maimonides' list.

Time is an accident consequent upon motion and is necessarily attached
to it. Neither of them exists without the other. Motion does not exist ex-

neither motion nor rest is predicated can possibly perceive temporal entities. Therefore God, may He be blessed, cannot

---

cept in time, and time cannot be conceived by the intellect except together
with motion. And all that with regard to which no motion can be found,
does not fall under time.

(The Guide, Pines tr., p. 237)

For a full discussion of the relationship between time and motion in Aristotle
and in the writings of his Jewish and Moslem successors, see Wolfson,
Crescas' Critique of Aristotle, pp. 93-98.

The former dogma is not on Maimonides' list of twenty-six propositions
since that list is confined to physics and metaphysics. However the dogma, viz.
that "actual knowledge is identical with its object" *(De Anima* 3.7, 431a1),
was acknowledged generally. Aristotle explains this dogma as follows:

Knowledge and sensation are divided to correspond with realities, potential knowledge and sensation answering to potentialities, actual knowledge
and sensation to actualities. Within the soul the faculties of knowledge
and sensation are *potentially* these objects, the one what is knowable, the
other what is sensible. They must be either the things themselves or their
forms. The former alternative is of course impossible: it is not the stone
which is present in the soul but its form.
It follows that the soul is analogous to the hand; for as the hand is a tool
of tools, so the mind is the form of forms and sense the form of sensible
things.

(De Anima, 3.8, 431b24-432a2, transl. W. D. Ross)

What is known of a thing is its form. The form expresses the nature of the
thing. In knowing that thing its form enters the soul. Hence, insofar as the
form of a thing is the thing, in knowing the subject (the soul) and the object
are one since they share a common form. The relation between the form of the
object and the form in the soul (i.e., the universal) and essences (which, as we
have seen, for Gersonides is the proper object of knowledge) is vital for understanding Gersonides' epistemology, but it need not concern us here. All
that is relevant to this argument is that from this conception of the relationship
of the knower and the known it follows that the knower and the known are the

possibly perceive temporal entities. Let us further add to this conclusion one well known[30] premise, namely that particulars are temporal,[31] and from this it necessarily follows that God, may He be blessed, does not perceive particulars.

The third way is that if it is postulated that God, may He be blessed, perceives such entities, then it would be thought that it

---

same kind of entity. Thus, if the object known is subject to motion, so the knower must be subject to motion.

In summary, what Gersonides is asserting here is the following: all temporal entities are subject to motion and rest (the second dogma). Hence, since the knower and the known are in some sense one (the first dogma), what knows temporal entities must itself be subject to motion and rest.

[29] This follows from Maimonides' proposition five, "Every motion is a change and transition from potentiality to actuality." If God is subject to the contraries of motion and rest then He is subject to change and must in some sense be potential. But the first mover necessarily does not change and is in no sense potential.

[30] Although the text reads יודע בה, (MS) suggests (צריך לומר) that the text should read ידוע, omitting בה.

[31] On Maimonides' list of premises the assertion that all particulars are temporal follows from propositions fifteen, five, and seven. Fifteen (see note 28) asserts that what is subject to time is subject to motion. Five asserts that what is subject to motion is subject to change. ("Every motion is a change and transition from potentiality to actuality.") Seven asserts that something is subject to change if and only if it is a body. ("Everything changeable is divisible. Hence everything movable is divisible and is necessarily a body. But everything that is indivisible is not movable; hence it will not be a body at all.") From these three premises it follows that all bodies are temporal. The missing link is that all particulars are bodies. Maimonides does not provide this link in his list of premises. Presumably Gersonides would regard it to be self-evident that matter is the principle of individuation so that all particulars are bodies. At least as regards this passage there is no distinction between being an individual and being a particular. However, as we shall see, the development of the text will show this identity to be problematic.

necessarily follows from this that the excellent would be perfected by the deficient. This is because knowledge is a perfection to the knower.[32] But this is utterly absurd,[33] and what necessarily leads to an absurdity is itself absurd. Therefore it is clear that God, may He be blessed, does not perceive such entities. This argument necessitates — so it is thought[34] — (the conclusion) that God, may He be blessed, knows only Himself, i.e. that He knows neither universals nor particulars.[35]

The fourth way is that if God, may He be blessed, had perception of these entities, it would be because (His) intellect ac-

---

[32] Perfection is used in this sentence in the sense of excellence of function. A knower insofar as he is a knower has the function of knowing. Excellence in knowing is knowing well. Knowing well consists in knowing truths. Consequently everything known perfects the knower as a knower.

[33] I.e., that the excellent is perfected by the deficient is absurd.

[34] By this expression Gersonides tells you that he considers this to be a sophistical argument.

[35] Whatever God knows perfects God as a knower. However, everything other than God is "less than" God. Hence if God knows anything besides Himself He would be perfected by what is less than Him. The argument depends on a shift in the understanding of the term, "perfection." Ṣ^{e}lēmūt (kamāl in Arabic, entelecheia in Greek) also means completeness or actuality. God as the first cause is the only entity who is totally actual. As such God is also the final cause of everything, i.e., that towards which everything tends. The argument presupposes a composite Platonic-Aristotelian cosmology in which everything in the universe is structured in varying levels of reality in which what occupies each level is more perfect than and is the perfection of the things occupying the level immediately below it. In such a cosmology the uses of these two senses of perfection — viz. that towards which something tends as a moral perfection and that through which a thing best practices its function where "best" is used with respect to skill and not necessarily as a moral grade — are constantly conjoined.

tuates itself by means of what it knows. Then it would seem[36] to follow necessarily from this that God, may He be blessed, is not one,[37] but is many, because of the multiplicity of the things perceived by which He is actualized. But this is utterly absurd, and what necessarily leads to an absurdity is itself absurd. Therefore, it is clear from this that God, may He be blessed, is without perception of these entities. This argument also necessitates — so it is thought — that God only knows Himself.[38]

[36] By this expression Gersonides tells you that he considers this to be a sophistical argument.

[37] The basic sense of "one" is "not composed of parts."

[38] In knowing an object that object, insofar as what it is is its form, becomes part of the knower. Hence if God knows anything other than Himself that object of knowledge is part of God. But if this is so then God is not simple. The argument is sophistical because, as Gersonides explains in the first treatise (see note 26), what the Active Intellect knows is the essence of things and their essence is their real unity. We discover the essence of things through abstracting their form from the matter by which they are differentiated. Because we know essences in this way (i.e., as universals), they never fully lose their plurality. However the Active Intellect knows essence as the blueprint or exemplar by which the sense particulars are created. Hence essence as known by the Active Intellect is free from any sense of plurality from that in which it is exemplified. Therefore, since the Active Intellect knows all things as unified, such knowledge entails no plurality in the Active Intellect. Since for Gersonides the Active Intellect is different from God, all that needs be added here is that if there is no plurality in the Active Intellect in its knowing sublunar natures as it knows them, how much the more so would this be the case with God.

It should be noted that although all of the discussion in this treatise is about God knowing particulars, the discussion in effect is really about how the Active Intellect knows particulars. However, Gersonides need not be understood here as contradicting his denial of the identity of the Active Intellect and God in the first treatise. In each discussion it can be understood that what applies here to the Active Intellect also would be true of God.

The fifth way is that particulars are infinite,[39] but knowledge is something encompassing and inclusive,[40] and knowledge can

[39] I.e., infinite in number. Concerning the total number of particulars in the universe — past, present, and future — their number is indefinite. It is clear that Gersonides intends at least this sense of infinite. However, he may mean infinite in another respect as well. In the *Physics* (3.4, 204a1-9) Aristotle distinguishes four senses of infinite. Two of the listed senses are "what admits being gone through, the process however having no termination" and "what naturally admits of being gone through, but is not actually gone through or does not actually reach an end." Numbers and sense particulars are infinite in these two senses, and, as we shall see, Gersonides discusses this argument in these terms at the end of his discussion of the aspects of plausibility of the position of the philosophers in this chapter.

[40] *Māqip* clearly here is a synonymn for *taklit* where the basic sense in this passage is to contain or limit. As used here it is synonymous with the Greek term, *peras*. Also the term, *taklit* is often used to express the Greek term, *telos*.

In this case the paradigm of knowing is defining which is a limiting or containing process since in designating what is defined as a member of one class the definiendum is excluded from other classes. However, the word *taklit* takes on other associations. These associations are worth noting here since they shed light on what we already have noted as the problem of what Gersonides means by essences, the proper object or objects of knowledge.

In *Metaphysics, Δ*.17, 1022a4-14, Aristotle distinguishes four senses of the term, "limit" (*peras*).

'Limit' means (1) the last point (*eschaton*) of each thing, i.e., the first point beyond which it is not possible to find any part, and the first point within which every part is; (2) the form, (*eidos* or *schema* or *morphe*) — whatever it may be, of a spatial magnitude or of a thing that has magnitude; (3) the end (*telos*) of each thing (and of this nature is that towards which the movement and the action are, not that from which they are — though sometimes it is both, that from which and that to which the movement is, i.e., the final cause); (4) the substance (*ousia*) of each

neither encompass nor include what is infinite. This argument necessitates that there can be no knowledge of particulars in their totality either by God, may He be blessed, or by anyone else.[41]

The sixth way is that if it is the case that God knows things subject to generation then the following dilemma is unavoidable. Either God has knowledge of these things subject to generation before they come to be, or He has knowledge of them only when

---

thing, and the essence (*ti en einai*) of each; for this is the limit of knowledge; and if of knowledge, of the object also.

As we already have seen, senses two and four correspond to the way that Gersonides uses the term *'eṣem*, and senses one and three correspond to Gersonides' use of the term *seder*. Given that the term *taklit* for Aristotle has all four senses, *taklit* thus provides the link by which *'eṣem* and *seder* are identified. The terms "form of a thing," "substance," "essence," "end" or "final cause," and "that which defines or limits a thing," i.e., the proper object of knowledge, are all one and the same thing, i.e., each of these terms with their different senses refers to a single entity.

Wolfson (*Crescas' Critique of Aristotle*, pp. 358-359) has argued that the identification in referent of the above indicated senses of "form" and "limit" is found in the writings of Ibn Rushd, specifically with reference to his *Middle Commentary on the Physics*, 4, i, 1, 8. It is quite likely that the source of Gersonides' understanding of essence (or form, or limit, or ordering) is Ibn Rushd's.

[41] Gersonides can accept this argument without any qualification. It excludes knowledge of particulars only insofar as they are particulars while at the same time affirming that there is knowledge of the essence of particulars. This affirms what Gersonides lists above as the second interpretation of Aristotle's position with regard to God's knowledge of particulars, which, as we shall see, is Gersonides' own position. This argument also entails the claim that with respect to knowledge of particulars there is no qualitative difference between God's knowledge and man's knowledge. As we shall see this contention is a basic issue between Gersonides and Maimonides.

they come to be and not before. If it is assumed that He has knowledge of them before they come to be, then His knowledge is related to what does not exist. (*123*) This is absurd, because the object of knowledge necessarily is a definite existent.[42]

Furthermore, (anyone who maintains) that He has knowledge of things subject to generation before they come to be cannot avoid the following dilemma: either He knows them according to their nature as contingent beings[43] so that the contradictory[44]

---

[42] This argument works only with God as the knower. Taken as a general argument the argument rests on the ambiguity of the word, "existent." The object of knowledge as the object of knowledge in some sense is, but that is not to say that it has anything more than a mental existence. In Aristotle's terms, where the object of a concept is not actual it is potential and as such it exists. However, no such argument can be used in the case of God's knowledge. Given the unity of knower and known, if the object of God's knowledge exists potentially, then in God too there would be potentiality. But this is impossible.

[43] In Maimonides' presentation of the basic presuppositions of Aristotelian science (*The Guide* 2. Intro.), the definition of a contingent being is given in proposition nineteen.

> Everything that has a cause for its existence is only possible with regard to existence in respect to its own essence. For it exists if its causes are present. If, however, they are not present, or if they become nonexistent, or if their relation that entails the existence of the thing in question has changed, that thing does not exist.
>
> (S. Pines tr.)

A contingent being is a being whose existence is dependent on the presence of a cause other than itself. As such a contingent being is the contrary of a necessary being. As stated in proposition twenty,

> Everything that is necessarily existent in respect to its own essence has no cause for its existence in any way whatever or under any condition.
>
> (S. Pines tr.)

of what He knows will be actualized remains a possibility,[45] or He knows perfectly which one of these contradictory alternatives will be actualized and its contradictory does not remain possible.[46] If we assume that He knows them according to their nature as contingent beings, it necessarily follows that His knowledge of these entities before they come to be changes with their coming to be. The reason for this is that both were possibilities which either could be actualized or could not be actualized before they came to be, but afterwards both of these alternate possibilities were eliminated.[47] Since the intellect is actualized by what it knows, it necessarily follows that God, may

---

Necessary beings are the cause of their own being.

As was noted above (note 3) the terms "necessary" and "contingent" are modal predicates ranging over things and not over propositions about things. It should be noted as well that Maimonides' proposition twenty-four states that every contingent being possesses matter. As Maimonides says, "Whatsoever is something in potentia is necessarily endowed with matter, for possibility is always in matter."

[44] The word "contradictory" is appropriate if we understand the opposing alternatives to be states of affairs expressed through contradictory propositions rather than objects.

[45] For example, God knows that a sea-battle will happen tomorrow although it is possible that it will not happen.

[46] For example, God knows that a sea-battle will happen tomorrow and there can be no doubt about it.

[47] Assume that God has pre-knowledge of a sea-battle. Consider the proposition, "A sea-battle will not take place tomorrow." Before the sea-battle it happens to be the case that this proposition is false but it need not be the case. However, after the sea-battle it is necessarily the case since once the sea-battle has occurred it is impossible that it not have occurred. Similarly before the sea-battle occurs it happens to be the case that the sea-battle will occur, but after the battle this proposition is undeniably, i.e., necessarily, true.

He be blessed, is in continuous flux. But this is absolutely absurd.

If we assume that God, may He be blessed, knows perfectly which one of the pair of possibilities will be actualized, then it would follow necessarily from this that nothing in this world is a contingent which either may or may not be actualized. Thus everything would be necessary. But this is absolutely absurd and nonsensical.[48] This being the case it is clear from this that it is absurd that God should have knowledge of these things subject to generation before they come to be.

If it is assumed that He has knowledge of them only when they come to be then His knowledge is in continuous flux. Since the intellect is actualized by what it knows, it would necessarily follow from this that the essence of God, may He be blessed, is in continuous flux.[49] But this is absolutely absurd.

---

[48] If there is no doubt that the sea-battle will occur then it is necessarily the case that the sea-battle will occur and it is impossible that the sea-battle will not occur.

[49] The total argument presupposes that the modal predicates modify not things but propositions about things. However, the fundamental understanding of these modal predicates for Gersonides' contemporaries and his predecessors is that these predicates modify things and not propositions. In this primary sense of the terms "necessary" and "contingent," the argument fails. A sea-battle, for example, is contingent because its happening depends on causes other than itself. If God knows the causes of the sea-battle and He also knows that these causes will be present tomorrow, then He knows that it is necessarily the case that the sea-battle will occur tomorrow and that the sea-battle is a possible or contingent sea-battle. This conjunction involves no contradiction once the two senses in which modal predicates are applied are kept separate. Following these two senses, Ibn Sina, for example, in his *Metaphysics* distinguishes between what is necessary in itself and what is necessary in virtue of a cause. Only God is necessary in the first sense whereas everything else

The seventh way is that if God, may He be blessed, knows these particulars, the following dilemma is inescapable: either He governs and orders them in good and perfect order, or He is imperfect and He is unable to order them, or He is able to order them well but He neglects and forgets them either because they are too lowly and base in His eyes or because of jealousy. It is clear that the latter two alternatives of the dilemma are false. This is because it is evident that God, may He be blessed, is not incapable of doing anything He desires to do and He does not withhold the gift of goodness and perfection from any existent insofar as is possible.[50] This is wonderfully exhibited in the science which deals with the creation of living things,[51] namely the greatness of (God's) power to place in them[52] as much goodness and perfection as is possible so that it is impossible that they could exist in a way more perfect than their present way. This being so, the only alternative that remains is that if He knows them God, may He be blessed, gave these entities a perfect and good ordering. But this is contrary to what the senses

---

may be said to be possible in itself but necessary with respect to its cause. Cf. Gerard Smith S.J., "Avicenna and the Possibles," *New Scholasticism*, 17 (1943), 340-353; Beatrice H. Zedler, "Saint Thomas and Avicenna," *Traditio*, 6 (1948), 105-159; and [Ibn Sina,] *Avicenna's De anima*, ed. by Fazlur Rahman (New York, 1959).

However, as we shall see when Gersonides considers this argument again in a slightly different form but in more detail later in this chapter, this understanding of contingency is too weak for Gersonides. As stated there the argument avoids the ambiguity of the different senses of the modal predicates and it is a valid argument.

[50] I.e., insofar as it is logically possible for Him to bestow the gift.

[51] Or, the science of animals. With either translation the meaning is the same, viz. the science of biology.

[52] In the living things or animals.

find (to be the case) with these particulars, i.e. that there is
found evil and much lack of order in them so that many evils
21c exist/for the good and many goods exist for the wicked.[53]

In their[54] opinion this is the strongest of their demonstrations
that God, may He be blessed, does not know particulars. It
seems that this is the argument that moved the Philosopher to
maintain that God, may He be blessed, does not know particulars. This is clear from what he said in his book the
Metaphysics.[55]

---

[53] The argument may be summarized as follows: either God knows particulars or He does not. If He does know them then either He orders them or
He does not. It is not the case that He does not order them because of God's
omnipotence and the evidence provided by biology. But neither is it the case
that He orders them, given the sense evidence that the world lacks moral order
or justice. Therefore, since none of the consequences of the assumption that
God knows particulars can be maintained, it follows that God does not know
particulars.

However, it might be objected that the argument is self-contradictory in the
following way: to deny that God orders particulars Gersonides cited the experience of disorder, and to deny that God does not order particulars he cited
the experience of order. In one case he is claiming that it is *a posteriori* the
case that there is no order, and in the other case he is claiming that it is *a
posteriori* the case that there is order. But these two claims are contradictory.

In fact the two claims are not contradictory. As Gersonides will argue subsequently, insofar as particulars have an essence they are ordered, and insofar
as any given particular is other than its essence, i.e., insofar as it is embodied
essence, i.e., insofar as it is material, it is subject to chance and not ordered.
Sciences such as biology testify to the order of particulars, but not insofar as
they are particular. In this respect sense evidence is against any order in particulars.

[54] I.e., in the opinion of the philosophers who with Aristotle deny that
God knows particulars.

[55] It is not clear what specific passage Gersonides had in mind. The

These are the arguments which we have extracted (*124*) either from the words of the philosophers or from the logical implications of their words to establish that God, may He be blessed, is without knowledge of these particulars.

There is an eighth argument by which it may be demonstrated — so it might be thought[56] — that God, may He be blessed, is without knowledge of these particulars. In (the writings of) some recent philosophers[57] we have seen (this argument) from which they necessarily conclude that continuous magnitude is divisible into what is indivisible. We have seen fit to mention it here because it is possible that it could be thought that this argument makes it clear that God is without conception of these particulars.[58] That is to say, if God, may He be blessed, knows all

---

question of God's knowledge is discussed in Λ.9, 1974b15-1075a11. The question of the moral order of the universe is discussed in Λ.10, 1075a12-1076a7. However, the two chapters are not connected in such a way that the latter is part of the argument for the former. On the contrary the argument given in *Metaphysics* Λ, chapter nine more resembles Gersonides' third argument above than it resembles this argument. It may be the case that what Gersonides here ascribed to Aristotle actually appeared in Ibn Rushd's *Long Commentary on the Metaphysics*.

[56] See note 34.

[57] The meaning of this term, *hamit^e'aḥērim* and its synonymn, *ha'aḥărônim* is used very broadly. It can refer to anyone — Moslem, Christian, or Jew — from the time of Maimonides and Ibn Rushd (12th century) to Gersonides' own time (14th century). It could very well be the case that Gersonides uses this general designation because his reference is to Christian philosophers. However, this is only conjecture. On this question, see Shlomo Pines, "Scholasticism after Thomas Aquinas and the Teachings of Hasdai Crescas and his Predecessors," *Israel Academy of Sciences and Humanities, Proceedings*, 1 (Jerusalem, 1967), no. 10, and Wolfson, *Crescas' Critique of Aristotle*, pp. 320-321.

[58] Gersonides feels that an explanation is necessary for presenting this

these things, it necessarily follows from this — so it might be thought — that the impossible is possible.[59] This is because it has been made clear already that continous magnitude is divisible into what is capable of division.[60] If it is assumed that God, may He be blessed, knows perfectly that into which it is possible that this magnitude *qua* magnitude is divisible, then there would be in magnitude parts known to God, may He be blessed, which are not divisible. The reason for this is that if they were divisible, God, may He be blessed, would not know perfectly that into which this magnitude could possibly be divided. But this is absurd, by which is meant that it is absurd (to claim that) there is in continuous magnitude *qua* magnitude indivisible parts.[61]

---

argument because he judges it to be totally false. But in introducing this set of arguments against God knowing particulars he told us that each of these arguments contains "some aspects of plausibility." (See note 22.)

[59] In other words, the argument given here is a *reductio ad absurdum*.

[60] In *De Caelo* 1.1., 268a7ff, and in the *Metaphysics* Δ.13, 1020a7 Aristotle defines a continuous quantity as that which is "divisible into things always divisible." In proposition 7 of Maimonides' list of twenty-six presuppositions of Aristotelian philosophy in *The Guide* (2. Intro.), Maimonides says, "everything changeable is divisible. Hence everything movable is divisible and is necessarily a body. But everything that is indivisible is not movable; hence it will not be a body at all." (S. Pines tr.)

As implied here and made explicit at the end of chapter four, this eighth argument may be summarized as follows. What is continuous magnitude, i.e., is a body, is divisible. If God has perfect knowledge of what is divisible then He knows all of its parts. To know all of its parts requires that God know the ultimate parts. But this is impossible since all of the parts of magnitude, themselves being magnitude, are further divisible. (See *Physics* 6.1, 231a20-232a23 for Aristotle's demonstration why magnitude is divisible into magnitudes.)

[61] Considering the ultimate parts that God knows, either they are ultimate, in which case God's knowledge that they are ultimate is correct, or they are not

Some recent philosophers have conjectured concerning this argument that from it it necessarily follows that continuous magnitude is divisible into what is indivisible. What brought them to this (conclusion) was that they first granted that God, may He be blessed, knows everything and is not ignorant of anything. Because of this it necessarily follows for them from this argument that continuous magnitude is divisible into what is indivisible.

These are the arguments which establish that God is without knowledge of any of these particulars. In themselves[62] they negate the view of those who believe that God, may He be blessed, knows these particulars.

What[63] the sages of our Torah, may their memory be blessed, postulated — that God, may He be blessed, knows these particulars — also has aspects of plausibility.

The first way is that because God, may He be blessed, is the

---

really ultimate, in which case God is mistaken. If they are ultimate then they are not divisible. But if this were so magnitude (i.e. that which is divisible infinitely) would not be divisible infinitely (i.e. would not be magnitude).

Concerning why magnitude must be divisible infinitely, Aristotle says the following:

> for if it were divisible into indivisibles, we should have an indivisible in contact with an indivisible, since the extremities of things that are continuous with one another are one and are in contact.

(*Physics* 6.1, 231b15-18, transl. by
R. P. Hardie and R. K. Gaye)

[62] Excluding the arguments that Gersonides tells us that they are spurious (see note 34), these arguments are all valid. But they are not the total story. They are thus only "aspects of plausibility." (See note 22.)

[63] (MS) introduces this paragraph with פני הראות לדעת חבמיים.

most perfect thinker, it is not proper that the imperfection of ignorance be related to Him, i.e. that He should be ignorant of anything.[64] This is because ignorance is a great imperfection, and he who chooses to attribute ignorance to Him in these matters rather than attribute to Him that He is incapable of ordering them with a good order[65] flees from one evil to fall into an even greater evil. The reason for this is that it happens to be the case with respect to the nature of a recipient that it could not possibly receive a greater portion of perfection, and that (therefore) this is not an imperfection with respect to God, may He be blessed.[66]

[64]   No doubt it is a primary notion that all good things must exist in God and that with regard to Him all deficiencies must be denied. It is almost a primary notion that ignorance with regard to anything whatever is a deficiency and that He, may He be exalted, is ignorant of nothing.

With these words Maimonides begins his defense of God's omniscience in *The Guide* 3.19. It should be noted that Maimonides distinguishes between the assertion that no imperfection can be attributed to God, concerning which there is "no doubt," and the assertion that ignorance is a deficiency, concerning which there is "almost" no doubt. Gersonides will grant that no deficiency can be predicated of God but he will argue that ignorance of particulars is not a deficiency.

[65] Gersonides' statement here is a paraphrase of *The Guide* 3.16 in which Maimonides introduces the related problems of Divine Providence (the topic of Gersonides' fourth treatise) and Divine Knowledge. As stated here Maimonides' "first way" relates specifically to what Gersonides previously listed as the seventh way of the Aristotelian philosophers.

[66] Gersonides' statement of the first way, paraphrasing Maimonides (see note 65), confuses together two separate arguments. The first is an argument that God must be perfect in all respects which would not be the case if God were ignorant of anything, even particulars. The second is a reply to an objection to this argument presented by Gersonides as the seventh way of the philosophers. The reply is that even if we grant this objection, better to say

The second way is that it is not proper to think that what the Creator has actuated should be concealed from Him. Rather, His knowledge of what He actuated is more perfect than the knowledge of anyone besides Him. This is because He knows by a single (act of) knowledge all that is subject to generation (and corruption) in what He actuated from the aspect of the disposition[67] which He has set upon it. However everyone else

---

that God ordered the sublunar world as well as He could rather than to say that God is ignorant of anything. The reason that the former statement is admissible is that while nothing other than God is absolutely perfect (something that can be said only of God), everything is as perfect as it is capable of being.

Gersonides judges this argument as well as the seventh way of the philosophers to have "aspects of plausibility." What this means is that his final statement of how and what God knows will have to reconcile the following claims: (1) God knows particulars but He does not know them as particulars. (2) What He knows He knows perfectly. (3) In no sense is His knowledge deficient. (4) Everything that is is as well ordered as it possibly could be. (5) There is an element of chaos or lack of order in the universe. (6) God does not know this element of chaos.

[67] The term, $t^e k \hat{u} n \bar{a} h$ or "disposition" is a translation of the Arabic, $hay \bar{a} t$ which in turn is a translation of the Greek *diathesis*. In Metaphysics Δ.19, 1022b1-3, Aristotle defines "disposition" as "the arrangement of that which has parts, in respect either of place or of potency or of kind." In addition to having this sense of arrangement with respect to place and potency and kind, the Hebrew term borrows from its Arabic source the connotations of "exterior," "appearance," and "form." Cf. H. A. Wolfson, "The Classification of Sciences in Mediaeval Jewish Philosophy," *Hebrew Union College Jubilee Volume* (*Cincinnati*, 1925), p. 302n, and *Crescas' Critique of Aristotle*, pp. 687-688.

Gersonides as well as Maimonides had stated in several places that God's knowledge differs from ours in that God knows through a single act of knowledge what we know through multiple acts. Gersonides here identifies this object of Divine Knowledge as the disposition of the thing. In the light of our earlier comments on *'eṣem* and *seder* the primary senses of the term, "dis-

besides Him acquires this knowledge from the product.[68] When he[69] sees a thing change[70] from the aspect of its endowed nature, then (his) knowledge of the thing that has changed (also) changes.[71] Thus things subject to generation acquire successive

---

position" in this context are form and arrangement. (See notes 13 and 40.) However it is clear that the sense of arrangement is broadened to be the arrangement as such and not arrangement as the term is limited in its range in Aristotle's context. Given the extension of the term to refer to the form of a thing, this change is understandable.

[68] Literally, what is made. What Gersonides seems to mean here is the following: every sense particular has an essence or nature or form or ordering (these terms all being understood as having a single referent). From this essence the thing "appears" in the sublunar world. Its appearance is through a succession of spatial-temporal states caused and determined by the nature. It is these appearances through which we first become acquainted with the thing in terms of which we deduce the essence of the thing. Hence the process of knowing for God and man is inverse. God knows the essence immediately and (for Maimonides as interpreted by Gersonides, but, as we shall see, not for Gersonides) by means of this essence God knows the spatial-temporal effects of this essence. We on the other hand know first through the senses these manifestations from which we deduce or abstract the essence.

On this picture the question arises, what is the relation between the essence we know and the essence God knows. For Maimonides there is none, for which reason Maimonides claims that no analogy can be drawn between our knowledge and God's. As we shall see, this answer cannot be acceptable to Gersonides.

[69] I.e., anyone other than God.

[70] Either come to be or pass away. *Hithadeš* could refer to both. In this case the primary picture is in terms of genesis, viz. the genesis of successive states of the sense particular. However, there is no genesis without corruption. The coming to be of one state of a thing is concurrent with the ceasing to be of another state.

[71] I.e., either comes to be or passes away or both. Any change in the object of knowledge will affect a corresponding change in the knower.

states of knowledge (*125*) and it is probable that, if the successive states of generation (and corruption of the thing known) are very great numerically, he will never have perfect knowledge of what proceeds from this (particular) product.

This being the case, and (it further being the case that) God, may He be blessed, is the Actuator of what exists in this totality, therefore He (must) know what is subject to generation by a perfect knowledge, unrelated to our knowledge. This is so because He knows by a single (act of) knowledge all that is subject to generation and corruption from the aspect of its endowed nature, (whereas) we know what is subject to generation by its changing.[72] Therefore, it is not proper that we should draw any

---

[72] Maimonides states the following in *The Guide* 3.21:

> A great disparity subsists between the knowledge an artificer has of the thing he has made and the knowledge someone else has of the artifact in question. For if the artifact was made in a way conforming to the knowledge of its artificer, the artificer only made it through following his own knowledge. With regard to the other one who looks at the artifact, comprehending it with his knowledge, his knowledge follows the artifact. ... For we know all that we know only through looking at the beings; therefore our knowledge does not grasp the future or the infinite. Our insights are renewed and multiplied according to the things from which we acquire the knowledge of them. He, may He be exalted, is not like that. I mean that His knowledge of things is not derived from them, so that there is multiplicity and renewal of knowledge.
>
> (Pines tr., pp. 484-485)

Gersonides, as we have noted above, often uses this analogy of the artificer to illustrate what it means to know the *seder* or *'eṣem* of a thing. However, Maimonides' illustration of his point is somewhat confusing. He asks us to consider an instrument and its movements. The inventor from knowing the instrument knows its movements whereas we come to know the instrument from

analogy between our knowledge and the knowledge of God, may He be blessed, by saying that if God, may He be blessed, has such states of knowledge, He would possess a plurality of cognitions and (thus) His essence would possess plurality. The reason for this is that what is known to us by a great number of states of knowledge is known to God, may He be blessed, by a single cognition, as was mentioned above. Indeed, He knows by a single cognition of these things what we could not possibly conceive by multiple cognitions. This is because our knowledge does not encompass the multiplicity of things subject to

---

the movements. The example is confusing because in this case both the inventor and the observers have direct knowledge of the thing. We differ only with respect to its functions. However, it is clear from Maimonides' continuation of the quote given above that he did not intend his example to apply only to knowing functions:

> On the contrary, the things in question follow upon his knowledge, which preceded and established them as they are: either as the existence of what is separate from matter; or as the existence of a permanent individual endowed with matter; or as the existence of what is endowed with matter; or as the existence of what is endowed with matter and has changing individuals, but follows on an incorruptible and immutable order. Hence, with regard to Him, may He be exalted, there is no multiplicity of insights and renewal and change of knowledge.

What God knows is a model of a thing in a single insight. This knowledge is such that to know the model itself is to know all of its functions. However, it is the model — which is one — and not the functions — which are many — that He knows. We never see the model but from the unfolding of the functions and/or manifestations of the thing in time and space, we determine our own model. As noted above (note 68), Gersonides, who basically accepts this account of the situation of divine and human knowing, will have to explain how our model and God's model are alike and different.

generation in the world from the side of the nature with which
God, may He be blessed, has endowed it.[73]

These are the two arguments which the Master The Guide,
may his memory be blessed, mentions in Part 3 of his honorable
book, *The Guide of the Perplexed,*[74] in order to establish that
God, may He be blessed, knows all of these particulars. It is
clear that this second argument, if it established that God, may
He be blessed, knows all of these entities subject to generation,

---

[73] Not only is the world constituted of an infinite number of individuals,
but there is an infinite number of propositions predicable of each individual
since relational statements can be made about any individual with respect to
another individual at least in terms of their spatial and/or temporal relations.
If God's knowledge includes all of these propositions, then we can never even
approximate in our knowledge what God knows. However even if we could
know all of these propositions, our knowledge still would be different from
God's in that we would know all this as an infinite conjunction whereas God
knows all this as a single judgment.

Gersonides himself uses this very argument in Treatise One to argue that
the Active Intellect and our acquired intellects are not identical. Hence there is
no question of Gersonides accepting the truth of what Maimonides here
claims. However, the force of this argument is to negate the validity of all of
the arguments of the Aristotelian philosophers. All of those arguments began
with an analysis of how we know, from which they concluded to what is the
case with God's knowledge. But, if Maimonides' argument be granted, it
follows that none of those arguments are valid since they falsely assume some
analogy between God's knowledge and ours. But Gersonides already has told
us that those arguments contain "aspects of plausibility." As we shall see, he
solves this dilemma by accepting Maimonides' premises but denying his conclusion. This argument certainly shows that God's knowledge is different from
ours. But to say that there is thus no analogy at all between our knowledge and
God's knowledge is to overstate the case. Just what this analogy is is one of
the more important problems that Gersonides will consider.

[74] 3.19 and 21. See notes 64 and 72.

negates some of the arguments by means of which the philosophers negated (the proposition) that God, may He be blessed, knows these particulars.[75] (However) some

[75] Cf. note 73. All of the arguments of the philosophers presuppose some analogy between God's knowledge and our knowledge. The force of this second argument of Maimonides is to negate this analogy.

Gersonides only notes here the second argument because, as he will explain subsequently, the first argument does not negate the arguments of the philosophers. What is confusing in his statement, however, is that he says that the second argument negates some and not all of the arguments of the philosophers. All of the arguments equally assume the stated analogy. Hence it is difficult to see on what grounds Gersonides claims that this argument applies to some but not to all of the arguments.

What Gersonides may have in mind here is the following: we already have noted that he did not consider all of the stated arguments of the philosophers to contain "aspects of plausibility." Concerning those arguments which are in this sense valid, this second argument is not an effective denial. The reason for this is that while the argument demonstrates that God's knowledge and our knowledge are different, it does not show that there is no analogy between them. (Cf. note 74.) However, concerning those arguments noted not to contain aspects of plausibility, this second argument of Maimonides is effective. The problem now is, however, in what way this second argument is effective. It would be strange to say that this second argument is effective simply because the spurious arguments are spurious anyway.

I would propose the following solution to this problem: in stating the first argument of Maimonides it was emphasized that to attribute to God ignorance of particulars is worse than attributing to God a not absolutely perfect ordering of the sublunar world. But Gersonides already has indicated that this reply to this objection will be that God knows particulars, but He does not know them as particulars. However, this reply is valid only in terms of those arguments which maintain the weaker interpretation of Aristotle's position listed in chapter one, viz. that God knows particulars in terms of their ordering and universal nature rather than as particulars. This defense does not apply to those listed arguments whose conclusion supports the strong interpretation, viz. that God knows only Himself and He does not know particulars in any way. Ger-

21d philosophers/ rejected the first of the above-mentioned arguments to establish that God, may He be blessed, knows all of these particulars by stating that it does not necessarily follow from our positing that God, may He be blessed, is without knowledge of these particulars that imperfection would be attributed to God. This is because not every lack is an imperfection.[76] Rather, it is an imperfection (only) in a being to

---

sonides tells us that the fourth argument has this strong conclusion and he indicates that it is a spurious argument. Similarly, the one other argument of Gersonides' predecessors noted to be spurious, the third, also has this strong consequence. Therefore what Gersonides may be claiming in this passage is that the arguments for the weak interpretation assume some analogy between God's knowledge and ours whereas the arguments for the strong interpretation presuppose that knowledge is univocally the same in both cases; this second argument of Maimonides does not prove that there is no analogy between these two instances of knowing but it does prove that knowledge is not univocal in both cases; hence while this second argument is not a valid refutation of all of the arguments of the philosophers, it is valid against the third and the fourth arguments which defend the strong interpretation of Aristotle's denial that God knows particulars.

[76] Gersonides deals with this point below in more detail. As an example of this point he says that lack of motion would not be considered an imperfection in God because only an imperfect being could possess motion; in other words there are perfections whose range is limited to imperfect beings. Such perfections are not applicable to perfect beings. Hence to consider the lack of them to be an imperfection in a perfect being is to commit a category mistake. It is a perfection of a knife to be sharp in the sense of cutting. But this is not a perfection of man. Similarly, since man is not sharp in this sense, it does not follow that he is in this sense dull. Neither of this pair of contrary predicates is appropriate in this context. In the same way neither motion nor its contrary, rest is appropriate to be predicated of God. The consequence of this argument, of course, is that neither knowledge nor lack of knowledge of particulars is appropriate to be predicated of God. To say that God is ignorant of particulars is as illformed as to say that God knows them.

whom such predication is appropriate,[77] (but it is) not (an imperfection) in a being to whom such predication is not appropriate.[78] For example, motion is a certain kind of perfection for beings which possess a soul.[79] Yet in saying that God, may He be blessed, is motionless we do not (attribute to Him) an imperfection. Rather it[80] is a perfection. Similarly they[81] say that it is not an imperfection that God, may He be blessed, is without knowledge of these particulars; rather (it is) a perfection, because His knowledge is of the noblest known entities (and) is not of the lesser known entities. Therefore Aristotle said in the statement recorded in Book Lambda of the *Metaphysics*[82] that he who cannot perceive multiplicity[83] is better[84] than he who can perceive (multiplicity).[85]

[77] Literally, "to him whose way is such that he may be predicated of this property."

[78] Because to predicate either the perfection or the imperfection of the thing in question would be a category mistake.

[79] I.e., an "anima vitalis."

[80] I.e., what we predicate here of God, viz. lack of motion. The reason this is a perfection is because lack of motion is not the contrary of motion. The contrary of motion is rest. Motion and rest are appropriate to be predicated of imperfect beings. Lack of motion is a perfection for God since its contrary is "motion or rest," i.e., the pair of predicates applicable only to imperfect beings.

[81] I.e., these Aristotelian philosophers.

[82] For the passage in question see Aristotle, *Metaphysics* Λ.9, 1074b, "... since it is better not to see some things than to see them." (Tredennick's translation, *Loeb Classical Library, Metaphysics*, Books X-XIV (Cambridge, Mass., 1935) p. 165.) (The source already was noted by Kellermann in his German translation, 2: 107.) It will be noticed that the Hebrew somewhat paraphrases the original.

[83] Literally, "many of the things."

[84] I.e., of a higher order of being.

[85] The first argument of Maimonides does not refute the claim of the

The Master The Guide, may his memory be blessed,[86] rejected all of the aforementioned arguments[87] and arguments similar to them. It was thought that it necessarily follows from them that God, may He be blessed, is without knowledge of these particulars on the grounds[88] that it is not proper to draw an analogy between our knowledge and the knowledge of God, may He be blessed. This is because just as the level of His existence, may He be blessed, is higher than the level of our existence, so the level of His knowledge is higher than the level of our knowledge. This necessarily follows since His knowledge is His essence, as the philosophers have explained. Therefore the Master The Guide, may his memory be blessed, (*126*) blames the philosophers for drawing an analogy between our knowledge and His knowledge, may He be blessed.[89]

---

philosophers, as Gersonides shows in this paragraph, but neither does he consider it to be spurious. It too has "aspects of plausibility." It shows (a) that God cannot be ignorant of particulars in at least some sense, and (b) the claim that God does not know particulars must be able to be reconciled with the dogma of God's absolute perfection.

[86] (MS) introduces this paragraph with ביאור דברי הרב המורה

[87] I.e., the arguments of the Aristotelian philosophers.

[88] Literally, "in saying."

[89] In *The Guide* 3.20, Maimonides states the following (note the close parallel between the Hebrew of Gersonides' summary of Maimonides' argument and the Hebrew of the Ibn Tibbon translation):

The philosophers ought to be blamed more strongly than anyone else with regard to this question. For they were those who have demonstrated that there is no multiplicity in His essence, may He be exalted, and that He has no attribute beyond His essence; but that, on the contrary, His knowledge is His essence, and His essence His knowledge. ... For the selfsame incapacity that prevents our intellects from apprehending His essence also prevents them from apprehending His knowledge of things as

It would necessarily follow from this analogy that God, may He be blessed, would be without knowledge of these particulars

they are. For this knowledge is not of the same species as ours so that we can draw an analogy with regard to it, but a totally different thing. And just as there is a necessarily existent essence from which — according to their opinion — every existent derives of necessity, or that — according to our opinion — produces all the things that are other than itself after they have been nonexistent — so do we say that this essence apprehends all that is other than itself; that in all the things that exist, nothing whatever is hidden from it; and that between our knowledge and His knowledge there is nothing in common, as there is nothing in common between our essence and His essence. With regard to this point, only the equivocality of the term "knowledge" occasions the error; for there is a community only in the terms, whereas in the true reality of the things there is a difference.

(Pines tr., pp. 481-482)

Maimonides' argument is that God's knowledge and God's essence are the same and since it already has been established that there is no analogy between God's essence and the essence of anything else, so there can be no analogy between God's knowledge and the knowledge of anything else. The claim that God's essence and knowledge are the same thing is based on Aristotle's *Metaphysics*:

... it must be of itself that the divine thought thinks (since it is the most excellent of things), and its thinking is a thinking on thinking. ... Since, then, thought and the object of thought are not different, in the case of things that have not matter, the divine thought and its object will be the same, i.e., the thinking will be one with the object of its thought.

(Λ.9, 1074b33-1075a4)

That there is no analogy between God and anything else is argued in *The Guide* in a section earlier than the one quoted above:

The subject of investigation and speculation is ... the question whether there is between Him, may He be exalted, and any of the substances created by Him a true relation of some kind so that this relation might be

in this world. But they themselves[90] have explained to us in
what way the term, "knowledge" is predicated of God, may He

> predicated of Him. It is clear at first glance that there is no correlation
> between Him and the things created by Him. For one of the properties of
> two correlated things is the possibility of inverting the statement con-
> cerning them while preserving their respective relations. Now He, may He
> be exalted, has a necessary existence while that which is other than He
> has a possible existence, as we shall make clear. There accordingly can be
> no correlation between them. ... For it is impossible to represent oneself
> that a relation subsists between the intellect and color although, ac-
> cording to our school, both of them are comprised by the same
> "existence." How then can a relation be represented between Him and
> what is other than He when there is no notion comprising in any respect
> both of the two, inasmuch as existence is, in our opinion, affirmed of
> Him, may He be exalted, and of what is other than He merely by way of
> absolute equivocation. There is in truth no relation in any respect be-
> tween Him and any of His creatures. For relation is always found be-
> tween two things falling under the same — necessarily proximate —
> species, whereas there is no relation between the two things if they merely
> fall under the same genus, namely color. If, however, two things fall un-
> der two different genera, there is no relation between them in any respect
> whatsoever, not even according to the inchoate notion of common
> opinion; ... How then could there subsist a relation between Him, given
> the immense difference between them with regard to the true reality of
> their existence, than which there is no greater difference?
>
> (1.52, 60b-61a)

For there to be any analogy between two things they must have something in
common. Yet even with things in the same genus where they are in different
species (i.e., non-proximate species), there is no valid analogy. How much the
more so would this be the case with things that do not even share a common
genus. But this is precisely the case with God and everything else. Since God
is the only necessary being and everything else is created, contingent being,
there can be no analogy between God and other things.

As will be noted below, what is problematic in this argument is the use of
the terms analogy (heqēš), equivocation (šittûp haššēm), absolute equivocation

be blessed, and of us, (viz.) in nominal equivocation,[91] as it is clear that with equivocals it is not proper to apply a demon-

---

(*šitùp gāmùr*), and nominal equivocation (*šitùp haššēm I^ebad*), (what in Aristotle's terminology is called "equivocal by change"). Maimonides tends to treat these four terms as equivalent. Yet they are quite different, and on that difference turns Gersonides' opposition to Maimonides' argument.

[90] I.e., the Aristotelian philosophers.

[91] Literally, "in equivocation of the name alone."

In chapter one of the *Categories* Aristotle distinguishes between equivocals and univocals. Two things are equivocal when they have only a name in common and the definition of being which corresponds to the name is different. Thus man and the picture of a man are equivocals because while they share an external form and they are both identified by the word, "man," they have being in different ways. Conversely two things are univocal when they have a name in common and the definition of being which corresponds to the name is the same. Thus with respect to being animals, men and oxen are univocal. Note first of all that the terms "univocal" and "equivocal" range over pairs of things and not over names of pairs of things. The names of the pairs are only signs or criteria by which the different pairs are distinguished. Note secondly that this general use of the term, "equivocal" corresponds exactly to Maimonides' term, "equivocal" (*šitùp haššēm*).

Aristotle distinguished three types of equivocals. First there are *equivocals by chance*. In this case the pairs of things have only the name in common. Their definitions are absolutely different. This sense of equivocal corresponds to what I have translated as "nominal equivocation" (*šitùp haššēm I^ebad*) and "absolute equivocation" (*šitùp gāmùr*). Second, there are *pros hen equivocals*. Two things are equivocal in this sense either because they have a common origin or because there is something to which they in some way refer. Maimonides does not use this sense of equivocation. However, as we shall see, Gersonides, as well as Maimonides' Moslem predecessors (cf. H. A. Wolfson, "The Amphibolous Terms in Aristotle, Arabic Philosophy and Maimonides," *Harvard Theological Review*, 31 (1938), 151-173, and H. A. Wolfson, "Maimonides and Gersonides on Divine Attributes as Ambiguous Terms," *Mordecai M. Kaplan Jubilee Volume* (N.Y., 1953), pp. 515-530) did use this expression. Gersonides uses the expression, "*mah šene'ĕmār b^eqòdem*

stration concerning one of them as a proof concerning the other.[92] By this argument[93] it was established, as far as he[94] was

---

ub^e'hur," "predication with respect to the prior and the posterior." Finally, there are *equivocals by analogy*. For such equivocation at least four related terms are necessary. In such equivocation the second is related to the first as the fourth is to the third. This strictly speaking is the proper use of the term, "analogy" (*heqēš*). However, this sense of equivocation does not have a significant role in the theories of either Maimonides or Gersonides.

While this three-fold distinction in the uses of the term, "equivocal" will be particularly important in Gersonides' objections to this argument of Maimonides (at least the first two of them), it is doubtful that Maimonides here recognizes that he is using the term "equivocation" equivocally since his phraseology in the argument lightly slides between the terms "analogy," "generally equivocal," "equivocal by chance" and "*pros hen* equivocation," as was noted above (note 89). Hence while the phraseology here is clearly that of equivocal by chance, Maimonides probably meant merely equivocal without distinguishing any senses of the term.

[92] Literally, "that there be taken the demonstration from some of them to others of them."

In the *Posterior Analytics* Aristotle says that in a valid demonstration the middle term "must be a single identical term unequivocally predicable of a number of individuals" (1.2, 77a9). The argument, "my coat is red; a red is a communist; therefore, my coat is a communist" is not valid because the term, "red" is used equivocally in the argument. The red called "red" in the major premise is not the same red that is called "red" in the minor premise. These two instances of red are equivocals by chance. However, while Maimonides' point here is perfectly intelligible with equivocals by chance, it is not clear that the same thing holds true for *pros hen* equivocals. That demonstrations involving this latter kind of equivocals is categorically different is seen in Aristotle's *Metaphysics* where Aristotle quite consciously constructs a number of demonstrations concerning *ousia* where the term, "*ousia*" is intentionally equivocal in this sense. (Cf. Joseph Owens, *The Doctrine of Being in the Aristotelian Metaphysics*. (Toronto: Pontifical Institute of Medieval Studies, 1951).) That the demonstrations here contain *pros hen* equivocals in no way is a violation of the rule of logic cited in the above passage from the *Posterior Analytics*.

concerned, that these arguments which the philosophers mentioned do not render impossible (the doctrine) that God knows all of these particulars. Since clearly it is not impossible, then clearly it is proper to posit that He knows them[95] in order to remove from Him the imperfection of ignorance.[96]

[93] I.e., Maimonides' over-all argument, viz. if God cannot know particulars then there is some analogy between God's knowledge and our knowledge; there is no such analogy; therefore, it is not the case that God cannot know particulars.

[94] I.e., Maimonides. By this phrase Gersonides indicates that he considers this argument to be spurious. As we already have noted the weakness of the argument is Maimonides' failure to distinguish the different senses of the term, "equivocal."

[95] I.e., particulars.

[96] This second argument of Maimonides is not an argument that God knows particulars. It is a refutation of the earlier arguments that God does not know them. Given that no rational argument can be presented for or against God knowing particulars (which is the consequence of this second argument, if it is valid) then Maimonides says we should follow the teachings of the Torah, which is what the first argument states, viz. that from the Torah we learn that God is in every respect perfect which further entails that no ignorance, including ignorance of particulars, can be attributed to God.

As we already have noted, Gersonides finds these arguments spurious. However, they are not without their "aspects of plausibility." We already have noted this aspect concerning the first argument. (See notes 73 and 85.) It remains to be seen what is the aspect of plausibility of the second. As already noted, Maimonides fails to distinguish *pros hen* equivocation and equivocal by chance. His conclusion in this second argument would follow if God's knowledge and our knowledge were equivocal by chance. But they are not. They are *pros hen* equivocals. Maimonides' argument has validity insofar as it shows us that these two instances of knowledge are not univocals.

What follows is a development of this second argument of Maimonides. In it Maimonides states five cases in which God's knowledge differs from ours. They correspond to the differences pointed out in the arguments of the

The Master The Guide, may his memory be blessed, granted
five cases[97] in which His knowledge, may He be blessed, is different from our knowledge. I mean to say that each one of these
five cases which are characteristic of the knowledge of God, may
He be blessed, according to his[98] view, could not possibly be
characteristic of our knowledge. I will now explain this to you in
discussing these five cases.

The first of them[99] is that that knowledge which is
numerically one is equal to and agrees with many different
species of things. It is proper that you should know that it is impossible for us to conceive[100] of a known plurality which is not
(naturally) unified. I mean to say that (we could conceive of this
case only) with a unity such that the one thing derives from the
other thing a level of perfection and fulfillment.[101] This is

---

Aristotelians for why God cannot know particulars. When Gersonides shows
that these differences make sense only as grounds for *pros hen* equivocation
and not chance equivocation, Gersonides then has laid out all the "data" that
he needs to propose his own solution to the problem of God's knowledge of
particulars.

[97] Literally, "accepted five things." These are five propositions stated by
Maimonides in *The Guide* 3.20 (pp. 482-483 of the S. Pines tr.) to illustrate
his second argument, viz. that no analogy can be drawn between God's
knowledge and our knowledge. In the text of *The Guide* each of these instances
of difference is stated in a single sentence. Gersonides takes each of these and
for his own purposes, as we shall see, elaborates them.

[98] I.e., Maimonides.

[99] I.e., the first of the five cases. As stated by Maimonides, the case reads,
"His knowledge, while being one, corresponds to many known things
belonging to various species."

[100] Literally, it is impossible that this be conceived in our knowledge.

[101] In the *Metaphysics* (Δ.6, 1015b16-1017a3), Aristotle gives us two different lists of different senses of the term, "one." The second list is intended to

because only in this way could a plurality of things become one
in number.[102] For example, our statement that man is corporeal,

---

be a summary of the first list, but it is not altogether clear how the two lists
correlate.

The first list notes the following different senses of what it means for two
things to be one: (1) things are one "by accident." In this sense two things are
one when they are accidents of the same substance, e.g. Coriscus and what is
musical, i.e., both terms are predicated of a single referent but the predication
in both cases is accidental, i.e., neither Coriscus nor musical are part of the
definition of what is both. (2) Things are one "by its own nature." Here what
is predicated of a thing is predicated essentially. Gersonides limits the range of
the term unity to this second sense since in the first sense any two things could
be called in some sense one, e.g. all particulars are part of the same universe.

Within this second category in his first list, Aristotle notes four different
senses. (2a) Two things are one because "they are continuous," so that the
elements of a piece of wood would be one in this sense, i.e., they constitute a
single substance. (2b) Two things are one when "their substratum does not
differ in kind" so that we can say that all juices are one in the sense that they
are composed of the same elements, water and air. (2c) Two things are one
when their "genus is one though distinguished by opposite differentiae." For
example, horse and man are one in this sense since both are animals. (2d) Two
things are one "when the definition which states the essence of one is indivisible from another definition which shows us the other." In this sense
everything that diminishes or increases is one. However, Aristotle adds an important qualification to this sense of unity. As it now stands anything that has
quantity and is continuous would be one in this sense. This would apply to all
sense particulars. But if this were the case there would be no distinction between natural oneness in this sense (2d) and accidental oneness (1). Hence
Aristotle states as a qualification, "While in a sense we call anything one if it
is a quantity and continuous, in a sense we do not unless it is a whole, i.e.,
unless it has unity of form." In other words, insofar as we are speaking of
natural unity, what is called one in this sense (2d) must be one already in one
of the other senses of natural unity (2), i.e., it must share a form in common.

Finally Aristotle says (3) that two things are one when "the *essence* of what
is one is to be some kind of beginning of number." By this he means that they

vegetative, sensitive, (and) rational,[103] refers to a subject which is numerically one. (This is so) even if the parts of the definition

must constitute the same numerical unit of measure. For example, all things that have weight are numerical with respect to weight. Insofar as they have the same weight they are one, i.e., the number signifying the weight of one is the same number signifying the weight of the other. In this sense number is predicated of classes of things so that for things derivatively to have the same number, e.g. one, they must belong to the same class.

Aristotle's second list consists of the following different senses. Things may be one (A) in number, when their matter is one (i.e., identical in reference), (B) in species, when their definition is one (i.e., identical in reference), (C) in genus, when the same (i.e. identical in reference) figure of predication applies to both, and (D) by analogy, when they are related as a third thing to a fourth. Again, it is not clear how these two lists correlate. However, I would suggest the following correlation: (A) with (2a), (2b), and (3), (B) with (2d), (C) with (2c), and (D) with (1).

What is problematic here is that (3) is clearly numerical unity from Aristotle's examples but what constitutes numerical unity is sharing a same class, which is identity of form. However, Aristotle tells us in his second list that numerical unity consists in identity of matter. By his second list (3) is more like what he describes (B), unity in species, to be. This confusion may explain why Gersonides' description of what he calls numerical unity (A) fits Aristotle's characterization of what Aristotle calls in his second list (B) unity in species. In any case Gersonides considers numerical unity to be possible only where there is a single form shared by the numerous things numbered.

[102] If we limit ourselves to Aristotle's first list of senses of unity (see note 101) then Gersonides' point is correct since (3) would be regarded there as numerical unity. In (3) things are numerable and numerically identical if they belong to the same class, and, as Aristotle explains in other places (e.g. *Metaphysics* A.1 and A.2), to belong to the same class is to share the same form and the form of a thing constitutes its perfection and fulfillment. However, from Aristotle's second list, Gersonides' claim here can be refuted. Aristotle tells us the following:

> The latter kinds of unity (senses A, B, C, D) are always found when the former are; e.g. things that are one in number [where their matter is one]

are many, since one part of the definition is perfected and fulfilled by the other.[104] However, concerning the many things of

___

are also one in species, while things that are one in species are not all one
in number; but things that are one in species are all one in genus, while
things that are so in genus are not all one in species but are all one by
analogy; while things that are one by analogy are not all one in genus.
                                                              (1016b32-1014a3)

In other words, while technically Gersonides is right in claiming that only
what is one in species can be numerically one, there are other senses of unity
than numerical unity, and things which are neither one numerically nor in
species nor in genus may be in some sense one (viz. D). Gersonides' reply to
this objection probably would be that in this very loose sense sensible particulars may be one but in this sense there is no knowledge of the thing since
to know a thing is to know its cause which is its form (*Metaphysics* A.1) and
hence oneness of knowledge cannot be oneness by analogy.

[103] This terminology was commonplace in medieval Jewish philosophy. For
example, Abraham Ibn Daud in his *Hā-Ĕmûnāh Hā-Rāmāh* notes the
following faculties of the soul *nepeš*: 1. vegetative (*simᵉḥiyût*), 2. animal
(*ḥiyûniyût*), and 3. human ('*ĕnôsiyût*). The terms that Gersonides uses, namely, *mᵉdabbēr*, *marᵉgis* and *nizôn* are to be understood as synonymous in this
context for Ibn Daud's names noted above. This difference in terminology (but
only in terminology) is not unusual, since there are several traditions in the
Moslem-Jewish philosophy for the names of these faculties. The vegetative
faculty involves nutrition, growth and generation. The animal faculty involves
sensation, feeling and motion. The rational faculty involes speech and the
various forms of rational activity discussed in note 25. Cf. *Hā-Ĕmûnāh Hā-
Rāmāh*, published with a German translation from the Hebrew by Simeon Weil
(Frankfurt a.m., 1852; Hebrew text only reprinted 1966 or 67), pp. 20-34 of
the Hebrew text.

[104] The preceding example of the unity of the three functions of the soul of
man and the body is ambiguous with regard to the two senses of mathematical
unity noted by Aristotle. (See note 102.) However this sentence makes it clear
that the required unity is a unity of form in the sense of (3) in note 102, i.e.,
multiple things are numerically one if and only if they form part of the
definition of a single substance, i.e., they are interrelated as parts of the form

which it is impossible that the one derives a level of perfection and fulfillment from the other — as is the case with particulars which, insofar as they are particulars, are infinite[105] — clearly it is impossible that they should be unified in our thought,[106] even if we should have knowledge of them. This is because they do not have any aspect in which they are unified. (Therefore) how much the more so (is it impossible) that they should become one in absolute simplicity, as is the case with the knowledge of God, may He be blessed, which is one in absolute simplicity since He is one in absolute simplicity.

That it is impossible that these particulars derive from each other the form and the perfection[107] is clear, since they proceed

---

or essence of the thing which is at the same time the end or final cause of that thing.

[105] Aristotle tells us that "art arises when from many notions gained by experience one universal judgment about a class of objects is produced" (*Metaphysics* A.1, 981a5). Knowledge consists in forming a universal judgment about a class of things of which experience makes us aware. But there is no actual knowledge of the particulars themselves. "When we come to the concrete thing, ... whether perceptible or intelligible ... — of these there is no definition, but they are known by the aid of intuitive thinking or of perception; ... but they are always stated and recognized by means of the universal formula. But matter is unknowable in itself" (ibid., 1936a2-9). What we know of a thing is its definition which consists of the universal and the form (ibid., A.2, 1036a28), but the particular itself is unknowable because matter is unknowable. Similarly, Gersonides argues here, particulars are incapable of numerical unity since that very matter which makes them particular also accounts for their number being infinite.

[106] Literally, in our knowledge.

[107] Aristotle tells us that knowledge of a thing consists in knowing the end of the thing (*Metaphysics* A.2). Furthermore the good, the end and the causes of the thing are the same (ibid., 982b10).

As we already have noted (note 105), what is known of the thing is its de-to what is not an end,[108] as it is impossible that some of them should be a form for others of them,[109] as is explained in the *Metaphysics*.[110] Furthermore, they[111] move cyclically, i.e. in species, although they do not move cyclically as individuals,[112]

---

finition. In *Metaphysics* Z.12, 1037b7-1038a35, Aristotle explains that this very definition of the thing, which we already have noted (*Metaphysics* A.2) to be the good of the thing, is also the unity of the thing. Hence neither the perfection nor the unity of a thing can lie in that thing as a particular. The unity and perfection is found in the form or definition which itself is not a particular.

[108] *Taklit* is used here in the sense of *telos*. (Cf. note 40.) The meaning is that no particular can in itself be an end. (Cf. note 107.) Hence if the end of particulars, through which they are naturally unified, lies in each other, then each proceeds to what is not an end so that its end is something that is not an end, which is absurd.

[109] Since no particular as a particular can be a form, the form being both the definition and the end of the thing.

[110] It is not clear if Gersonides has a specific passage in mind or not. He may simply mean the *Metaphysics* as a whole, referring to the kinds of passages that we have noted from the *Metaphysics* in notes 101, 102, 105 and 107. The argument that follows somewhat resembles Aristotle's discussion in *Metaphysics* I.2, 994a-994b. But the resemblance is very superficial. Both the Aristotle passage and Gersonides' passage are arguments for the necessity of a final cause where that cause cannot lie within the particulars themselves. However, beyond this the resemblance of the two passages vanishes. The Aristotle passage is an argument against an infinite regress of causes. The Gersonides passage, on the other hand, is against explaining the causal process with particulars in terms of cyclical movement. I can find no passage in the *Metaphysics* where a discussion exactly in these terms occurs. It also should be mentioned that Gersonides' reference here may be to the commentary on the *Metaphysics* of Ibn Rushd rather than directly to Aristotle's own words.

[111] I.e., the multiple particulars which are not as particulars naturally unified.

[112] No individual in the sublunar world has cyclical motion. However it is

and clearly it is impossible with things that move cyclically that one of them should be at the level of the form and the perfection of all of the rest, since, if this were so, the one thing would be at the level of the form for itself.[113] But this (consequence) is absolutely absurd. For example, (consider) the accidents *A, B, C* (which) are subject to generation. They proceed in cyclical movement to a different end so that *B* would be the perfection of *A*, and *C* would be the perfection of *B*, and furthermore *A* would become the perfection of *C*.[114] Therefore *A* is the perfection of *A*,[115] and by this (line of reasoning) clearly *B* is the perfection of *B*, and *C* is the perfection of *C*.

---

not the case that no individual *per se* has cyclical motion, e.g. the movement of the sun is cyclical. (Cf. *De Generatione et Corruptione*, 338b6-11.) It is not clear what Gersonides means here by species as distinct from individuals. He may have the following in mind: natural phenomena like rain and showers have individually rectilinear motion, but Aristotle tells us (ibid.) that the occurrence of such phenomena is cyclical. In other words, the individual drops of water that fall on a given place fall with rectilinear motion, but the rain itself, which is a specious term in this case, occurs cyclically.

However, the meaning of the whole passage is not clear in this context. It is an argument for final causes and not an argument for why particulars lack natural unity. In fact the argument has nothing to do with particulars at all, as Gersonides tells us in this sentence. Perhaps the point is that which is indicated in note 110, viz. that the unity of a thing lies in its final cause and the final cause must be other than the particulars themselves.

[113] I.e., something would be its own form and therefore its own perfection, the perfection and the form of a thing being one and the same thing. (Cf. note 107.)

[114] Since *C* moves to *A* completing the circle *A* to *B* to *C* to *A*.

[115] Since the perfection of a thing is that to which it proceeds and *A* ultimately proceeds to *A*, therefore *A* is its own perfection. The same holds true for *B* and *C* respectively.

But it is impossible that we should conceive this to be the case, namely that a non-unified plurality could be one in absolute simplicity and (*127*) oneness. (Therefore) the Master The Guide, may his memory be blessed, said that in this case the knowledge of God, may He be blessed, and our knowledge are different. It is possible for him to say this given that the term, "knowledge" is predicated of God, may He be blessed, and of us in nominal equivocation.[116]

---

[116] Cf. note 91. Gersonides should be understood as speaking here and in the other four cases to follow "with tongue in cheek." As laid out by Gersonides, Maimonides' argument reads as follows. God's knowledge is different from ours. Therefore God can know particulars as particulars. The reason that God's knowledge is different from ours is that (Case 1) God knows what naturally is not unified as unified which could not be the case with human knowledge. But the reason why God's knowledge must differ from ours in this respect is because God knows particulars. In other words, Maimonides begs the question. Since God knows particulars then His knowledge is radically different from ours from which it follows that God knows particulars.

Maimonides could reply that these five cases are illustrations of the difference and not arguments. But the illustrations are irrelevant if they already presuppose the very thing in question, namely knowledge of particulars. Maimonides must find examples of God's radically different knowledge which do not entail or presuppose divine knowledge of particulars as particulars.

Gersonides' point beyond this logical one is that in all five cases the doctrine that God knows particulars as particulars leads to absurdities and that the defense of this dogma makes the claim that God knows in any sense unintelligible. But this is exactly what Maimonides means when he says that divine predicates are absolutely equivocal. Gersonides' reply is that such equivocation is itself unintelligible. Maimonides is correct to point out that human and divine predicates are equivocals, but they are not absolutely equivocal.

Of all the five cases explicated by Gersonides, the explanation here is the least intelligible. However, the form of argument indicated in this first argument runs clearly through all five. In the latter four his point is presented with greater clarity.

The second of these cases in which the knowledge of God, may He be blessed, and our knowledge differ, according to the view of the Master, may his memory be blessed, is that His knowledge, may He be blessed, is connected with non-existence.[117] It is proper that you should know that/ it is necessary that he[118] posit this difference between His knowledge, may He be blessed, and our knowledge, since he[118] posited that God, may He be blessed, knows all particulars.[119] Therefore, it would necessarily follow that He knows that they[120] are now non-existent, but that they will come into existence at such and such a time, and that at such and such a (later) time they will cease to exist. Therefore, His knowledge of this non-existent event[121] exists now in actuality although the known upon which that knowledge depends is non-existent.

It is impossible that we conceive of this.[122] This is because the

---

[117] If God knows particulars and His knowledge is unchanging although the particulars themselves are always changing, i.e., coming into existence and going out of existence, then God must know a given particular before it has come into existence and/or when it has gone out of existence, i.e., when it does not exist. Thus God's knowledge is connected with an infinite number of non-existent objects of knowledge. Maimonides expresses this second difference as follows: "In the second place, it (i.e., God's knowledge) may have as its object something that does not exist." (Cf. note 97.)

[118] I.e., Maimonides.

[119] Cf. note 116. By this statement Gersonides indicates that Maimonides begs the question concerning God's knowledge of particulars.

[120] I.e., the particulars.

[121] Or, accident.

[122] Gersonides is again speaking tongue-in-cheek. Cf. note 116. What Maimonides finds to be a case of absolute equivocation is more properly a case of *pros hen* equivocation. Maimonides must claim that this is absolute equivocation because if God knows particulars as particulars then what it

known and the knowledge are one in number. (Thus) it necessarily follows that when the known is non-existent, the knowledge would be non-existent. Therefore it necessarily follows[123] in the case of our knowledge that if the knowledge of a thing exists in actuality, the known upon which the knowledge depends would exist.

One may not reply[124] that our knowledge is actual, but that the known is non-existent, as is the case with many mathematical figures of which we have knowledge that have no existence at all outside of the soul.[125] (One may not say this) because[126] we already have explained in Treatise One of this

---

means to say that God "knows" is completely unintelligible. What proceeds is a demonstration of why this case of knowing is inconceivable, i.e., unintelligible.

[123] From the numerical identity of the known and the knowledge.

[124] This expression, w^e'ēn l'ōmēr šeyo'mar is used consistently to identify an objection against a point that Gersonides has just noted. His reply to the objection immediately follows the statement of the objection.

[125] In *Metaphysics* M.2, Aristotle tells us that mathematical objects neither exist in sensible things (1076b1) nor exist separately (1076b12-13). Generally the objection is an objection to the reference theory of meaning which is assumed in this instance both by Maimonides and Gersonides, i.e., what a term means is its object with the consequence that for a term to have meaning entails that the term refers to an existent object of some kind. The objection arises not only from knowledge of mathematicals, but, as Gersonides will explain further on (in his discussion of case four), the objection arises from the case of non-existent particulars. Gersonides' theoretical objector claims that such entities have only mental existence. As Gersonides will explain in his reply, this is not a correct interpretation of Aristotle's claim concerning mathematicals. As we shall see later, the answer that he gives here concerning mathematicals also applies to the question of the knowledge of non-existent particulars.

[126] The term, "*ki*" following the statement of an objection indicates the beginning of Gersonides' reply to the stated objection.

book[127] that our knowledge is dependent upon the intelligible ordering which these things have[128] in the soul of the Active Intellect.[129] This ordering exists perpetually in His soul.[130] But it is

[127] Chapter 6, pp. 36-48. There Gersonides states the following:

> This is because if these multiple conceptions were not unified in the soul of the Active Intellect, the Active Intellect would be complex because its conceptions are complex and they are its essence, because the intellect and the conception (or intellection) are numerically one thing, as was explained. And it already was explained above that the Active Intellect is numerically one, so that this change is not possible. Therefore it is clear that the Active Intellect knows all these orderings from the aspect by which they are one, and in this way the Active Intellect is one. However, it happens that the hylic intellect does not conceive from the aspect in which these orderings are numerically one except in a far removed degree since its reception of the conceptions from the Active Intellect is joined to the senses.
>
> (pp. 37-38)

What the Active Intellect knows is the orderings (cf. notes 13, 14, 26, 33, 38, and 40) of things. This includes all things, actual and/or possible existent particulars and mathematicals. We conceive (as opposed to perceive) them in the same way. The difference, however, between us and the Active Intellect is that as conceived by the Active Intellect these orderings are unified. Hence the multiple orderings which we conceive have a single referent (although each presumably keeps its distinct sense; this point is never explained; if it were we would have a clear distinction between sense and reference), namely the single order which is both the content of the Active Intellect and the Active Intellect itself.

[128] Literally, which is found for these things.

[129] I.e., the intelligence whose sphere is the moon who governs or "orders" the sublunar world.

[130] In *Metaphysics* M.3, Aristotle tells us that the term, "exist" has many senses (1077b16). Not only do some concrete particulars exist, but also mathematicals exist, since they are objects of knowledge. But the sense in

impossible that the Master The Guide should maintain that the
knowledge of God, may He be blessed, of these things subject to

which they exist is different from the sense in which sense particulars exist.

> For as there are many propositions about things merely considered as in
> motion, apart from what each such thing is and from their accidents, and
> as it is not therefore necessary that there should be either a mobile
> separate from sensibles, or a distinct mobile entity in the sensibles, so too
> in the case of mobiles there will be propositions and sciences, which treat
> them however not *qua* mobile but only *qua* bodies, or again only *qua*
> planes, or only *qua* lines, or *qua* divisibles, or *qua* indivisibles having
> position, or only *qua* indivisibles. Thus since it is true to say without
> qualification that not only things which are separable but also things
> which are inseparable exist (for instance, that mobiles exist), it is true
> also to say without qualification that the objects of mathematics exist,
> and with the character ascribed to them by mathematicians. And as it is
> true to say of the other sciences too, without qualification, that they deal
> with such and such a subject — not with what is accidental to it ... but
> with that which is the subject of each science ... so too is it with
> geometry; if its subjects happen to be sensible, though it does not treat
> them *qua* sensible, the mathematical sciences will not for that reason be
> sciences of sensibles .... Thus, then, geometers speak correctly; they talk
> about existing things, and their subjects do exist; for being has two forms
> — it exists not only in complete reality but also materially.
>
> (*Metaphysics* M.3, 1077b24-1078a31)

If a proposition is true it must refer to something which exists, and in the case
of an affirmative true proposition the object of the referred to state of affairs
must exist as well. Yet Aristotle tells us that while the propositions in sciences
such as mathematics, physics and metaphysics are true, none of which consider
particulars as particulars since even physics prescinds its subject matter from
accidental characteristics concerning which there is no scientific knowledge,
only particulars exist. Aristotle's solution is to distinguish two senses of
existence, existence in complete reality and material existence. Presumably a
single thing can exist both ways simultaneously. But what exactly is this

generation is dependent upon the intelligible ordering which they have in Himself[131] because He[132] exists perpetually.[133] If

---

"existence in complete reality"? The objector, in this case, remembering that for Aristotle universals have no objective existence, considers this to be mere mental existence. But then is it not strange that Aristotle calls such subjectivity existence in "complete reality"?

As we already have seen (cf. note 127), Gersonides has a different account. Material things have an essence ('eṣem) which is their form (ṣûrāh). It is what the material thing is, i.e., it is the definition of the thing. It also is what it means to say that different things are numerically one. (Cf. notes 101, 102, 104 and, 105.) Things are one when they have the same form. (In this way the sense of "one" as identical is combined with the sense of "one" as equivalent. Two things are "one" in the sense of equivalence if and only if all propositions about one have the same (i.e., identical) truth value as all propositions about the other. Two things are "one" in the sense of identity if they are one and the same thing. On this account two things, different materially, are one in the sense of equivalence if and only if they are essentially one, i.e., they have the same form or essence, in the sense of identity.)

This form may exist in the material world, i.e., in combination with matter. When it does the form is also the end or telos of the thing formed from the combination of the form in question and matter. (Cf. note 107.) This form may be spoken of then as the order (seder) of the thing. Insofar as a thing is material it is unintelligible for matter itself is unintelligible. (Metaphysics Z.10, 1036a9.) (This is why there is no science of things considered with their accidental characteristics.) Things are intelligible only insofar as they have an intelligible structure which is insofar as they are ordered. But since the order or ordering of the thing is that thing prescinded of matter and besides matter the only remaining principle of the thing is its form, the order and the form of the thing are the same.

But form, as we have seen, not only exists in matter. It exists also conceptually in the human mind (in which case it is called a universal) and it exists objectively unified with all other forms as the content of the Active Intellect. Hence objective scientific statements are possible even about things that do not have material existence. Such entities have "complete reality," i.e., they are the forms existent in the Active Intellect as a single entity. These are the

(this) would be assumed,[134] He could not know particulars as particulars; rather He would know them in terms of their in-

---

proper referents of scientific statements. Hence even mathematicians "talk about existing things, and their objects do exist."

Gersonides walks a tight rope between nominalism and realism. The nominalist claims that only concrete things are real and that universals are simply mental constructs. Common sense supports the nominalist but alas he must somehow account for the objectivity of knowledge. One way of doing this is to reject the reference theory of meaning, but Gersonides, following Aristotle, did not take this path. The realist, overwhelmed by the problem of objective knowledge, asserts the reality of universals. The charge against him is that his overpopulation of the universe defies common sense. To the world of sense particulars Gersonides adds one entity, the Active Intellect. This entity is the objective reference of all scientific propositions. It is a single indivisible entity which is all forms in a unified way.

The resemblance of Kant's Transcendental Unity of Apperception to Gersonides' Active Intellect cannot go unnoticed. But there are important differences. In the first place Gersonides' world of sense particulars is a real world; it is not mere phenomena. Secondly, the Active Intellect is not hypothesized only as a necessary condition for the truth of scientific propositions. It also functions within a cosmological schema as the intelligence of the sphere of the moon in a way which would have been somewhat unintelligible to Kant. To be sure this schema of Gersonides has many difficulties. But it has the advantage of avoiding the associations of subjectivity to which Kant's Transcendental Unity of Apperception fell victim. This is because Gersonides' Active Intellect is not only a necessary condition of thought.

[131] Or, in his soul. The literal expression "in his soul" is idiomatic generally for "himself." This is all the more so the case here where God and His soul are identical.

[132] Or, it, i.e., the soul.

[133] This point will become clearer in the fourth case. Since God is not subject to change, his ideas are not subject to change. If God knows particulars *qua* their ordering which consists of eternal essences or forms, there is no difficulty. But Maimonides wants to maintain that He knows particulars as par-

telligible ordering which they have in His intellect, which is the aspect in which they are not particular.[135] Therefore he[136] decreed that in this case also the knowledge of God, may He be blessed, and our knowledge are different. This is possible in his[136] view, may his memory be blessed, since the term, "knowledge" is applied to us and God in absolute equivocation.[137]

It is proper that you should know that, on the basis of the second argument which we mentioned by which the Master The Guide, may his memory be blessed, established that God, may He be blessed, knows particulars as particulars, it would seem from the reasoning that he intended that the knowledge of God, may He be blessed, of these particulars be dependent upon the intelligible ordering of the world in His soul, according to the nature which is implanted upon it.[138] Therefore he said that the

---

ticulars, and, as will be explained in the discussion of the fouth case, this is not conceivable without God Himself being subject to change.

[134] I.e., that His perpetual, unchanging intellect knows these particulars.

[135] Which is how Gersonides maintains that God knows them. But in what sense is this knowledge of a particular? How by knowing the order of a thing do you know that thing at all? Yet Gersonides tells us that in some sense this is knowledge of the particular. But this seems strange. I understand what it means to know that Charley and Frank are instances of the form man. But how in knowing the form man do I know Charley or Frank? If only what we would call universal can be known, how are we to understand what it means to know an individual through the universal? Once Gersonides applies his Divine epistemology developed in this book to the problem of providence (*The Wars of the Lord* 3.6, and Treatise 4) a solution emerges. It is implicitly premised, as we shall see in our discussion of chapter six, on a distinction between particulars and individuals where an individual is that which is capable of unique reference and a particular is a material individual.

[136] I.e., Maimonides.

[137] See note 116.

[138] Literally, according to the nature which is "ennatured" upon it. The

Creator's knowledge of what He created is more perfect than the knowledge of anyone else, since the things subject to generation in that created thing[139] are dependent on His knowledge. (That God's knowledge is more perfect than anyone else's knowledge) is because He made that created thing[139] in such a way that the changing things in it should come into and go out of existence and the knowledge of the men who investigate it[139] is dependent upon the things subject to generation.[140] This being so, it might be thought that he contradicted himself. This is because, according to what was stated in this argument, it seems that he held the view that God, may He be blessed, is without knowledge of particulars (*128*) as particulars, but that He knows the intelligible ordering which they have in His soul.[141] It is proper that it be said to remove this doubt that the Master The Guide, may his memory be blessed, did not intend to explain to us how God, may He be blessed, knows things on the basis of this argument. This is because it is impossible for man to apprehend this, as the Master The Guide, may his memory be blessed, states many times.[142] Rather he intended to explain by this

---

"it" refers to the world. On the point made in this sentence, cf. notes 13, 26, 29, 40, 67, 129, and 130. God has a single, perpetual act of knowledge which entails that His object of knowledge is a single object. Yet the only way in which particulars can be so unifed is not insofar as they are particulars but only insofar as they have an intelligible ordering i.e., insofar as they are their form which itself is not a particular.

[139] I.e., the world.

[140] See *The Guide* 3.21, pp. 484-485 of the Pines translation. Also see the discussion of this passage in note 72.

[141] Cf. notes 130 and 135.

[142] For example,

If we knew how it comes about (viz. that everything is revealed to His knowledge), we would have an intellect in virtue of which an ap-

argument that God, may He be blessed, knows things and that
there is a great difference between His knowledge and our
knowledge, and that thus it is not proper that we should draw an
analogy between our knowledge and His knowledge, as did the
philosophers. This is clear to anyone who investigates well what
the Master The Guide, may his memory be blessed, said there
concerning this matter.[143]

---

prehension of this kind might be had. This, however, is a thing that in
what exists belongs only to Him, may He be exalted, and it is His
essence.

> (*The Guide* 3.21, p. 485
> of the S. Pines tr.)

[143] At the end of his discussion of God's knowledge, Maimonides tells us
the following:

> Understand this then. For I say that this is something most extraordinary
> and a true opinion; if it is carefully studied, no mistake or distortion will
> be found in it, nor will incongruities be attached to it; and no deficiency
> is ascribed through it to God. No demonstration at all can be obtained
> with regard to these great and sublime notions, either for our opinion —
> that of the community of those who adhere to a Law — or for the
> opinion of the philosophers, even if one considers all the differences
> among the latter with regard to this question. And with regard to all
> problems with reference to which there is no demonstration, the method
> used by us with regard to this question — I mean the question of the
> deity's knowledge of what is other than He — ought to be followed. Un-
> derstand this.

> (*The Guide* 3.21, p. 485)

Maimonides tells us that this discussion contains no contradictions, and that
the method used here should be noted carefully. However, concerning the first
part of his claim, Gersonides notes what might be considered a contradiction
in his argument, viz. that he maintains that God knows particulars as particulars but the consequence of asserting that God knows them as one is that

The third of these five cases is that His knowledge, may He
be blessed, encompasses the infinite from the respect in which it

---

He knows particulars insofar as they are their intelligible ordering and not insofar as they are particulars.

In his introduction to *The Guide* Maimonides lists seven causes of contradictory and contrary statements in any book. The sixth cause is the
following:

> The contradiction is concealed and becomes evident only after many
> premises. The greater the number of premises needed to make the con-
> tradiction evident, the more concealed it is. It thus may escape the author,
> who thinks there is no contradiction between his two original
> propositions.
>
> *(The Guide* 1. Intro., p. 18)

The objector considered here is saying that Maimonides is guilty of this kind
of contradiction concerning his second argument. But, as we already have
noted, Maimonides explicitly tells us that he is sure that no such contradiction
is present. How then are we to explain the contradiction? After listing these
seven causes for contradictions Maimonides tells us that "Divergencies that are
to be found in this Treatise are due to the fifth cause and the seventh" (ibid.,
p. 20).

Maimonides characterizes the seventh cause as follows:

> In speaking about very obscure matters it is necessary to conceal some
> parts and to disclose others. Sometimes in the case of certain dicta this
> necessity requires that the discussion proceed on the basis of a certain
> premise, whereas in another place necessity requires that the discussion
> proceed on the basis of another premise contradicting the first one. In
> such cases the vulgar must in no way be aware of the contradiction; the
> author accordingly uses some device to conceal it by all means.
>
> (Ibid., p. 18)

Some matters must be concealed from the masses. Therefore the author in different places will use contrary premises in order to mislead the masses. This is
one possible way of interpreting this passage, but it is not the one that Ger-

is infinite.[144] It was necessary that he[145] should believe this, since he posited that God, may He be blessed, knows particulars

---

sonides accepts. Rather he accounts for the apparent contradiction in terms of Maimonides' fifth cause.

> The fifth cause arises from the necessity of teaching and making someone understand. For there may be a certain obscure matter that is difficult to conceive. One has to mention it or to take it as a premise in explaining something that is easy to conceive and that by rights ought to be taught before the former, since one always begins with what is easier. The teacher, accordingly, will have to be lax, and, using any means that occur to him or gross speculation, will try to make that first matter somehow understood. ... Afterwards, in the appropriate place, that obscure matter is stated in exact terms and explained as it truly is.
>
> (Ibid., pp. 17-18)

Maimonides lists the five cases of difference between God's knowledge and our knowledge in 3.20. His assertion that there is no analogy between God's knowledge and our knowledge of any kind is a consequence drawn at the end of the discussion in 3.21. Gersonides reads the contradiction involved here to be of this kind. The statement of the second case involves an implied explanation of how God in fact knows. Maimonides is aware of this implication but, in order not to confuse his student unnecessarily, he lets this go until the student is already for this matter to be set straight.

There is no question that a contradiction is involved here. Maimonides is claiming that we can know nothing about how God knows and to prove this point he assumes something about how God knows. But, as Gersonides has told us, this second case is not to be read as a statement of how God knows. It is only an illustration for pedagogic purposes to enable the student to see how it can be said that God's knowledge and our knowledge are different. Maimonides would be guilty of a contradiction in his thought if at the end of his lesson he did not "set the record straight." Gersonides himself uses this same method, as he tells us that he will do in his introduction to this book. (The seventh cause of why this book has the particular order that it has, pp. 9-10 of the Leipzig, 1866 edition.) Concerning the seventh cause of Maimonides see note 6.

as particulars, and this is the aspect in which they are infinite. It
is impossible that we conceive of this matter.[146] This is because
knowledge insofar as it is knowledge necessitates that the known
be something limited and contained, but knowledge can neither
encompass nor limit the infinite.[147] Therefore the Master The
Guide, may his memory be blessed, said that in this matter also
the knowledge of God, may He be blessed, is different from our
knowledge. This is possible for him (to say) since knowledge is
predicated of Him, may He be blessed, and us in absolute
equivocation, as was said.[146]

One may not reply[148] that our knowledge also encompasses
the infinite since definitions and universal judgments contain an
infinite number of individuals.[149] (One may not say this)
because[148] this statement, when one examines it, is not correct.
This is because with repect to definitions and universal
judgments individuals are not known as individuals, which is the
respect in which they are infinite. Rather they are known from

---

[144] "In the third place, it may have as its object something that is infinite"
(*The Guide* 3.20, p. 483 of the Pines translation). Since God knows particulars He knows what is numerically infinite. See note 105.

[145] I.e., Maimonides.

[146] Cf. notes 91, 116 and 122.

[147] Literally, "that which is without limit." "To encompass" and "to limit"
are synonymns in this context. Hence the sentence is a simple tautology, viz.
God cannot limit what is without limit. See note 40.

[148] Cf. notes 124 and 126.

[149] The objector reads propositions like "all men are mortal" or "man is a
rational animal" to refer to all men. In other words, propositions have
referents and the referent of universal propositions and definitions is the members of the class referred to rather than the class itself. In other words, expressions such as "all x" are to be understood as distributively referring to any
x rather than collectively referring to every x.

the respect in which they are one, which is (their) common nature.[150] This is self-evident.

One may object that our knowledge encompasses the infinite since we can know concerning continuous quantity that it is divisible into what is divisible *ad infinitum*,[151] and that also we know concerning number that it is augmentable into what is augmentable *ad infinitum*.[152] We reply to him that we have this

---

[150] Given that all meaningful propositions must have a referent, we may designate the referent of general terms to be what the objector designates, namely the members of a class, or the class itself. Usually when the class is taken as the referent we opt for realism, i.e., we assert the reality of universals. But Gersonides accepts neither of these positions. The referent of a general term is neither a reified class nor the members of the class expressed distributively. It is rather that which they all are which, as it exists in the soul of the Active Intellect, is a single entity, viz. the essence or form or intelligible ordering of these things.

[151] "... it is plain that everything continuous is divisible into divisibles that are infinitely divisible. ... The same reasoning applies equally to magnitude, to time, and to motion" (*Physics* 6.1, 231b15-19).

[152] This argument is discussed at length at the end of chapter four. Since any magnitude is composed of an infinite number of parts, continuous magnitude being infinitely divisible, in knowing a magnitude we know what is infinite. Similarly, since the number of numbers is itself infinite, since given any number *n* there is always an *n* + 1, in knowing number generally we know what is infinite. The example with magnitude comes from Aristotle, as noted in note 151. As Gersonides will explain in chapter four, it is discussed at length by Ibn Rushd. But the extension of this example to number is not found in either. It appears to be Gersonides' own addition to the objection.

It might be objected that actually these two cases of magnitude and number are very different. In referring to any magnitude I am referring to what has an infinite number of parts. But in referring to a number this need not be the case. In the first example we are speaking of specific instances of magnitude. In the second example we are speaking of the class of numbers and not specific numbers. However, in Gersonides' defense it could be said that on Gersonides'

knowledge also from the respect in which the parts are one, (and) not from the aspect/ in which the parts are many.[153] This is because we do not have this knowledge of the parts in such a way that (we know), for example, one (part) is a *zeret*,[154] and another is half of a *zeret*, and another is a fourth of a *zeret*, which is the aspect in which they are many. Rather from the aspect in which each one of them is continuous magnitude we know that every continuous magnitude is divisible.[155] The same

2b

---

terms the reference to a specific magnitude is as much or as little a class reference as is the reference to number in general, since the referred to magnitude consists of an infinite number of magnitudes. Therefore, just as the general term, "number" may refer to numbers 1, 2, ..., n, $n + 1$, ..., so any term designating a given magnitude may be really a general term referring to an infinite list of magnitudes.

[153] Again Gersonides rejects both usual interpretations, viz. that the referent of general terms is either the members of the designated class or the class itself. Rather the referent is the form which determines the class. This form in one sense is the members of the class because the form is "in" the members and it is that which any given member "is" by definition. Yet it is also the class itself since it is what those members "share in common." But to say this is only to speak metaphorically. The form is an independent, individual entity, existent in the soul of the Active Intellect, which "causes" both the class (the universal) and the members of the class but is distinct from both of them.

In the light of this theory of knowledge, it is clear why Gersonides in considering Maimonides' second case understands numerical unity in the sense of identity of form rather than in the sense of identity of matter. Cf. notes 101, 102, and 104. A statement about numbers in general is not a distributive statement nor a collective statement about a class of classes. Rather it is a statement about a form of forms. Cf. note 130.

[154] A "zeret" is the distance from the little finger to the thumb of a spread, average-sized, adult hand.

[155] Literally, capable of division, i.e., in knowing the form of continuous magnitude we know what is true of every continuous magnitude.

thing holds for numbers because we do not have knowledge of numbers, for example, from the aspect in which one (number) is twenty and another is twenty-one and another is twenty-two, which is the aspect in which they are many. Rather from the aspect in which each one of them is a number we know that every number is augmentable.[156]

The fourth of these five cases is that the knowledge of God, may He be blessed, of things[157] which will come to be in the

[156] I.e., in knowing the form of number we know what is true of every number.

[157] The context makes it clear that by "things," (*d^ebārim*), Gersonides means "states of affairs." Otherwise to speak here of contradictories (*sôt^erim*) would seem strange. For example, both "chair" and "red" have opposites, viz. "non-chair" and "non-red," but these are not contradictories. However, the proposition that "some chairs are red" has a contradictory, viz. "no chairs are red." However, as Gersonides uses the term, "contradictory," there may not be a clear distinction drawn between contradictories and contraries. The reason for this is that the states of affairs that he is considering all have definite subjects. Thus the proposition expressing the fact that this chair is not red might be considered by Gersonides to be the contradictory and not merely contrary of "this chair is red."

Similarly Aristotle says concerning propositions with definite subjects the following:

It is evident also that the denial corresponding to a single affirmation is itself single; for the denial must deny just that which the affirmation affirms concerning the same subject, and must correspond with the affirmation both in the universal or particular character of the subject and in the distributed or undistributed sense in which it is understood. For instance, the affirmation "Socrates is white" has its proper denial in the proposition "Socrates is not white."

(*De Interpretatione* 7, 17b36-18a2)

Although Aristotle clearly distinguishes contraries and contradictories with

future does not necessitate that the known will be actuated; rather its (*129*) contradictory[157] remains possible.[158] It was necessary that he should believe this since it was impossible for him to negate the nature of the contingent.[159] This is because

---

propositions whose subject is universal or indefinite, with propositions like "Socrates is white" he indiscriminately speaks of their "proper denial."

[158] What Gersonides here presents as the fourth case is given by Maimonides as his fifth case.

In the fifth place, it is in accordance with the opinion of our Law that God's knowledge, may He be exalted, does not bring about the actualization of one of the two possibilities even though He, may He be exalted, knows perfectly how one of them will come about.

(*The Guide* 3.20, pg. 483 of the Pines tr.)

[159] Consider the two possible states of affairs, "a sea-battle will occur tomorrow" and "a sea-battle will not occur tomorrow." These two events are related in such a way that if one is true the other must be false. Maimonides here claims that God knows which is true and which is false while at the same time it remains true that these are possible and not necessary states of affairs.

The issue involved here is more than a question of God's knowledge of future contingents. Also in question is the logical status of propositions concerning future contingents. The logical issue is raised by Aristotle in *De Interpretatione* 9, 18a26-19b37. Consider the stated disjunction of the above two possible states of affairs. This disjunction is necessarily true. But, argues Aristotle, since the truth value of complex propositions is determined solely on the truth value of their simple components, this would lead to the conclusion that the components themselves must have a necessary value, which would have the further consequence that all apparently matter of fact truths are really necessary truths. This latter conclusion, however, is unacceptable to Aristotle who rejected any doctrine of absolute determinism. In his words, "Yet this view leads to an impossible conclusion; for we see that both deliberation and action are causative with regard to the future" (ibid., 19a6).

Aristotle's solution to the logical problem is that propositions concerning future contingents do not have a definite truth value. While it is true that "a

both Philosophic Thought and the Torah necessitate that there should exist in this world contingent entities. This being the case, it necessarily follows that when it is posited that God, may He be blessed, knows things which will come to be in the future, the contradictory of that thing which according to the knowledge of God, may He be blessed, will be actualized may (instead) be actualized, and what God, may He be blessed, knows will be actualized will not be actualized.[160] The reason for this is that if

---

sea-battle will occur tomorrow'' is either true or false and there is no third alternative, which value this proposition has cannot be assigned until the sea-battle does or does not occur on the next day. However, this solution will not do in the case of a God who knows such states of affairs. God must know today the definite truth value of this proposition, "a sea-battle will occur tomorrow." Furthermore its actual occurrence or failure to occur cannot affect this knowledge, since God is not subject to change.

[160] Consider two contradictory states of affairs with a single definite subject, Fa and $\sim Fa$. As indicated in note 157, as expressed by Gersonides the reading of $\sim Fa$ is ambiguous. It can be read either as "a is not F" or as "it is not the case that a is F." Gersonides would probably consider these two readings to be synonymous.

In general Fa and $\sim Fa$ are logically related in the following way: it is necessarily the case that (hereafter this phrase will be expressed simply by "N" preceding the proposition) Fa is true or Fa is false. N (Fa if and only if $\sim Fa$).

To say that Fa and $\sim Fa$ are contingent propositions entails the following additional claims: $\sim N(Fa)$, $\sim N(\sim Fa)$, $Fa \supset \sim N(Fa)$, $\sim Fa \supset \sim N(\sim Fa)$. In other words, whether Fa or $\sim Fa$ are true or false, neither is necessarily true and neither is necessarily false. But how could this be the case if we assume that God knows the truth value of Fa or $\sim Fa$?

Assume that Fa is true and that God knows this. Since God's knowledge is not subject to change and God knows eternally what He knows, it therefore follows that it has always been the case that Fa is true and $\sim Fa$ is false. But if this is so, then Aristotle's solution to the dilemma of future contingents (cf.

what God, may He be blessed, knows will be actualized without any doubt would be actualized, then its contradictory would in no way be possible, which would negate the nature of the contingent. It is from this (conclusion) that the Master, may his memory be blessed, fled.[161]

---

note 159) will not work, since propositions about future contingents will have definite truth values assigned to them before the event.

In effect what Maimonides is doing here is rejecting this consequence. It may be the case that God knows that Fa. But as Aristotle said Fa does not have a definite truth value until Fa occurs. Otherwise, as Aristotle argues, Maimonides believed that it would not be possible to defend the claim that not every event is pre-determined, a claim which Maimonides (as well as Gersonides) believed to be essential to maintaining a belief in human choice.

[161] As expressed by Gersonides the problem turns on the ambiguity of the expression, "without any doubt." A proposition is necessarily true if and only if there is no doubt that it is true. But what constitutes sufficient grounds for there being no doubt as to the truth of proposition? Aristotle's answer to this question is that if it is not possible for a contrary state of affairs to obtain then there is no doubt concerning the state of affairs in question.

Note that the problem here concerns the state of affairs itself and not our knowledge of that state of affairs. It may very well be the case that we are in considerable doubt about a given state of affairs whose occurrence is itself beyond any doubt, that is to say, inevitable and unavoidable.

However now we must ask, when is it not possible for a contrary state of affairs to obtain. Consider our sea-battle. After the sea-battle occurs it is certainly not possible for the sea-battle not to have occurred. Does this mean that it not merely happens to be the case that the sea-battle occurred but that it was necessarily the case that it occurred? We find ourselves faced with a class of propositions which at one time have no definite truth value and at another time have a definite truth value necessarily but at no time do they merely happen to have a definite truth value. In fact there is no class of propositions which merely happens to have a definite truth value.

Aristotle suggests a solution to this problem. He says that if a given state of

But it is not possible that we conceive of this. The reason for
this is the following. Suppose that the Master The Guide, may

---

affairs has no possibility at all, then we may call its contradictory necessary.
Hence our sea-battle is not necessary since its contradictory has some
possibility. But if we add to this that God always has known that the sea-battle
would take place then it is not correct to assert that there ever was any
possibility that the sea-battle would not occur, since God was always in the
knowing situation concerning the sea-battle which we were in only after the
fact.

Ibn Sina solves this problem by distinguishing two senses of necessity. (See
note 49.) Some things (namely, the existence of God) are necessary in themselves and other things (namely, every fact concerning everything and anything
other than God) are necessary in virtue of a cause. What it means to say that
future contingents are contingents is that while they are necessary in virtue of
their cause they are not necessary in virtue of themselves. Thus it certainly was
determined by a series of causes originating with the creation of the world that
the sea-battle would occur, but there is nothing about the sea-battle itself considered independent of its causes that could tell you whether or not it would
occur. Hence the fact that the sea-battle would occur is a contingent fact.

However Ibn Sina's method of preserving contingency pays too great a price
for either Maimonides or Gersonides (or at least as Gersonides understood
Maimonides). For them to say that an event is contingent is to say that its
non-occurrence is a real option and on Ibn Sina's account there are no real
options.

As Gersonides later explains, the reason for preserving the sense of contingency as a real option is religious. Maimonides maintained that only if there
are real options in choice can responsibility for choice be assigned, and only if
responsibility can be assigned are the commandments intelligible. Gersonides
believed (as he will explain later) that this was the real motive for Maimonides
maintaining his strange (in the opinion of Gersonides) doctrine of divine
predication. In other words Gersonides considers the doctrine of divine
predication to be a consequence of Maimonides' theory of divine knowledge,
and Maimonides adopted this theory (equally strange in the opinion of Gersonides) because he felt that on no other terms could he preserve the intelligibility of the commandments.

his memory be blessed, intended that (when) God, may He be blessed, knows that a given alternative from a set of possibilities[162] will be actualized, He (also) knows that (that alternative) may not be actualized, but that (instead) its contradictory may be actualized. And it is proper that it be thought that he did intend this. Then (assuming this interpretation) we would not call anything like this "knowledge." Rather it would be called "opinion."[163] This is self-evident. The reason for this

[162] Consider the fact that "John weighs 10 pounds." The truth of this fact entails the denial of an infinite number of other facts, namely, "John weighs 1 pound," "John weighs 2 pounds," ..., "John weighs n pounds," "John weighs $n + 1$ pounds," .... This whole series of facts constitutes a set of possibilities. A set of possibilities are a conjunction of possible states of affairs related in such a way that the truth of any one of them entails the falsity of all the others.

[163] Gersonides here is considering one of two possible interpretations of what Maimonides meant when he stated this fourth case. Gersonides tells us here that he considers this to be the proper interpretation of what Maimonides wanted to say but since this interpretation leads to a strange consequence he raises immediately after this discussion a second interpretation whose consequences turn out to be equally peculiar. The strangeness in this first interpretation is that the term, "knowledge" as applied to God turns out to be literally what is called "opinion" when applied to man. If I say that I believe that a sea-battle will occur tomorrow but of course it is possible that it will not, then I properly would characterize my state of belief as a state of opinion and not of knowledge, i.e., properly speaking I am of the opinion that a sea-battle will occur tomorrow but I do not know that it will occur.

Again there is a certain ambiguity in the statement of the argument. If we eliminate from our consideration knowledge of logical truths, what does it mean to know a proposition? Better, how is the line between knowing matters of fact and having an opinion about them drawn? Both Plato and Aristotle said that in the former case I can give an account of what I know whereas in the second case I cannot. That the given fact does happen to be the case is

is that when we say that we have knowledge that a specific one
of a set of possibilities will be actualized, then it is not possible
for us[164] that it will not be actualized. If we suppose that what
we think will be actualized might not be actualized, then we call
this "opinion," not "knowledge." I mean to say that we then
say that we are of the opinion that this alternative will be actualized, but we do not say that we know that this alternative
will be actualized. If what we thought would be actualized is not
actualized, then this thought is for us "error," not "knowledge."[165] This is self-evident.

---

irrelevant, since opinions can be correct as well as false and still not be
knowledge. But what does it mean to give an account? Suppose, for example,
that I work for an American political polling organization and my sample poll
has led me to the conclusion that a certain candidate will win a certain election
two weeks from now. Am I not justified in saying that I know that he will
win? Gersonides, as well as Maimonides, would say no. There are all kinds of
correct opinions. Some are more justified than others. (For example, I say that
so and so will win based on my poll and you say that so and so will win based
on your reading of the bumps on the candidate's skull.) But since none of
these stated reasons "necessitate" what they justify, the views based on these
reasons are not knowledge. But what does it mean to "necessitate"? Assume
that I can specify an n-set of conditions such that these conditions are
necessary and sufficient conditions for a given event A to occur. If I know that
these conditions obtain and I know that these conditions are necessary and
sufficient conditions of A, then and only then can I say that I know that A. But
on these terms there is no possibility that A will not occur since if there were
such a possibility my given set of conditions either would not be necessary or
they would not be sufficient, in which case I only would have an opinion and
not knowledge.

[164] Gersonides is speaking "with tongue in cheek." It is not possible for us
to claim that we know that A where A happens to be false, although,
presumably God could make such a claim.

[165] Assume that I believe that A. I know that A if and only if A is true and I

Suppose that the Master The Guide, may his memory be blessed, intended that God, may He be blessed, knows clearly which alternative of a set of possibilities will be actualized and He does not know that it is possible that it would not be actualized, although the matter is so in itself. i.e. that it is possible that that matter would not be actualized and its contradictory would be actualized. Then (on this second interpretation) we would not call anything like this "knowledge." Rather it is called "error," i.e. when the contradictory of what is judged to be actualized is (itself) actualized (then this is called "error"). This is self-evident.

This being so, it is clear that, according to this doctrine, what is to us the opposite of knowledge is knowledge for God, may He be blessed. This is because error is the opposite of knowledge, and opinion also in some way is the opposite[166] of knowledge. Therefore the Master, may his memory be blessed, judged that in this case also the knowledge of God, may He be blessed, differs from our knowledge.[167] This difference between

---

am aware of the causes (i.e., the necessary and sufficient conditions [cf. note 163]) of A, and I am aware that these causes are the causes (i.e., the necessary and sufficient conditions) of A. I am of the opinion that A if and only if A is true. (Opinion here is used by Gersonides to refer only to true opinion.) I am in error that A if and only if A is false.

[166] That A is contingent entails that it is possible that A not occur. But on this interpretation while God knows that A, He does not know that A need not occur. More accurately, God believes that A must occur since He knows A. But He is wrong. As noted above, (note 165) three conditions obtain in a state of knowledge. Where the first does not, the state is called "error." In this sense knowledge and error are opposites. When the conjunction of the latter two do not obtain the state is called "opinion." In this sense knowledge and opinion are opposites.

[167] See notes 116 and 122. Gersonides is speaking with tongue in cheek.

the two (uses of the term) "knowledge" is possible, according to the Master, may his memory be blessed, because the (term) "knowledge" for him[168] is predicated of Him, may He be blessed, and of us in absolute equivocation.

One may not reply[169] that the Master, may his memory be blessed, intended by this that God, may He be blessed, does not judge by His knowledge which alternative of a set of possibilities will be actualized. (One may not say this) because[169] he[170]

---

[168] The equivocation in this case however is not properly characterized as absolute. Since the term, "knowledge" as predicated of God turns out to be the opposite of what the term means when it is predicated of us, namely "opinion or error," it is not altogether different from what we mean by "knowledge" since at least in this one case the range of application is the same. For example, "fat" and "thin" have more in common than do "fat" and "red," precisely because they are opposites.

[169] See notes 124 and 126.

Although Gersonides presents his remarks here in the form of an objection they in effect constitute a third interpretation of Maimonides' fourth case. The first interpretation (which Gersonides tells us is the correct one) is that God knows that given any possible state of affairs A which will occur (1) A will occur and (2) A is possible. On this interpretation God's knowledge turns out to be opinion. The second interpretation is that (1) God knows that A will occur but (~ 2) He does not know that A is only possible. On this interpretation God's knowledge turns out to be error. Given the two claims involved in knowing a contingent particular (1 and 2), there remains a third possible interpretation, viz. God knows (2) that A is possible but (~ 1) He does not know that A will occur. This third interpretation is what is considered here in the form of an objection.

Gersonides may raise this discussion as an objection rather than as an interpretation because, as he notes below, Maimonides' language makes it clear that this interpretation was not intended. It is the least possible of the three interpretations of Maimonides' words.

[170] I.e., Maimonides.

believed that God, may He be blessed, knows the alternative which will be actualized by way of unity[171] with (perfect) clarity. This is clear from his language in mentioning this distinction.[172] But if we were to accept this (interpretation), then it is clear that (in this case) also we cannot conceive of this. This is because we do not call anything like this "knowledge." Rather we call it "perplexity"[173] and "confusion." This is because we say that we are confused and cannot conjecture if this alternative of a set of possibilities will be actualized or that (other) one or that (third) one, and (concerning this) the greater the number of alternatives the greater the confusion. But "perplexity" and "confusion" is (*130*) the opposite of "knowledge." How much the more so (is this the case) when it is posited in this way, namely that there is found with something subject to generation an almost infinite number of contradictory alternatives, for example, a thousand years prior to its (actually) coming into existence. This is because when it is posited (that) each of the intermediary events[174] may either be or may not be, and if it is not it is

[171] God knows everything in a single act of knowledge with a single object of knowledge. Cf. notes 26, 130, 138, and 150. To know in this way is to know in a manner more perfect than the way in which we know multiple facts in conjunction but not in unity.

[172] Cf. note 158.

[173] Gersonides is playing on the title of Maimonides' work which is intended to be a "guide for the *perplexed* (*nᵉbôkim*)."

[174] I.e., those events which bring about and determine the nature of the particular event in question. For example, A occurs only if B occurs only if C occurs, ..., only if Z occurs. If Z is the first cause, then B through Y are the intermediary events.

Consider an event A which involves only one intermediary event, B. B is itself contingent. Instead of B there are B^1 through B^3 alternate possibilities. Given no question of the initial cause, then the chances are four to one that A

possible that such and such (instead) will or will not be, then, when the case is structured in this way, it will be found to be true, concerning the final event which comes to be by the intermediacy of these other events, that if (that final event) is actualized it will be (so) from an infinite (number) of contradictory alternatives. But we would call anything like this absolute perplexity and confusion, i.e. there is confusion as to whether one thing or something else will come to be from the infinite alternatives. This is because there would be less confusion and perplexity when the contradictory alternatives are numerically less.[175]

Therefore the definition[176] which best individuates an object from others besides it is that which gives the most complete knowledge of the thing, even though it does not individuate (the thing) completely.[177] For example, one would say concerning a

---

will occur. The greater the number of alternate possibilities to B the less the chances are the A will occur.

Again consider this same event A with two intermediary events, B and C. C also is contingent. Now the chances that A will occur have been even further reduced. Hence the greater the number of necessary intermediate events and the greater the number of alternatives in the sets of which each of these intermediary events are parts, the less the chances are that A can occur.

[175] Gersonides assumes that all of the events constituting a given set of possible events are equally possible. This need not be the case. For example, it may be possible that my yet-to-be-born son will have blond hair or black hair but these are not equal possibilities given my and my wife's genetic history.

[176] Literally, "the answer." This paragraph of the text should be regarded as a footnote on the functions of definitions as knowledge of a thing where this knowledge is conceived as the means by which the number of multiple states of affairs to which a contingent being is possibly subject is narrowed.

[177] The more data that a definition gives the fewer things that are able to qualify for that definition. For example, if I say that Socrates is a Greek

boat that it is a substance of wood, made through (the employment of) a craft, hollowed out, (and) uncovered./ Each one of these specifications increases the knowledge, since it removes confusion from everything included in the individuation which preceded it, which is not included in it, even though not one (of these particular predicates alone) completely individuates the boat from other things.[178]

---

philosopher, you might confuse him with others, e.g. Aristotle and Plato. Once I add that Socrates is a Greek philosopher who was snub-nosed and drank hemlock, these others are excluded. However, not all possible others are excluded since there may be other people who were Greek, philosophers, had snub noses and drank hemlock.

Note that this sense of definition does not necessitate that the list of predicates be only essential predicates. With individuals, since it is their matter that individuates them, a list of predicates which individuates a particular from other particulars will contain necessarily some non-essential characteristics, notably spatial-temporal predicates.

Would it ever be possible to fully individuate a particular by such a list of characteristics? Presumably yes. My social security number individuates me, i.e., I am the only individual who can have that number. Also if we assume an infinite list of characterizations which include every possible fact about a given individual that too would individuate him. But Gersonides says no. The reason for his denial is that ultimately a thing is individuated by matter and matter cannot be stated. Such characterizations as the ones noted here are perfectly all right for practical purposes. For example, it is sufficient to say that Socrates is a snub-nosed, Greek philosopher who drank hemlock in order to individuate Socrates from everyone else of whom we know. But in principle it is not possible to state a definition which would individuate Socrates from all possible other individuals. This relatively small list is adequate with Socrates only because we know relatively few Greek philosophers. But we do not know — nor need we consider for practical purposes — all possible Greek philosophers, of whom there is an infinite number.

[178] Assume a very small universe in which there are initially only two possibilities, a and b. a gives rise only to possibilities c and d, and b gives rise

The fifth of these five cases[179] is that the knowledge of God, may He be blessed, does not change with the generation of any

---

only to possibilities *e* and *f.* Now there are four possibilities: *c, d, e, f.* But if we know which of the two initial possibilities would occur, *a* or *b,* the field of four present possibilities would be narrowed to two. Similarly, the more that I know about a thing the fewer possibilities I can entertain concerning that thing. For example, because I know that John is a man and not a frog I know that he will speak words and not croak. But I do not know if John is king of Babylonia or not. Once I learn that John lives in the twentieth century and Babylonia has not existed for some time, this possibility for John's future also is eliminated.

It is in this sense that knowing the definition of a thing is knowing its cause. More specifically, however, knowledge is limited to only certain kinds of information about things, namely those kinds of predicates which in modern terms we would call "dispositional predicates." For example, from the information that a boat is made of wood and is hollowed out I can assume that under normal circumstances it will float on and not sink under water.

Gersonides here is hinting at a way in which God may know particulars as individuals although not as particulars. God cannot know any particular as a particular for the reasons already discussed. (See notes 13, 26, 105, 130.) His knowledge necessarily is limited to universal judgments. But universal judgments can be understood in two senses. They may be judgments about universals or they may be general judgments. Unfortunately in Hebrew no distinction is made between these two. The same term is used for both, namely *k*[e]*lal.*

Consider for the moment general judgments. While no general judgment can ever totally individuate anything if to individuate means to exclude all possible references (this is true even with spatial-temporal references since we always may assume two universes which are in every way the same except that they are not identical), yet for practical purposes individuation among known actual entities is possible through only general statements. My social security number is a case in point. This number is an abbreviation of a lengthy statement of numerical positional relationships in which my name (i.e., my number) occupies a unique place. In this way someone working in the social security office has no difficulty distinguishing me from millions of other people although

of these things subject to generation and corruption of which He
has knowledge prior to their[180] occurrence, even though the ob-

---

he does not know me in any way as a particular (i.e., he would not recognize
me if he were to pass me on the street).

Let us now assume for the moment that the propositions that God knows
about universals (i.e., the forms) are expressible in general judgments. As a
judgment about universals this infinite set of general judgments is a single
judgment. It then is intelligible to say that while God cannot know a particular
he may know an individual. In other words, God may be able to individuate a
given boat from other boats although He will not know the boat as a particular
boat, i.e., He cannot see it.

If this is in fact how God, according to Gersonides, knows individuals, then
God certainly knows them differently from the way in which we know them.
But the difference is understandable. It is not a case of absolute equivocation.

It is worthy of note that while the Hebrew does not distinguish between
"general" and "universal," it does distinguish between individual ('*iši* or
*y*e*hidi*) and particular (*p*e*rāṭi*), and except for this present paragraph Gersonides has been discussing knowledge of particulars, not individuals.

[179] What Gersonides lists here as the fifth case is given by Maimonides as
the fourth case. (See note 158.)

> In the fourth place, His knowledge undergoes no changes in its ap-
> prehension of things produced in time. And yet it might seem that the
> knowledge that a thing will exist is not identical with the knowledge that
> it already exists; for there is in the latter case a certain surplus, namely,
> the fact that what had been in potentia became actual.
>
> (*The Guide* 3.20, p. 483)

These last two cases obviously are related and somewhat similar. Perhaps this
is the reason for the change in order from Maimonides' presentation, i.e., Gersonides confused the two cases. But Gersonides' discussion of the two cases
shows that he saw them as significantly different so that such a simple confusion would be unlikely. One possible answer is that Gersonides' discussion
of this case presupposes his discussion of the previous case. Gersonides thus
may have intentionally changed the order of these last two cases because he
believed that the case presented here (Maimonides' fourth) logically presupposes the case previously considered (Maimonides' fifth).

ject to which His knowledge is connected changes. The reason for this is that it[181] was at first a possibility and afterwards an actual existent.[182] It was necessary that he (Maimonides) believe this, since the knowledge of God is (identical with) His essence, as is made clear in (several) places concerning which there is no doubt.[183] Since His essence does not change, it necessarily follows that His knowledge will be changeless.

[180] I.e., these things subject to generation.

[181] I.e., any given thing subject to generation which God knows.

[182] Consider the contingent particular state of affairs A, "this sea-battle is occurring at 10:30 AM, January 16, 1984." So stated the fact that A is timeless since the time reference is included in the statement of the fact itself. It is a fact such as this which was considered in the last case. The problem growing out of God knowing such a fact was not so much a problem of God's knowledge as it was a problem of the nature of the world, i.e., for God to know such propositions has the consequence that everything is determined.

The facts considered in this case are slightly different. Consider the following two facts about A, A^1 ("That A is a possible state of affairs") and A^2 ("That A is an actual state of affairs"). These two facts are not eternal. Prior to 10:30 AM, January 16, 1984, A^1 is true and A^2 is false. After this time A^2 is true. (The status of A^1 after this time is not clear. Properly it is false since what is actual is not possible. Maimonides' statement of the case, however, suggests that he interpreted the matter differently since he says that in this latter instance there is "a certain surplus." In other words, on Maimonides' account, after the stated time A^2 is true in addition to rather than instead of A^1 being true. The reason that God did not previously know A^2 is because before the given time A^2 was false.) The problem growing out of God knowing A^1 and A^2 is more of a problem of God's knowledge than it is a problem of the nature of the world. However as argued by Gersonides the problem of knowledge discussed here presupposes the problem of the nature of the world discussed in the previous case.

[183] For example,

According to our opinion — that is, the opinion of people who say that His knowledge is not something super-added to His essence — it is truly

When we study this matter, it becomes evident that our intellect and our wisdom could not possibly conceive of this (case). This is because the Master The Guide, may his memory be blessed, previously states[184] that God, may He be blessed, knows that this thing which is subject to generation will be non-existent at such and such a time and afterwards will exist at such and such a time, and afterwards it will cease to exist at such and such a (later) time. This is the case with every single entity in the world that is subject to generation. When the thing subject to generation is generated (God's) knowledge is not increased, and what He did not know was not generated. Rather what was known previously that it would be generated in fact did come to be. This being the case, it is clear that God, may He be blessed, knows, according to this assumption, everything that will be generated and everything that was generated.

This (fifth case) also must necessarily be believed by anyone who would flee from ascribing ignorance to God, may He be blessed, of these matters. This is because ignorance of what has undergone generation is a greater ignorance and imperfection than ignorance of what will undergo generation.[185] This is self-evident.

---

necessary that His knowledge should differ from ours in substance, just as the substance of the heavens differs from the substance of the earth.

(*The Guide* 3.20, p. 483)

[184] In case two.

[185] Since in the former instance the alternative to ignorance is knowledge whereas in the latter instance the alternative is only opinion. See Gersonides' case four. However Maimonides certainly can reply to this that what God knows (using the symbolism of note 182) is A and not A^1 or A^2. But Gersonides may reply that A^1 and A^2 are as much facts about the world as is A. Furthermore, A entails A^1 and A^2. Hence if God knows the first but not the

This being the case, the following dilemma is unavoidable: either He knows that the alternative from a set of possibilities which He knew would be generated has been generated, or He knows that (*131*) the actualized alternative from a set of possibilities has been generated, even though it is different from that alternative which He knew would be generated prior to the generation of this actualized alternative.[186] If we say that He knows the alternative from the set of possibilities which He knew would be generated, then it necessarily follows from this that much of His knowledge of these things belongs to the class of what we call "error" rather than "knowledge." The reason for this is that since it is possible that the alternative which He knows will be actualized may not be actualized, then it will happen with many of these things that the alternative which God, may He be blessed, knows will be actualized will not be ac-

---

other two then God is in the unfortunate situation of knowing certain propositions while not being able to discern their simple entailments. God therefore would suffer from a defective ability to draw inferences.

[186] Consider a pair of alternative possibilities (a) "John exclusively sucks his thumb at t^1" and (b) where (b) is any possibility so related to (a) that (a) is true if and only if (b) is false. For example, facts such as "John exclusively sucks his middle finger at t^1" or "John puts his hands in his pockets at t^1," etc., qualify as instances of (b). Assume that at some time before t^1 God knows that (a). Since (a) is a contingent and not a necessary state-of-affairs (as discussed by Gersonides in case four), at t^1 either (a) or (b) will be the case. Assume that at t^1 (b) occurs. Either God knows this fact or He does not. The first horn of the dilemma stated by Gersonides assumes that at and after t^1 He does not know (b). (Cf. note 20.) The second horn of the dilemma assumes that He does. As we shall see the first horn preserves the changelessness of God's knowledge at the cost of its truth, while the second horn lacks even this virtue.

tualized. But anyone who thinks that what has not been actualized has been actualized without a doubt errs.[187]

If we say that He knows that the alternative which becomes actual from the set of possibilities has been generated, even though it is different from the alternative which He had known would be generated prior to the actualization of this alternative, then there is no doubt that this is the generation of knowledge and it is a change in the knowledge of God, may He be blessed.[188] It is from this (conclusion) that the Master The Guide, may his memory be blessed, fled by proclaiming this basic doctrine of the knowledge of God.[189]

One may not reply[190] that the particular which God, may He be blessed, knew would be actualized before the generation of the thing subject to generation is without a doubt the alternative which was actualized.[191] (One may not say this)[190] since if the

[187] This horn of the dilemma preserves the claim that God's knowledge cannot undergo change. What He knows once He must know always. Now assume that God knows (using the symbolism of note 186) (a). Of necessity (a) is contingent and since (a) is contingent, as was argued already in Gersonides' fourth case, it is possible that (b) will be the case rather than (a). Hence there will be times when God knows (a) but (b) is the case. In these cases the purported proposition known by God will be false. In other words, God is mistaken.

[188] Here God knows that (b) (using the symbolism of note 186) at t^1 even though previously He knew that (a). In this case God's knowledge is constantly changing, i.e., God is constantly receiving new knowledge.

[189] Namely that the term, "knowledge" is predicated of God and of us in absolute equivocation. Cf. note 161.

[190] Cf. notes 124 and 126.

[191] The objection shifts the question from a consideration of the nature of God's knowledge to a consideration of the nature of what God knows which returns us to the situation involved in Gersonides' case four rather than case five.

case were so posited then everything would be necessary and there would be no contingency in this world at all.[192] This is the falsehood from which the Master The Guide, may his memory be blessed, fled.[192a] Therefore, he decreed that the contradictory of what God, may He be blessed, knows will be actualized possibly may be actualized.

This being the case, it is clear that we cannot conceive of this matter in any way. This is because "knowledge" such as this either is what we call "error" or it is subject to generation and change. It is neither changeless nor free of generation, as it was proclaimed as a basic doctrine (by Maimonides). This is a matter completely inconceivable to us since the like of this which is called "unchanging knowledge" with reference to God, may He be blessed, is called with reference to us either "error" or "generating and changing knowledge." Each of these is the opposite of unchanging knowledge. This is because error, for us, is the opposite of knowledge and generating and changing knowledge is for us the opposite of unchanging knowledge.

Since it is not possible for us to conceive of this matter, The Master The Guide, may his memory be blessed, decreed that in this case also the knowledge of God, may He be blessed, is different from our knowledge. This is possible for him since the (term) "knowledge" is said of God, may He be blessed, and of us in absolute equivocation.[193]

The Master The Guide, may his memory be blessed, believed,

---

[192] As Gersonides argued at length in his case four. In other words the case discussed here arises and is valid only by first presupposing Gersonides' previous case. See note 179.

[192a] See note 61.

[193] Cf. notes 116 and 122.

because of the exalted level of the knowledge of God, may He be blessed, that we are not able to comprehend how and in what way He knows, and that our trying to know how this is is as if we tried to become Him,[194] our comprehension being His comprehension. For this reason (according to Maimonides) great absurdities were generated for us in our investigation of this question of how God, may He be blessed, knows things. This is because the nature of this knowledge necessitates that it be inconceivable to us and incomprehensible.

[194] Since knower and known are in some sense one. This is particularly the case here where God's knowledge and God's essence, i.e., God, are one.

In Which We Shall Investigate Whether or Not the Arguments of the Guide, may his Memory be Blessed, Logically Suffice.

It is proper that we should investigate whether (or not) what the Master The Guide, may his memory be blessed, mentions in order to refute all of these arguments which the philosophers who disputed with him could have raised logically suffices. (We should do this) before we investigate (the following:) whether or not these above mentioned arguments[195] to establish their[196] view are correct, and if they are correct whether or not what (the philosophers claimed that it) necessarily follows from them does (in fact) necessarily follow.[197] The reason for this[198] is that if what the the Master, may his memory be blessed, argued in order to refute these arguments[196] logically suffices, then it would not be necessary to investigate them in another way. Thus we say that the (proper) method for investigating (this question) is to investigate first if our knowledge and His knowledge, may He be blessed, can possibly be equivocal in such a way that there

---

[195] I.e., of the philosophers.

[196] I.e., of the philosophers.

[197] This is the topic of chapter four. Gersonides will grant the validity of the arguments of the philosophers but he will modify their conclusion. In other words the arguments of the philosophers show that God does not know particulars as particulars, but from this it does not follow that God does not know particulars at all.

[198] I.e., the reason for considering the arguments of Maimonides first before the arguments of the philosophers.

would be between them the kind of difference which the Master, may his memory be blessed, mentions — namely that the knowledge of God, may He be blessed, is the opposite of our knowledge, in such a way that what is for us opinion or error or confusion is knowledge for God, may He be blessed — or if the equivocation between them is such that this kind of difference is impossible.[199]

We say that it would appear that this view of the Master The Guide, may his memory be blessed, concerning the knowledge of

[199] As stated in chapter two, Maimonides asserts that the term, "knowledge" with reference to God and man is absolutely equivocal and he states five cases of difference between our knowledge and God's knowledge to illustrate that difference. As Gersonides analysed those cases it turned out that what Maimonides calls "knowledge" with reference to God is, depending on the particular interpretation applied, what is literally called with reference to us "opinion" or "error" or "confusion." In other words the predicate, 'knowing' as instantiated by God is synonymous with the compound disjunctive predicate, "having an opinion or being mistaken or being confused" as instantiated by us. As such these cases are not illustrations of absolute equivocation at all. (Cf. note 168.)

But this is not a proof that the term, "knowledge" is not predicated of God and of us in absolute equivocation since these five cases were only illustrations. The most that was shown is that the illustrations were inadequate, a contention which would be quite acceptable to Maimonides since given the doctrine of absolute equivocation of divine predicates no illustration in principle could be adequate. Only a direct attack on the doctrine of predication itself could be adequate. It is such an attack that Gersonides will present in this chapter. Basically his argument is that divine predicates must be understood as *pros hen* equivocals rather than as absolute or merely nominal equivocals. (Cf. note 91.) Finally, given that divine predicates are *pros hen* equivocals Gersonides will argue that the five cases are more than misleading illustrations. They in principle are not correct since they describe situations which cannot be reconciled with *pros hen* equivocation.

God, may He be blessed, did not result from speculative foundations. This is because Philosophical Thought[200] rejects this (position), as I shall explain. Rather it would appear that the Torah[201] put great pressure on him in this matter.[202] However,

[200] The term, "*ha'iyûn*" is used here in contrast to the term, "*torāh*." As "Torah" is to be understood as an abbreviation for the various doctrines of Rabbinic tradition so the term, "Philosophic Thought" is an abbreviation for the various conclusions of speculative-demonstrative-scientific thinking. It is not to be understood as a personification. "Philosophic Thought dictates that *p*" does not mean that there is some divine entity whose name is Philosophic Thought who decrees *p*. Rather it means that anyone who reasons correctly, i.e., who begins with self-evident premises and makes no mistakes in forming his inferences by accepted principles of procedure in scientific demonstration, must conclude that *p*.

[201] Cf. note 2.

[202] In other words, Maimonides reached his conclusion concerning divine predicates not because Philosophic Thought (cf. note 200) necessitates this conclusion but rather because he felt that on no other terms could he maintain a view of divine predication in agreement with the basic dogmas of Judaism.

At the end of his discussion of God's knowledge, Maimonides tells us to note the method that he employed in discussing this question. (*The Guide* 3.21, p. 485. Cf. note 143.) The method as described by Maimonides is the following: given any proposition *p*, if it is the case that on the basis of Philosophic Thought alone one cannot opt between *p* and ~*p*, but that the Torah dictates *p*, then one should conclude that *p*. In this case *p* is that God knows particulars as particulars. The reason that Philosophic Thought cannot settle between this *p* and ~*p* is that there is no relation between God's knowledge and our knowledge, and Philosophic Thought can make judgments only on the basis of such a relation. (Maimonides uses this same procedure with the proposition that the world was created *ex nihilo*. Gersonides judges Maimonides to be as mistaken in that issue as he is in this issue. See Treatise Six of *The Wars of the Lord*.)

Gersonides here is claiming the following: Philosophic Thought leads to the conclusion that God cannot know particulars as particulars. But Maimonides

whether (or not) this view is necessitated by the Torah is what we will investigate after we have completed this investigation into what Philosophic Thought decrees concerning it.[203]

That Philosophic Thought rejects what the Master The Guide, may his memory be blessed, posited, concerning the knowledge of God, may He be blessed, will be clear from what I will say. It

---

believed such a conclusion to be contrary to the dictates of the Torah. Therefore he introduced his doctrine of absolute equivocation of divine predicates so that he could claim that there is no way for reason to judge this issue. Gersonides' words carry the implication, which becomes more and more spelled out as the text continues, that in doing this Maimonides was intentionally working some "intellectual magic," i.e., that his move is not intellectually honest and Maimonides knew that it was not.

At least in part Gersonides' accusation against Maimonides rests on his interpretation of what Maimonides notes as the seventh cause for contradictions in a text which Maimonides tells us is a cause of contradiction in his own text. (Cf. note 143.) There are several ways of interpreting Maimonides' meaning in this case. One interpretation is that Maimonides is trying to protect himself against any possible charges of intellectual inadequacy, i.e., if you (the reader) should find any contradictions in my (Maimonides') work it is not that I (Maimonides) made a mistake, but I have a hidden doctrine which you (the reader) must work to discover. However, in greater fairness to Maimonides' integrity one may grant that Maimonides does have a hidden doctrine as he in fact here tells you that he does. But the problem now is just what that hidden doctrine is. With respect to the two most notable cases in *The Guide*, viz. God's knowledge of particulars and creation *ex nihilo*, two contrary interpretations are possible. Given what Maimonides in honesty found to be an irreconcilable conflict between Philosophic Thought and Torah, either Maimonides perverted the Torah in favor of Philosophic Thought and his hidden doctrine is that the true readers will reject the Torah in favor of Philosophic Thought at this point, or Maimonides perverts Philosophic Thought in favor of the Torah. Gersonides clearly takes this latter interpretation to be the correct interpretation of Maimonides' intention.

[203] The question discussed in the final chapter, chapter six, of this treatise.

would seem that His knowledge, may He be blessed, is equivocal with our knowledge by priority and posteriority. I mean to say that the term, "knowledge" is said of God, may He be blessed, priorly and of any other being posteriorly. This is because He has His knowledge from His own essence, whereas the knowledge of other beings is caused by His knowledge,[204] and in the case of anything of this kind the term is said of it[205] priorly and of the other things of which it is said it is (said) posteriorly.[206]

Similarly it is proper that the case will be the same with the terms, "existent," "one," "entity"[207] and with other terms of

[204] The essences in the intellect of God are the cause of the things that exist in this world. In this sense they are prior to the things in this world. The essences that we know, however, which are called "universals," are formed by abstraction from the things of this world. In this sense our known essences are posterior to the things in the world. In other words, there is the-F which is the model by which F-things are created and it is from these F-things that we come to know F. Except for the additional characteristic that every the-F in the intellect of God is a single thing, namely the intellect of God, whereas in our intellect each F is distinct, Gersonides in no other way characterizes the differences between the-F, F-things, and F. It is important to note, however, that in some way the "F" in all three instances is the same.

It is of interest to note in this connection that this description which is the basis for rejecting Maimonides' analysis of divine predication in general and divine knowledge in particular is given by Maimonides himself in *The Guide* 3.21. Cf. notes 26, 67, and 71.

[205] I.e., the primary thing, i.e., that of which the predicate is essentially applied which is the source from which other things are designated by the same predicate.

[206] Cf. footnote 91.

[207] "*H'eṣem*" here is a translation of the Greek term, "*ousia.*" All of the problems associated with an English translation of this Greek term equally ap-

the same order, i.e., they are said of God, may He be blessed, priorly and of other beings posteriorly. This is because His existence, His oneness, and His entity[207] belong to Him essentially,[208] and from Him emanate the existence, the oneness, and the entity of every existing thing. And concerning anything so described, the term (in question) is said of it[209] priorly, while concerning other things whose predication essentially is determined in such a way that they are designated by this term, the term is said of them posteriorly.[210] All of this is clear to him

---

ply to its Hebrew synonymn. At the same time it designates substance, essence and being. Father Joseph Owens suggests as a translation for this term the word "entity" which combines and expresses these different senses. (See J. Owens, *The Doctrine of Being in the Aristotelian Metaphysics* (Toronto: Pontifical Institute of Mediaeval Studies, 1951), Introduction.)

[208] God being a necessary being is what He is in virtue of Himself and not in virtue of anything else. In other words, that God is a necessary being means that what He is (His essence) is the necessary and sufficient condition of everything that is true of Him. Hence with God all predication is essential predication (that is, if any predication at all is appropriate). Cf. note 43 and Maimonides' distinction between contingent (premise 19) and necessary (premise 20) beings in *The Guide* 2. Introduction.

[209] I.e., that to which the predicate is applied essentially and primarily.

[210] Aristotle explains what *pros hen* equivocation is in *The Metaphysics*. (See J. Owens, *The Doctrine of Being*, pp. 264-275.) Different things are called derivatively by the same name as something that is described by that term primarily either when the primary thing is the origin of the derivative things with respect to the characteristic in question or when the derivative things refer to the primary thing with respect to the characteristic in question. For example, a given color is called "healthy" because an individual having that color is a sign that he is healthy. Similarly a knife is called "medical" when that knife is used in the practice of medicine. In this same passage Aristotle tells us that two different things are called "good" in this sense of equivocation. Similarly, Aristotle's often repeated statement that "being

who studies this book, and it will be fully explained in the fifth treatise of this book.

This being the case,[211] it would seem that there is no difference between the knowledge of God, may He be blessed, and our knowledge except that the knowledge of God, may He be blessed, is more perfect than our knowledge. This is because this is the case with terms applied priorly and posteriorly. If the case is as we have posited, it being clear that the knowledge (*133*) which is most perfect is more true[212] in precision[213] and clarity,[214] then it would seem to follow necessarily from this that the knowledge of God, may He be blessed, is more true (than our knowledge) in precision[213] and clarity.[214] Therefore it is impossible that His knowledge should be designated as what with reference to us is opinion or error or confusion.

It is clear in another way[215] by Philosophic Thought that the knowledge of God, may He be blessed, is not different from our knowledge in the way that the Master, may his memory be

---

(*ousia*) is said in many ways" in the *Metaphysics* is to be understood in terms of this kind of equivocation. (J. Owens, ibid. and note 91.)

[211] I.e., that divine predicates are *pros hen* equivocals.

[212] Cf. note 22 for an example of how different statements can be partially true. Once partial truths are admitted there is no difficulty in stating that different statements are more or less true than other statements.

[213] For example, God's knowledge is more precise than ours because He knows things as their cause whereas we have knowledge only as an effect of the things caused by God. Cf. notes 71 and 204.

[214] Cf. notes 26 and 204. The essence that God knows is different from the essence that we know and the essence that God knows is clearer than the essence that we know.

[215] What follows is Gersonides' second demonstration on the basis of Philosophic Thought that divine predicates are not absolutely equivocal but are *pros hen* equivocals.

blessed, maintained. This is because it is clear that we derive matters[216] that we affirm of God, may He be blessed, from matters[216] that are (affirmed) of us. I mean to say that we affirm of God, may He be blessed, that He has knowledge because of the knowledge found in us.[217] For example, because what we conceptually know existing in our intellect is a perfection of the intellect, otherwise impossible,[218] as an actual intellect, we affirm that God, may He be blessed, has knowledge, from the point of view that it is clear to us beyond any doubt concerning Him that He is an actual intellect.

[216] I.e., states of affairs or propositions.

[217] Gersonides here uses Maimonides' own words against him. In *The Guide* 1.26 Maimonides tells us the following:

> everything that all men are capable of understanding and representing to themselves at first thought has been ascribed to Him as necessarily belonging to God, may He be exalted.

(Pines tr., p. 56)

Given the espistemology presupposed by both Maimonides and Gersonides (see note 26) such a doctrine as this would follow necessarily. All of our concepts have their source in sensation, but there can be no sense experience of God.

Maimonides uses this claim as a basis for his doctrine of the absolute equivocation of divine predicates. He argues that since our predicates have reference essentially to what is found in this world and there is no relationship between God and this world, all predicates are equally appropriate and inappropriate. As we shall see Gersonides will use this consequence noted by Maimonides as a *reductio ad absurdum* argument against Maimonides (Gersonides' third and fourth arguments in this section).

[218] I.e., possessing conceptual knowledge is what perfects the intellect, which is for Gersonides equivalent to saying that actual concepts are what perfects the actual intellect. In other words, conceptual knowledge is a necessary condition for the perfection of the intellect, i.e., an intellect is perfected only if it possesses conceptual knowledge.

Now it is self-evident concerning any predicate when it is affirmed of a certain thing on the basis of its existence in some
other thing,[219] that it is not said of both things in absolute
nominal equivation. This is because between things which are
absolutely equivocal there is no analogy. For example, just as it
is not possible to say that man is rational because body is continuous, so this (above case) is not possible even if we posit one
term for (both) "rational" and "continuous" said of both in absolute equivocation.[220] This is self-evident.

[219] This clause constitutes a description of *pros hen* equivocation. Hence the
present sentence is a tautology, i.e., it states that *pros hen* equivocation is not
absolute or chance equivocation. Cf. note 91.

[220] Gersonides' illustration is misleading. What he wants to say is that
where two things are absolutely equivocal no inference can be made from one
to the other since to be absolutely equivocal entails that the two are in no way
comparable. However what is absolutely equivocal (if you can speak that way
in this instance) in his example is not the subjects of the two propositions but
the predicates. But Gersonides' case does not apply to equivocal predicates. In
fact to speak of equivocal predicates is not really unintelligible. Consider, for
example, the predicate, "continional" which ranges over the range of the
predicates "rational" and "continuous," i.e., "continional" and the compound
predicate "rational or continuous" are the same predicate. Now contrary to
what Gersonides seems to be claiming here, it is perfectly admissible to say
that man is continional because body is continional. This proposition can be
justified on the grounds that since all men have bodies and all bodies are continional therefore all men will be continional. To be sure we may deny this entailment (viz. we might claim that given the doctrine of immortality it is not
the case that all men have bodies), but this denial is very different from the
kind of denial intended here by Gersonides.

Again, the problem is not with Gersonides' meaning. The difficulty is his
example. An alternate example could be "man is rational because elephants
have sensation." Both claims are correct but the compound proposition cannot
be said not because there is no logical relationship between the two predicates

This being so, it is clear that the (term) "knowledge" is not said of (both) God, may He be blessed, and us in absolute equivocation. And since it is also impossible that it[221] should be said of (both) God and us univocally,[222] then it is clear that the only remaining alternative is that it[221] is said of Him, may He be blessed, and us priorly and posteriorly. Similarly this is clear with the other things[223] which are said of (both) God and us.[224] Therefore, it is clear that there is no difference between the knowledge of God, may He be blessed, and our knowledge except that the knowledge of God, may He be blessed, is immeasurably more perfect,[225] and this kind of knowledge is truer in level and clarity.[226]

In general, the equivocation between His knowledge, may He
3a be blessed, and our knowledge is/ like the equivocation between His essence and the essence of our acquired intellect. This is because the knowledge and the knower are numerically one,[227] as

---

but because the relation between the two subjects is too remote to justify such an entailment as is expressed by the term, "because."

[221] I.e., the term, "knowledge."

[222] Literally, "in agreement."

[223] I.e., predicates.

[224] Gersonides' argument that the term, "knowledge" is a *pros hen* equivocal with reference to God and us is a disjunctive syllogism. In other words, given any predicate applied to both God and us, it is either univocal in meaning or absolutely equivocal or *pros hen* equivocal; it is neither univocal nor absolutely equivocal; therefore, it is a *pros hen* equivocal. Gersonides here asserts that this argument is valid equally for every divine predicate.

[225] Literally, "more perfect is wondrous measure."

[226] Cf. notes 212, 213, and 214.

[227] On the unity of knower and known see note 38. On the sense of mathematical unity employed here, see notes 101, 102 and 104.

was explained above.[228] Just as His essence is more perfect than
the essence of our acquired intellect, so is it essentially the case
with His knowledge (as compared) with our knowledge.[229]

This (conclusion) — i.e., that the knowledge of God, may He
be blessed, is not different from our knowledge in the way mentioned by the Master The Guide, may his memory be blessed —
is clear by Philosophic Thought in another way.[230] Concerning
the things[231] that we investigate whether they are affirmed of or
negated from God, may He be blessed, it is clear that we judge
those predicates to have a single meaning (both) in the affirmation and in the negation. For example, when we investigate
whether God, may He be blessed, is a body or is not a body, it is
clear that the term, "body" has for us in some way a single
reference in both of these alternatives.[232] The reason for this is

[228] In the beginning of Gersonides' presentation of Maimonides' view in
chapter two. Note the first quotation from *The Guide* in note 89.

[229] In *The Guide* 3.20 (see the first quotation in note 89), Maimonides tells
us that the philosophers should have known better than to assert some form or
relation between God's knowledge and our knowledge since God's knowledge
and His essence are the same thing. Gersonides here takes Maimonides' charge
with which he introduces his doctrine of absolute equivocation in refutation of
the position of the philosophers and turns it against him. The relation between
God's knowledge and our knowledge is exactly that of God's essence as an actual intellect and our essence as an acquired intellect, viz. *pros hen*
equivocation.

[230] Gersonides' third proof.

[231] I.e., predicates.

[232] I.e., the same meaning. Gersonides presupposes the reference theory of
meaning. Cf. notes 26 and 125.

By "in some way" Gersonides may mean that the meaning of the term
predicated in both the affirmation and the negation is neither univocal nor absolutely equivocal as applied to both God and us, i.e., it is *pros hen* equivocal.
However, Gersonides would have to maintain that as the term is used with

that if the term, "body" in the negative one of these alternatives were said by us (*134*) in absolute equivocation with what would be said of Him in the affirmative, these alternatives would not be conceived by us to be contradictory.[233] This is self-evident. For example, just as no one would say, "I will investigate whether the wall is body or is not colored"[234] so this cannot be said even if the same term is posited for body and color. This is because such alternatives as these would not be contradictory.[235]

---

reference to a single subject, either God or us, the term would have to be used univocally in both the affirmation and the negation. In other words, the term, "good," for example, is a *pros hen* equivocal with respect to "God is good" and "man is good," but the term must be univocal with respect to "God is good" and "God is not good." An alternative interpretation of "in some way," and for this reason perhaps a better interpretation of "in some way," is that while the term, "good" in "God is good" and "God is not good" is univocal, i.e., used the same way in both cases, we know this term as a *pros hen* equivocal since no divine predicate is for us unequivocal.

[233] For propositions to be contradictory they must be such that one is true if and only if the other is false. (Cf. note 157.) However, with propositions of the form *Fa* and $\sim Fa$, these are contradictory only if both "*a*" and "*F*" are identical in both propositions. In the second argument Gersonides made this point with respect to propositions of this form where the subject, *a*, in both cases was not the same. In this argument Gersonides concentrates on the situation where the predicate, *F* is not the same.

[234] The proposed speaker intends the strong sense of disjunction, i.e., (*Fa* or $\sim Ga$) where one and only one of the alternatives can be true. Gersonides' point is that with a proposition such as "the wall is body or the wall is not-colored" both alternatives may be true or both alternatives may be false, and the truth value of one entails nothing about the truth value of the other.

[235] Gersonides repeats the same point that he made in the second argument concerning positing a single term for two unrelated predicates. There the point was a confusion. (Cf. note 220.) His point is in terms of equivocal predicates but there he was speaking of equivocal subjects. Here however there is no such confusion. For example, assume the term, "bolor" to mean "body or colored"

This being so, and it (further) being clear that when we
negate from God, may He be blessed, the things[236] affirmed of
us, no given predicate refers to Him, may He be blessed, and to
us in absolute equivocation,[237] so (also) is it the case when we
affirm of Him things[236] affirmed of us.[238] For example, we say
that God, may He be blessed, is motionless[239] since if He had

---

so that a thing is "bolor" if it is either a body or colored. To translate the sentence in question as "the wall is bolor or the wall is not bolor" would not be
correct since where the wall is colored but not a body the original statement
would be false (i.e., the wall is neither body nor not-colored) but its translation would be true. Nor would we be any better off claiming that a thing is
bolor if it is both a body and colored for when the wall is neither a body nor
colored the original statement would be false while its translation would be
true.

There is however one difficulty with Gersonides' example. If black and white
are considered to be colors, it might be objected that every body has a color
and something is colored only if it is a body, i.e., something is a body if and
only if it is colored. Then the propositions "the wall is not colored" and "the
wall is a body" would be truth-functionally contradictory. The problem,
however, is with the example and not with Gersonides' point. Where the
predicates are such that to say "*Fa*" entails nothing concerning "*Ga*," the
statement "*Fa* or ~ *Ga*" in the strong sense of disjunction is false. Furthermore, where a term is absolutely equivocal, which is the case that Gersonides has in mind when he speaks of a single term being posited for two
predicates, the predicates referred to must be so, i.e., there is no relation between them at all, including a relationship of logical entailment.

[236] I.e., the predicates.

[237] What was proved in the second argument.

[238] The point of the last paragraph was the following: given any predicate,
F, *F* must have the same meaning in both "god is *F*" and "God is not *F*."
Gersonides is now arguing that since *F* is not asserted with absolute
equivocation in the statement, "God is not *F*," it follows from the preceding
paragraph that *F* cannot be asserted with absolute equivocation in the
statement "God is *F*."

[239] Again the example is confusing. Motionless as used here is a negative

motion He would be body, because this is a necessary entailment of motion as motion.[240] Now it is clear that the term, "motion" in this proposition is not applied in absolute equivocation with the term, "motion" applied to what is (known) to us.[241] The reason is that if this were so, there would be no proof here that God, may He be blessed, is motionless. This is because the motion that would entail necessarily that He would be body is the (same) motion which is applied to what is (known) by us.[241] But the motion which is said of Him in absolute equivocation would not entail necessarily that He would be body.[242]

---

rather than an affirmative predicate, i.e., as stated by Gersonides the accepted argument is that since God is not subject to motion therefore He is motionless.

[240] In *The Guide* 2. Intro. premises five and seven of the Aristotelian philosophers read as follows:

(5) Every motion is a change and transition from potentiality to actuality.

(7) Every changeable is divisible. (*Physics* 6.4) Hence everything movable is divisible and is necessarily a body. But everything that is indivisible is not movable; hence it will not be a body at all.

(Pines tr., p. 236)

[241] I.e., the term, "motion" applied to God in "God is motionless" refers to the same motion that is found among everything that either has or does not have motion in the physical world.

[242] Consider M (the predicate, "possessing motion" whose range is everything excluding God) and M^1 (a predicate whose range is God). It is argued that anything that has M is a body, God is not a body, therefore God is not M. But it does not follow because God is not a body that God is not M^1. Since M and M^1 are entirely different predicates, we can make no statement about one on the basis of the other. It is logically possible that something is M^1 and not a body although it is impossible for something to be M and not a body. In general terms, let $-^1$ express divine predicates as opposed to all other predicates. Thus, given any two predicates f and g, which exhibit some logical

This being so and it (further) being clear that the predicates which we negate from God, may He be blessed, are not said of Him, may He be blessed, and of us in absolute equivocation,[243] it is clear that the predicates which we affirm of Him, may He be blessed, are not said of Him, may He be blessed, and of us in absolute equivocation. This is because it would be uncertain at first, according to the capability of our thought, whether these predicates should be affirmed of or negated from Him, may He be blessed, prior to a full investigation. (Only) afterwards could we affirm them of or negate them from Him.[244]

In general, if the things[244a] that we affirm of Him, may He be blessed, are said of Him, may He be blessed, and of us in absolute equivocation, (then) not one of the terms for things which are (known) to us would be more appropriate in negation from God, may He be blessed, than in affirmation, or (more ap-

---

relation R, it does not follow that because $R(f, g)$ that $R(f^1, g^1)$ is the case. But we only know predicates such as f^1 and g^1 on the basis of predicates such as f and g.

[243] Cf. note 238.

[244] Gersonides has argued that no predicate f can be affirmed or negated of God if that predicate as applied to God is absolutely equivocal with that predicate as applied to everything else. Cf. note 238. He gave an example of this with the negation of a predicate (motion) of God. He now asserts again that as in the example negations are not asserted of God in absolute equivocation, neither are affirmations so asserted. In his example the negation of the predicate, motion with respect to God (i.e., God is motionless) is concluded from an affirmative use of that predicate with respect to His world (i.e., anything subject to motion is a body). Gersonides now adds that the case is the same where the affirmation of some predicate with respect to God is concluded from either an affirmation or a negation of that predicate with respect to this world. Cf. note 242.

[244a] I.e., the predicates.

propriate) in affirmation than in negation. This is because someone could say, for example, that God, may He be blessed, is body, without meaning by this term, "body" something which has quantity but (rather) something which is absolutely equivocal with what we call (ordinarily) "body." Similarly it could be said that God is unknowing, since in this proposition the term, "knowledge" would not designate[245] with regard to Him what it designates when we call something "knowledge."[246]

One may not reply[247] that we negate corporeality from Him because it is a deficiency with reference to us, and that we affirm knowledge of Him because with reference to us it is a perfection.[248] (One may not say this) because[247] the term,[249] "cor-

---

[245] Cf. note 232.

[246] The general conclusion elaborated here already has been drawn at the end of the preceding paragraph. (Cf. note 244.) Gersonides' development here of this conclusion serves as a transition into his fourth argument from Philosophic Thought against the doctrine of absolute equivocation. The point is that since terms have a meaning when used as predicates with reference to God totally different from that which they have when used as predicates with reference to anything else, none of the rules of usage in the latter case apply to the former case and we have no way to determine alternate rules of usage in the former case independent of the latter case.

[247] Cf. notes 125 and 127.

[248] Maimonides states this in *The Guide* 1.26:

One has ascribed to Him, may He be exalted, everything that in our opinion is a perfection in order to indicate that He is perfect in every manner of perfection and that no deficiency whatever mars Him. Thus none of the things apprehended by the multitude as a deficiency or a privation are predicated of Him. Hence it is not predicated of Him that He eats, drinks, sleeps, is ill, does an injustice, or that He has any similar characteristic. On the other hand, everything that the multitude consider a perfection is predicated of Him, even if it is only a perfection in relation

poreality" is not a deficiency, which is what we negate from
Him.²⁵⁰ Rather its meaning is a deficiency. Similarly it is not the

------

to ourselves — for in relation to Him, may He be exalted, all things that
we consider perfections are the very extreme of deficiency.

(Pines tr., p. 56)

Gersonides does not present this objection as an objection of Maimonides, and
indeed Maimonides does not state this position as his own. Rather he is
describing what in fact the multitude do in affirming and negating predicates of
God, and particularly for Maimonides to describe any practice as the practice
of the multitude does not recommend that this procedure should be followed.
He himself notes as does Gersonides that this procedure is arbitrary.

There is, accordingly, no difference between, on one hand, predicating
eating and drinking of God, may He be exalted, and, on the other,
predicating movement of Him. However, in accordance with *the language
of the sons of man,* I mean the imagination of the multitude, eating and
drinking are considered in their opinion as a deficiency with reference to
God, whereas motion is not considered as a deficiency with reference to
Him; and this notwithstanding the fact that only need obliges recourse to
motion.

(ibid.)

But Maimonides does indicate nonetheless a certain respectability to this
procedure, namely that insofar as these positive predicates indicate not that
God has a given property but that "He is perfect in every manner of perfection," such predication is legitimate.

²⁴⁹ I.e., terms or words are themselves arbitrary. Only the things that terms
refer to can be either perfections or imperfections.

²⁵⁰ Gersonides here casually introduces a new but major criticism of
Maimonides' theory of divine attributes. To describe divine predicates as absolutely equivocal is to misunderstand what a predicate is. Predicates are
properties of things, but predicates are never themselves absolutely equivocal.
Only terms can be absolutely equivocal. In other words, at the very foundation
of Maimonides' doctrine there is a fatal confusion, viz. the confusion of terms
and what those terms mean.

term, "knowledge" which is a perfection, but its meaning. The proof (for this) is the fact that if we designate[245] by the term, "corporeality" what is designated[245] (ordinarily) by the term, "knowledge," and (if we designate) by the term, "knowledge" what is designated (ordinarily) by the term, "corporeality," (then) corporeality would be a perfection for us and knowledge a deficiency.[251]

Furthermore, we neither affirm nor negate anything of God, may He be blessed, unless we first investigate whether or not the existence of that thing is or is not appropriate to Him, may He be blessed,[252] without considering in this our investigation whether or not that something is a perfection with reference to us. This being the case, it is clear that Philosophic Thought rejects (the view that) the term, "knowledge" is said of both Him, may He be blessed, and of us in absolute equivocation.[253]

[251] Since words are themselves arbitrary symbols.

[252] Cf. note 244.

[253] Gersonides' main point in this argument can be stated as follows: a sign that a term is intelligible is that there are rules governing the use of that term. In other words, a term has meaning only if there are some contexts where it is correct to employ it and other contexts where it is not correct. But where a term indiscriminately is appropriate or inappropriate in all contexts the term is nonsense. For example, if I say that "strawberries are sidrap" but you have no idea what "sidrap" means (i.e., you do not know what kind of things are and are not sidrap and of those things which may or may not be sidrap you do not know how to tell whether they are or are not sidrap), the whole sentence "strawberries are sidrap" is unintelligible. (The same example applied to the preceding argument two would be "sidrap is red." For any term in a sentence to be untelligible ["is" is intelligible in the sense that there are rules for its use] renders the whole sentence unintelligible.) And this is precisely the case with all statements about God. The statement "God is F," no matter what F is, is unintelligible first (by the second argument) because the

(*135*) It is clear in another way[254] that Philosophic Thought
rejects what the Master The Guide, may his memory be blessed,

---

term, "God" as employed by us is unintelligible, and second (by this third
argument) because "*F*" is understood to be absolutely equivocal which is to
say that the "*F*" used in this sentence has no relation to anything that we understand.

Against this argument (or rather, against the second and third arguments
incorporated in the above summary), Maimonides may reply as follows: in
The Guide 1.58, Maimonides tells us that "every attribute that we predicate of
Him ..., if the attribute is intended for the apprehension of His essence ...,
signifies the negation of the privation of the attribute in question" (Pines tr.,
p. 136). In other words, when we say that God is good we mean that God is
not bad or when we say that God has knowledge we mean that God is not
ignorant, etc. In other words all formerly affirmative statements about God
really are disguised negative propositions. To be sure this procedure can never
yield adequate knowledge of God. Maimonides himself asserts this: "Negation
does not give knowledge in any respect of the true reality of the thing with
regard to which the particular matter in question has been negated" (*The
Guide* 1.59, p. 139 of the Pines tr.). But on one hand no one can claim
properly to have adequate knowledge of God. "All men, those of the past and
those of the future, affirm clearly that God, may He be exalted, cannot be apprehended by the intellect, and that none but He Himself can apprehend what
He is" (ibid.). On the other hand, although negative knowledge is never
adequate knowledge it is nonetheless in some sense knowledge.

At the beginning of *The Guide*, 1.60, Maimonides gives what he calls a
"parable" to show that such knowledge of God through negative judgments is
in fact knowledge. He posits two situations through which a person comes to
know what a ship is. The first situation is through affirmative attributes, the
description of which closely parallels the ship example that Gersonides gave
above at the end of his presentation of Maimonides' "fourth way." (*The Wars
of the Lord*, p. 130 of the Leipzig edition; cf. note 178.) The second situation
is through negative attributes. In other words, whereas in the first situation a
person learns what a boat is by learning that it is a body consisting of timber
which is hollow, and oblong, in the second situation a person learns that it is
not an accident, not a mineral, not a living being, not a plant, not a natural

posited on the question of the knowledge of God, may He be blessed. This is because even if we assume that the knowledge of God, may He be blessed, is absolutely equivocal with our knowledge it is impossible that contradictions should be included in this knowledge, namely that it[255] should be without generation and without change while it is generating and changing.[256] However, the Master The Guide, may his memory be blessed,

---

body, etc. Although the process of learning is somewhat longer in the second case than it is in the first, nonetheless Maimonides asserts "He (the individual learning through negative statements) has, as it were, attained equality" with one who has represented the ship through positive assertions.

In any case Maimonides would claim against what Gersonides has argued here that this negative understanding of divine predicates renders these predicates intelligible. That this reply is not adequate is what Gersonides will argue in his fourth argument. In other words, the force of the next and final argument when combined with the second and third arguments is that even the above interpretation of absolute equivocation cannot render Maimonides' theory of divine predication intelligible.

[254] Gersonides' fourth proof.

[255] I.e., this knowledge, which is God's knowledge.

[256] Gersonides' fourth argument, stated in its entirety in this one sentence, contains the following line of reasoning. Let us assume for the moment that the kind of predication that Maimonides asks us to accept with reference to God is intelligible. To be sure, divine predicates are a different kind of entity from any other kind of predicates. But how different? These predicates will differ in use from other predicates, but certainly the difference cannot be so great that not even the law of non-contradiction has application to indicative sentences in which the terms expressing these predicates are incorporated.

Maimonides at this point might object and say, "Why not? This is precisely what it means to say that these terms for divine predicates are absolutely equivocal, i.e., nothing that is affirmatively true of what we know within the range of our other uses of language will be affirmatively true of our extension of this language to speech about God." Gersonides, as is clear in this context, would consider such a response from the point of view of Philosophic Thought

accepted these contradictions with regard to this knowledge,[257] as we explained,[258] from what he posited as a fundamental principle of this knowledge.[259]

---

to be absurd. But why? Gersonides does not tell us, but it is not difficult to construct his argument from what he says here and from what he has said in the previous three objections.

What in effect Maimonides is proposing that we do is the following. He suggests first of all that language about God cannot be included properly in ordinary language. (In Maimonides' terms, "in *the language of the sons of man*" [*The Guide* 1.26].) However, secondly, our ordinary language can be expanded to include "God-talk" if and only if the predicates in this case are understood to be absolutely equivocal. But, Gersonides may reply, this extension is not admissible. Language is intended to communicate but in order to do that not only must the language be subject to grammatical rules, it also must be subject to logical rules. However, in a language where not even the law of non-contradiction applies, there are no logical rules. But such a language is utterly unintelligible. (It must be noted that Maimonides' defense of his doctrine of predication rested on statements about God being in some sense intelligible. Cf. note 253.)

That the law of non-contradiction does not hold for statements about God with Maimonides' proposed interpretation can be shown generally and specifically. Gersonides' explicit demonstration is specific. In one sense his discussion of the five ways in chapter two and the whole of chapter three are a statement of this argument. Consider the predicate term, "knowledge." On Maimonides' interpretation of the term it is synonymous with "ignorance or error or confusion." Hence we may apply either term to God, i.e., on Maimonides' interpretation of a language of God-talk, that language includes as compatible the sentence, "God has perfect knowledge" and the sentence, "God is either ignorant or mistaken or confused." Certainly these two sentences are contradictory. But in a language which formally admits contradictory sentences, all sentences are admissible. Such a language is no language at all.

Gersonides' second and third argument entail implicitly a general argument which makes the same point made in the specific argument noted in the

Furthermore, he (himself) fled from relating the term, "ignorance" to God, may He be blessed.[260] Because of this he said that He knows everything. But its meaning[261] remained for him[262] in accordance with what was explained that he[262] posited as a fundamental principle concerning the knowledge of God, may He be blessed, namely that such knowledge as this is called "ignorance" by us, (and) not knowledge.[263]

---

preceding paragraph. On Maimonides' interpretation of positive predicates within this language of "God-talk" (cf. note 253), given any predicate F, F is to be read as "not not-F" where "not-F" is the opposite of "F." But what is the meaning of "F" in the "not-F" of the explanatory clause? This too must be read as "not not-F." But again the same question arises about the "F" contained in the new explanatory clause, and so on *ad infinitum*. The regress is inadmissible since if at no point can a definite account be given of any predicate in the system, the meaning of these predicates remains sufficiently indefinite that they are indistinguishable from their contradictories (in Gersonides' sense of the term). (Cf. footnote 44.) For example, we can say that God is good because what we mean by this is that God is not bad in human terms. But it is equally intelligible to say that God is bad because what this means is that God is not good in human terms, which literally is the case. In other words, God is both good and bad in this system. It cannot be objected that this statement is misleading because in the sentence, "God is both good and bad" the predicates appear as contraries but they are not since they are not used in the same sense. This is precisely the point. No two terms can ever be used in the same sense if no term can be given a positive account. Hence in principle the system cannot admit contradiction.

[257] I.e., the knowledge of God.

[258] I.e., the discussion of the "five ways" in chapter 2.

[259] Cf. notes 72, 89 and 257.

[260] *The Guide*, 3.19. Cf. note 64.

[261] I.e., the meaning of "God knows everything."

[262] I.e., Maimonides.

[263] In his discussion of the "five ways" that our knowledge and God's knowledge differ in chapter two.

However, the Torah[264] forced the Master, may his memory be blessed, to hold this kind of belief concerning the knowledge of God, may He be blessed, as we already have mentioned.[265] Having been of the view that Philosophic Thought/ greatly disputes this belief, he said what he said concerning the knowledge of God, may He be blessed, in order to rid himself of all of these arguments[266] and to establish what the Torah, according to him,[262] affirms of Him. But we will investigate this after we have concluded our investigation here.[267]

There is, in a certain way, an aspect of plausibility[268] to what the Master The Guide, may his memory be blessed, said, (namely) that the term, "knowledge" is said of (both) God, may He be blessed, and us in absolute equivocation. This is that clearly there is no relation between God, may He be blessed, and existing things; therefore, it is not possible that anything should be said of Him which is said of His created things, except in absolute equivocation.[269] Furthermore it is not proper that any at-

---

[264] Cf. note 2.

[265] Cf. notes 6 and 202.

[266] I.e., the arguments of the philosophers presented in chapter two.

[267] I.e., after refuting Maimonides' view by Philosophic Thought we will look to see if in fact this interpretation of Maimonides is the correct interpretation of the Torah. This "investigation" is presented in chapter six of this treatise.

[268] Cf. note 22.

[269] Cf. the quotation from *The Guide* 1.52, 60b-61a reproduced in note 89. Because God is the only necessary being and everything else is a created and therefore contingent being, (cf. notes 43 and 208 on the distinction between necessary and contingent being), and a distinction in terms of being is the broadest possible kind of distinction, i.e., there are no more general genera in which this distinction in being can be incorporated as a species difference, it

tribute should be predicated of God, may He be blessed, it being the case that any predicate entails necessarily complexity,[270] be it

_____

follows that there is no relation between God and anything else. If, Maimonides argues, no analogy can be drawn between things of the same genus but of non-proximate species, how much the more so would this be the case here where the genus is non-proximate.

[270] Maimonides presents this second general argument for this position in the following words:

There are many things in existence that are clear and manifest: ... To this category belongs the denial of essential attributes of God, may He be exalted. For that denial is a primary intelligible, inasmuch as an attribute is not the essence of the thing of which it is predicated, but is a certain mode of the essence and hence an accident. If, however, the attribute were the essence of the thing of which it is predicated, the attribute would be either a tautology — as if you were saying man is man — or the attribute would be a mere explanation of a term — as if you said that man is a rational living being. For being a rational animal is the essence and true reality of man, and there does not exist in this case a third notion, apart from those of animal and rational, that constitutes man. For man is the being of which life and rationality are predicated. Thus those attributes merely signify an explantion of a term and nothing else. It is as if you said that the thing denoted by the term "man" is the thing composed of life and rationality. It is then clear that an attribute may be only one of two things. It is either the essence of the thing of which it is predicated, in which case it is an explanation of a term. We, in this respect, do not consider it impossible to predicate such an attribute of God, but do consider it impossible in another respect, as shall be made clear. Or the attribute is different from the thing of which it is predicated, being a notion superadded to that thing. This would lead to the conclusion that that attribute is an accident belonging to that essence.

(*The Guide* 1.51, pp. 112-113 of the Pines tr.)

All attributes are of two kinds. Either they are accidents of a subject, in which case they tell us something about the subject, or they are essential predicates,

a qualitative or a substantive attribute.[271] Thus, it also is clear
that when any attribute is predicated of God it is predicated of

---

in which case they tell us what the subject is. Only the latter kind of predicates
are admissible in the case of God. The former are not because such predication
entails complexity in the subject and God is a simple substance. Yet even these
latter predicates are admitted in only a special sense, namely in the sense of
absolute equivocation, i.e., negative predication is admissible literally but
positive predication is admissible only in the sense that what is being said
properly is a double negative and not an affirmation. (Cf. note 256.) The
reason that the former kind of predication, viz. accidental, entails complexity
in the subject is the following: what the proposition, "a is F," where "F" is an
accident of "a," asserts is that the property F is *in a*. Hence "a" contains at
least two parts, "F" and those properties which express what "a" is.

It may be objected that this argument presupposes a doctrine of exclusive
internal predication, i.e., all predicates of a thing are to be understood as internal predicates, but given a doctrine of external predicates the argument
collapses. For example, the statement, "a is F" may be read as follows: there
is a relation, namely the relation of predication or exemplification, which holds
between "a" and "F." On this reading "F" is true of "a" but "F" is not contained in "a" so that the statement "a is F" in no way entails complexity in
the subject "a."

In a sense Maimonides at times recognizes that there are statements that
literally can be made about a thing which do not entail a property being in-
ternally predicated of a thing, i.e., that are not read in such a way that one
thing, viz. a property, is said to be contained in another thing, viz. a subject.
In *The Guide* 1.53, Maimonides considers five kinds of affirmative attributes
none of which are admissible with reference to God since they entail attributing complexity to God. At the conclusion of this argument Maimonides
says the following:

> He, may He be exalted, is one in all respects; no multiplicity should be
> posited in Him; there is no notion that is super-added to His essence; the
> numerous attributes possessing diverse notions that figure in the Scrip-
> tures and that are indicative of Him, may He be exalted, are mentioned in
> reference to the multiplicity of His actions and not because of multiplicity

Him, may He be blessed, and us in absolute equivocation. This
is because it[272] designates in Him, may He be blessed, a quality

---

subsisting in His essence, and some of them, as we have made clear, also
with a view to indicating His perfection according to what we consider as
perfection.

(Pines tr., p. 119)

Maimonides grants two contexts in which affirmations may legitimately be
made of God. One context is in terms of the use of terms which are absolutely
equivocal (cf. notes 253 and 256) in which multiple positive attributes affirm
only one thing, namely that God is supremely perfect (as is discussed by
Maimonides in *The Guide* 1.26.) (cf. note 248). To this we shall return
momentarily. The second context is in terms of actions. In other words, when
some action is predicated of a subject it does not mean that the action resides
in the subject. In other words, an external relation holds between a subject and
its actions.

In any case Maimonides still can argue that accidents cannot be predicated
of God without using directly the doctrine of internal predication. Maimonides, as well as his predecessors and followers in the Moslem-Jewish medieval
tradition, might reply that to say that God is a necessary being is to say that
He is necessary in every respect, i.e., anything that is true of Him is
necessarily and not contingently true of Him. But if external relations are applicable to God they would of necessity be contingent. (To be necessary means
to follow exclusively from the nature of the thing in question. Hence for a
predicate to be related externally to a thing while still being a necessary
predicate of the thing is a contradiction in terms.) However, it should be noted
that the force of this argument is to make even action predicates, if admissible
at all, internal predicates of a thing. It might well be objected that this use of
the term, "necessary" is unreasonably extended. It makes perfectly good sense
to say that it happens to be the case that such and such is true (as an external
relation) of a necessary being without denying that the necessary being is
necessary, i.e., something that exists in virtue of itself and not in virtue of an
external cause.

Maimonides' comments above concerning essential predication contain a
number of points worthy of note. As mentioned above in essential predication

which is in itself the essence of what is described.[273] The Master
The Guide, may his memory be blessed, already explained this

---

you say what a thing is. Given a reference theory of meaning (cf. note 125)
such predication is a curious thing. If I say that "a is b" then on this theory of
meaning "a" and "b" mean the same thing so that "a" and "b" are in-
terchangeable in all contexts without changing the meaning of the statements
containing them. Hence "a is b," "a is a," and "b is b" are all equivalent in
meaning. As Maimonides notes, they are "tautologies." But clearly not all
statements of the form "a is b" where "b" is an essential predicate are like
this. One common exception is when you say "a is F and G," "F" expressing
a genus and "G" expressing a specific difference. But no such example has
relevance to God since if God contains a genus and a species God would be
complex, i.e., God would be "composed of" F and G. But even in this case the
above curious situation obtains, namely that since "a" is "F and G," "a" and
"F and G" are mutually substitutable in all contexts, making the statement "a
is F and G" a tautology.

The problem is that "a is b" seems to provide information whereas "a is a"
and "b is b" do not. Maimonides' answer to the problem is that in such contexts as these where the kind of predication involved is essential predication,
the predication is "an explanation of a term." In other words, in saying "a is
b" we are not asserting anything about a and b. This we could not do since a
and b means the same thing, i.e., they are the same thing. Rather we are
speaking of the words "a" and "b" and the relation described is a relation of
terms rather than of things.

As we shall see subsequently, this explanation of Maimonides will play a
central role in Gersonides' argument that the simplicity of God, on even the
extreme interpretation of simplicity employed by Maimonides, does not entail
the doctrine of absolute equivocation of divine predicates.

[271] As used in this context 'in^eyan means non-essential or that relating to
quality which is therefore an accident. Nòsē' means substratum, i.e., that in
which qualities inhere. The term, "quality" as I use it here does not
correspond to Aristotle's use of the term as one of the nine categories of accidents. Rather it is used more broadly for all the categories of accident as
distinct from the first category of substance.

(matter) at length in his honorable book *The Guide of the Perplexed.*[274]

After this argument it would seem to follow necessarily[275] that attributes which are predicated of (both) Him, may He be blessed, and us are predicated in absolute equivocation. But the above arguments which we have presented on this (question)[276] necessarily entail that these attributes[277] may not be said (of God and us) in absolute equivocation. Thus, would that I knew how the matter could be like this![278]

We say that with a good deal of reflection it will be apparent that there are predicates[279] which are said[279] of God, may He be

[272] I.e., the term for what is predicated of God.

[273] God is simple, i.e. is not composed of parts. Therefore any predicate which is essentially true of God is God. In other words, given any predicate *F*, if it is true to say that "God is *F*" then God and *F* are one and the same thing.

[274] 1.50-55. Cf. note 270. This argument is discussed at length by Wolfson in "Maimonides and Gersonides," p. 525.

[275] Cf. note 36. While Gersonides admits the validity of the two arguments presented above he will deny their conclusion. In other words, given that there is no relation between God and anything else and given that God is simple in every way, it does not follow that all predication of God must be absolutely equivocal. Rather what follows is that divine predicates are *pros hen* equivocals.

[276] Namely the four arguments in chapter three against Maimonides' position.

[277] Rather the names or terms of these attributes, since words and not things are what are said.

[278] In other words, this is an impossible conclusion. Gersonides often uses this phrase to conclude his statement of a dilemma which he is about to solve.

[279] Literally, "attributes which are said." However, attributes cannot be said although attributes can be possessed and the names of terms for attributes can be said. Gersonides does not always keep clear the distinction between the

blessed, and other beings priorly and posteriorly which do not
necessarily entail that there is complexity in Him. The reason
for this is that not every statement that is said of something in a
certain manner necessarily entails complexity in that thing.
Rather, it indeed necessarily will entail complexity in it[280] if the
one part[281] is related to the other part[282] as the subject of
existence.[283] However, if it[281] is not related to it[282] as a subject in
existence, even though it is a subject in the statement,[283] it[284]
does not entail necessarily that there is complexity in it.[280] For

---

terms for attributes and the attributes themselves. For that reason in such contexts I translate *tō'ar* as "predicate," a term which by itself is equally vague
with respect to this distinction.

[280] I.e., in the thing which is the subject of predication.

[281] I.e., that part of the sentence which expresses the subject.

[282] I.e., that part of the sentence which expresses the predicate.

[283] Cf. Wolfson, "Maimonides and Gersonides," p. 526. What we have
translated here as "subject in existence" and "subject in the statement" Wolfson identifies with Aristotle's distinction between real and nominal definitions
respectively.

In the *Analytica Posteriora* 1.10, Aristotle distinguishes between the
existence and the meaning of subjects of the mathematical sciences in particular. In making this distinction he tells us that where what is stated are the
essential attributes of the subject, e.g., in the case of mathematical definitions
as well as in the case of definitions in the other sciences (astronomy is mentioned by name) "only the meaning is assumed" (76b5-7). Aristotle must
make this distinction since he claims that such statements are true while their
subjects do not exist. (Cf. note 125.) That definitions are somewhat unusual
linguistically, particularly given Aristotle's reference theory of meaning, is
noted by Aristotle at the end of this chapter where he states that "all
hypothesis and illegitimate postulates are either universal or particular,
whereas a definition is neither" (*Analytica Posteriora* 1.10, 77a3-4). In other
words, whereas everything that exists is particular and what characterizes
something that exists is universal, definitions are neither.

The reason why Aristotle makes this above judgment is clear. Consider the

example, when we say about a certain redness that it is a red
color, it does not follow necessarily because of this that the red-

---

proposition, "a unicorn is a single-horned horse." What is asserted here is an
identity relation. As such the right hand clause cannot be read as a universal
that is true of the left hand term for then the identity would be false. The ontological status of the referents of both parts of this statement must be the
same. But the referents are not particulars. "A unicorn is a single-horned
horse" is different from "the unicorn is the single-horned horse." The former
is true while the latter is false since there are no unicorns. Similarly, for
Aristotle, the term, "a unicorn" is different from the term, "all unicorns."
Hence Aristotle would not read the above definition to be synonymous with
the statement, "if anything is a unicorn then it is a single-horned horse." The
latter is a statement about all unicorns whereas the former is a statement about
"a unicorn." But what exactly is "a unicorn" if it is not simply an abbreviation for a collection of a certain kind of creature? According to Aristotle
it is an "essential nature." Hence definitions are statements about essential
natures which are neither universals, i.e. characterizations of existing things,
nor particulars, i.e., existing things. These essential natures are "meanings" as
opposed to "existents."

In the *Analytica Posteriora* 2.10, Aristotle elaborates this analysis of
definition as follows: "... definition is (a) an indemonstrable statement of
essential nature, or (b) a syllogism of essential nature differing from demonstration in grammatical form, or (c) the conclusion of a demonstration giving
essential nature" (94a10-13). The first kind of definition is "a statement of
the meaning of the name, or of an equivalent nominal formula" (ibid. 2.10,
29-30). In this case no existence claim is made. All that is given is how to use
a term. This is what Wolfson has called "a nominal definition." But the last
two cases of definition differ from the first in that they do state something
about the world. The second is "a formula exhibiting the cause of a thing's
existence" (ibid. 93b39-40) while the third is "the conclusion of the demonstration embodying essential nature" (ibid. 94a8-9). These two are not different. Rather the third is an abbreviated expression of the second. In the
second kind of definition what is stated is the essential nature of a thing in the
sense of essence discussed in notes 26 and 125. It is a statement of the cause
of a thing where cause is understood primarily as final cause which is that

ness in question would be composed of color and redness. This
is because color is not something existent as a subject for red-

---

towards which a thing, insofar as it is potential, tends to be actually. Such a
definition is a disguised causal statement. In other words the definition, "*a* is
b" and the statement "*b* is the cause of something becoming *a*" express identical propositions. Such a case is a case of what Wolfson calls "a real
definition." Again, the third kind of definition differs from the second only in
that, using the same example, whereas "*b*" in the second case is a complex
statement of causes in which the last cause in this chain is what "*a*" is identified with, in the third case only this last, proximate cause is stated as "*b*."
For example, the definition of thunder as the noise of fire being quenched in
the clouds" can be abbreviated "noise in the clouds" (ibid. 94a4-9).

In the case of a definition of the form "*a* is *b*" where "*a*" is the subject of
existence as well as the subject of the statement, i.e., in the case of a "real
definition," it is not clear what is the status of "*b*." Is it a complex of universals describing "*a*" where "*a*" and not "*b*" is what exists or is "*b*" itself a
special kind of existent, and if "*b*" does exist, does it exist as a series of causal
events, as the description in the *Analytica Posteriora* 2.10 leads you to believe,
particularly from the examples given, or, in keeping with the description of
definition given in the *Analytica Posteriora* 1.10, is it a special kind of entity
neither particular nor universal but nonetheless existent? Whatever Aristotle's
intention, Gersonides, and probably his Moslem-Jewish predecessors, would
apply this last interpretation to what Aristotle called a "real definition." (Cf.
notes 13, 14, 26, 35, 40, 67, and 68.) What is given in this case is the essence
of a thing which is a single thing existent in the Active Intellect by which the
thing defined is ordered and therefore exists.

There is one further feature of real and nominal definitions that needs to be
noted which becomes clear in Gersonides' subsequent discussion. In keeping
with the reference theory of meaning, in the case of real definitions the stated
proposition "pictures" reality in that there is a one-to-one correspondence between the parts of the sentence and the things in the world. This feature,
however, is not the case with nominal definitions. As Gersonides discusses
these two kinds of definitions this "picturing" feature with its corresponding
assumption of formal coincidence between the parts of the sentence and the
parts of that to which the sentence refers becomes a sign (although not a
criterion) of which kind of definition a given definition is.

ness. Rather (*136*) it is a subject only in the statement.[285] This also will be the case if individuations bring about what they

[284] I.e., the statement in question.

[285] In *De Interpretatione* 11, Aristotle tells us the following:

> I do not apply this word 'one' to those things which, though they have a single recognized name, yet do not combine to form a unity. Thus, man may be an animal, and biped, and domesticated, but these three predicates combine to form a unity. On the other hand, the predicates 'white,' 'man,' and 'walking' do not thus combine. Neither, therefore, if these three form the subject of an affirmation, nor if they form its predicate, is there any unity about that affirmation. In both cases the unity is linguistic, but not real.
>
> (20b15-21)

Aristotle's main concern here is to tell us something about when multiple things may properly be called one and when they may not be called one. But in doing so he illustrates for us the difference between a subject in a statement, what Aristotle here calls "linguistic," and a subject in existence, what Aristotle here calls "real." Aristotle gives us two examples. The second is a case of accidental predication, e.g., "John is a walking, white, man." In some sense (what Aristotle calls "one by accident," cf. *Metaphysics* Δ.6, 1015b16-1017a3 and note 101) "walking," "white," and "man" are one, namely they belong to the same subject, but this is not a proper sense of one. The claim of unity here is "linguistic" and "not real." The first is a case of definition. For example, "man is domesticated, biped, animal." In this case the right hand clause in some sense (namely, identity) is what man is. In such a case, namely where identity rather than predication statements are involved, the assertion of unity is proper. But again this unity is linguistic and not real. The reason for this is that man in this context is a single thing and not a compound of three things, namely domesticated, biped and animal. (The case is different with a statement like "Man is a rational animal" where "rational animal" is understood to be the real and not the nominal definition of man. Cf. note 283.)

   This first example of Aristotle, where the identity asserted is linguistic but nonetheless a real unity is asserted, corresponds to the example that Gersonides gives here. A given hue of red is a simple sensation. As a sensation it

bring about.[286] (For example) if you would say that "it is a color intermediate between black and white, leaning more towards black than white," then all of them[287] designate only one simple thing. The plurality of conditions and individuation (only) serve to explain which of the simple colors is this color.[288]

---

is a single thing. Yet it is also a red and because red is a color it is also a color. But that is not to say that because this hue is both red and a color it is complex.

The same point may be made in another way. "Red" expresses a universal which is exemplified by this color. "Color" expresses a second level universal which is exemplified by the universal red. But universals do not exist. Hence to say that this hue is red and a color is to speak of conceptual relations rather than of existent entities.

It should be noted for the sake of clarity that by "linguistic" Aristotle (and Gersonides as well) does not mean the word or the physical sentence. Rather what is intended is what the word or sentence means. In Aristotle's language, sentences such as these are "addressed not to the spoken word, but to the discourse within the soul" (*Analytica Posteriora* 1.10, 76b24-25). However, at the same time this is not to say that Aristotle, as well as Gersonides, proceeded with a clear distinction between the term, the meaning of the term, and the referent of the term. We have had an ample number of examples to see that this is not the case.

[286] I.e., in cases of propositions where something named which is an individual is uniquely expressed through a complex series of predicates. Such an example is the ship example given at the conclusion of Gersonides' discussion of the fourth of the five "ways" in chapter two. (Cf. note 178.) In all such cases the subject is a subject in the statement but not in existence.

[287] I.e., all of the predicate terms.

[288] This example of propositions which individuate as opposed to statements of definitions is the creation of Gersonides rather than of Aristotle. The concern with such statements is one of the unique aspects of Gersonides' philosophy in relation to his Jewish and Moslem predecessors. However, the general point is the same in this context as the point that Aristotle had made (cf. note 285). The hue in the example is expressed by a conjunction of two

This also is essentially the case with things which have no (real or existent) subject, i.e., that the statement which is said concerning them[289] does not designate complexity in them. To illustrate, if we say of that intelligence which moves the sphere of the sun, for example, that "it is the intelligence which conceives of a certain nomos[290] by which that sphere's movements are ordered," (then) this sentence would not designate complexity (in the subject). This is because the term, "the intelligence" is a subject only in the sentence, not in existence.[291] Even though the (term) "intelligence" may be said of what is other than separate intelligences, in this case[292] they[293] do not

---

complex relations (a three-termed relation of being-intermediate-between and another three-termed relation of being-closer-to-than) and three terms (a variable for the color hue in question, black and white). Yet the hue itself is a simple thing.

[289] I.e., concerning those things which have no existent subject. Subject here is to be understood in the sense of substrate. As his example will show Gersonides specifically intends intelligences which are disembodied forms, i.e., they are not material entities where there is a form *in* matter. He does not mean non-existent entities.

[290] Cf. note 13.

[291] Intelligences are simple, existent forms. Hence complex identity or individuating statements concerning them necessarily involve subjects in the statement and not subjects in existence. However, for the purposes with which Gersonides is using this example, namely to refute Maimonides' theory of absolute equivocation based on the claim that any other form of predication entails complexity in God, the example is poor. In this example, what is predicated of the subject is a series of statements of the actions of the subject, but, as we have seen (cf. note 270), Maimonides' theory admits such predication in a sense (not explained by Maimonides) other than absolute equivocation.

[292] I.e., the case quoted involving separate intelligences as the subject.

[293] I.e., the separate intelligences. The point is that all of the separate in-

agree in subject and differ in (their) differences. Rather (it is the case that) we state in the sentence which one it is of the simple entities that the term, "intelligence" comprehends (to which we are referring).[294] The reason for this is that concerning these intelligences, some of them differ essentially from others of them without any agreement between them in anything. The reason for this is that if it were so,[295] (then) they would be complex entities (and) not simple entities. Indeed, the way in which (these) intelligences differ is the same way in which the objects of their conception differ.[296] This being the case, it is clear that when some (one) attribute or multiplicity of attributes is predicated of God, may He be blessed, these attributes do not

---

telligences are distinct yet they all are separate intelligences. In other cases of this sort where multiple things are called by a common name although they are individually different, we may say that they share some form in common in virtue of which they are one, expressed through a genus term, while there are also in these things other elements through which they are different, expressed either with reference to their matter or with reference to a formal specific difference (e.g., men and dogs are animals but the former is rational whereas the latter is not). But this cannot be the case with separate intelligences each of which is a single form and none of which is material.

[294] In a statement such as the one above about the intelligence which moves the sphere of the sun, we are not defining the intelligence. Rather we are giving a description which in this case is a verbal formula by which the listener will be able to pick out which individual among a collection of individuals is being referred to by a given name. The case is the same in the color example given above.

[295] I.e., that these intelligences could agree in one respect while differing in another. Cf. note 293.

[296] Since intelligences know forms or essences independent of sensation, the forms or essences that they know are in every way free of a material principle. Thus the objects of their knowledge, like the separate intelligences themselves, differ only formally, but are equally simple.

entail necessarily complexity in Him, because He has no subject.[297] Therefore, all of these attributes in Him do not designate
anything but a simple entity.[298]

It still can be demonstrated that the predicates which are said
of God, may He be blessed, are said of Him priorly and of other
existent entities posteriorly even if we grant that there is no
relation between God, may He be blessed, and His creatures.[299]
This is because one will find such cases among the terms which
are said priorly and posteriorly. For example, the term,
"existent" is said of the entity[300] priorly and the accidents
posteriorly, as has been explained in the *Metaphysics*.[301] But it is

[297] God being simple has no substratum other than Himself. Subject here is
used in the two senses of subject in a proposition and substratum. Thus, given
any predicate, F, to say that "God is F" is not to say that God is something
excluding F in which F inheres since that something is God and, if F is God,
and God is simple, that F and the something also are one and the same thing.

[298] The point may be expressed simply as follows: given that any predicate,
F as the referent (i.e., meaning; cf. footnote 125) of the term, "God" is God,
so the referent of the sentence, "God is F" is God and not some state-of-
affairs in which God is a participant.

[299] In the previous argument Gersonides defended his doctrine of divine attributes as *pros hen* equivocals against the second noted "aspect of
plausibility" of Maimonides' argument, namely that God is absolutely simple.
Now Gersonides defends his doctrine against the first noted "aspect of
plausibility," namely that there is no analogy between God and anything else.

[300] In this context I prefer the term, "entity" as a translation for the Hebrew
'eṣem which is a literal translation of the Greek, *ousia*. For the reasons why
this one term lends itself to a number of English translations, depending on
context, including "essence" and "being" as well as "entity," see note 207.

[301] In a sense this point is the central theme of the whole of the *Metaphysics*
(Cf. Joseph Owens, *The Doctrine of Being*, pp. 264-275). Passages specifically
related to Gersonides' claim are B.3, 998b22; H.6, 104a35-1045b7; Δ.28,
1024b10-15; Γ.2, 1003a33-1003b8; Z.1, 1028a10-30; Z.4, 1030a31-

clear that there is no relation between entity and accidents.[302]
It is proper that you should know that in this world there are

---

1030b4; and Δ.7, 1017a6-1017b10. This passage in the Gersonides' text is discussed at length by Wolfson in relation to its Aristotelian sources in "Maimonides and Gersonides," p. 528.

The two passages from the *Metaphysics* which most closely parallel in language what Gersonides is saying here are the following:

> There are many senses in which a thing may be said to 'be' but all that 'is' is related to one central point, one definite kind of thing, and is not said to 'be' by mere ambiguity. ... So, too, there are many senses in which a thing is said to be, but all refer to one starting-point; some things are said to be because they are substances, others because they are affections of substances. ...
>
> (*Metaphysics* Γ.2, 1003a33-1003b8)
>
> There are several senses in which a thing may be said to 'be,' as we pointed out previously in our book on the various senses of words; for in one sense the 'being' meant is 'what a thing is' or a 'this,' and in another sense it means a quality or quantity or one of the other things that are predicated as these are. While 'being' has all these senses, obviously that which 'is' primarily is the 'what,' which indicates the substance of the thing. Clearly then it is in virtue of this category that each primarily, i.e. not in a qualified sense but without qualification, must be substance.
>
> (*Metaphysics* Z.1, 1023a10-30)

That the sense of the many senses in which things are said to be is *pros hen* equivocation where the term is applied primarily to substance and derivatively to everything else is clear from the following quotation:

> For it must be either by an equivocation that we say these *are*, or by adding to and taking from the meaning of 'are' (in the way in which that which is not known may be said to be known), — the truth being that we use the word neither ambiguously nor in the same sense, but just as we apply the word 'medical' by virtue of a *reference* to one and the same thing, not *meaning* one and the same thing, nor yet speaking ambiguously; for a patient and an operation and an instrument are called

attributes which necessarily must be predicated of God, may He be blessed. For example, if you say that He is an entity,[300] the term, "entity" cannot be said of Him and other things univocally. Rather it is said priorly and posteriorly. This is because (where) a (certain) thing determines the way in which a given attribute is predicated of everything (else) of which that attribute is predicated, because of what they have acquired from it essentially and primarily, it is more fitting that it[303] should be

---

medical neither by an ambiguity nor with a single meaning, but with reference to a common end.

(*Metaphysics* Z.4, 1030a31-1030b4)

It is worthy of note how this last passage quoted from the *Metaphysics* lends itself to the interpretation that this kind of equivocation was the tool employed to solve the kinds of problems involved in a reference theory of meaning that subsequently led Frege to make a distinction between sense and reference. That such problems are implicit in many of Gersonides' discussions already has been noted several times. (See notes 125, 130, 150, 283, and 293.)

[302] Properly Gersonides is not really claiming that there is no relation between entity and accidents. There certainly is, namely a relation of dependence since accidents exist in and therefore are dependent on entities or substances. Rather what is claimed is that entity and accident are sufficiently different that they share nothing in common, i.e., they are entirely different kinds of being, which is the greatest possible difference.

It should be noted, however, that this qualification cannot be used by Maimonides as a defense against what Gersonides is arguing here. Maimonides would have to say as well concerning God and the world that a dependence relation is true of them, namely the world depends on God for its existence. Maimonides' point also in claiming no relation between God and the world must be that they are entirely different kinds of being. In any case, whatever was Maimonides' intention, his arguments for the denial of relation between God and the world are valid only to establish this latter weaker sense of denial and not to establish the former stronger sense of denial.

[303] I.e., the initial thing called by the given predicate term primarily and

called by that term.[304] Now God, may He be blessed, determines all other things to be characterized as entities.[305] This is because He caused them to acquire their being.[306] Thus it is more proper that He should be called "entity."[300] Furthermore, (this is so) because His essence exists from His essence[307] while all other existent things (exist because of) something other than themselves,[308] and what exists and persists from its own essence is

---

essentially in terms of which everything else referred to by the given predicate term is derivatively so called.

[304] I.e., by the name or term for the attribute in question. This is a straight forward description of *pros hen* equivocation. Cf. notes 91, 23, and 301.

[305] This sentence can be understood in several senses, all of which are compatible with Gersonides' language and the point that he is making. One, since everything other than God is a created thing they derive their existence ultimately from God. Hence God, who derives His existence from nothing else, is the primary instance of an existent thing, i.e., an entity. Two, as Gersonides will elaborate subsequently, since God is a necessary being whereas everything else is a contingent being (cf. notes 43 and 208), God is the primary instance of being, i.e., entity. Three, the cause of the existence of everything else is the essence (in the sense discussed in note 26) of the thing. This essence is what the thing is. But in another sense it is not since, as a created, contingent, caused thing, it derives its essence from a source other than itself. (In the case of material things we can say that the thing is its essence "embodied." As already noted the situation is more problematic with separate intelligences. [Cf. note 293.]) Only God in a primary sense is his essence, i.e. entity. Since the term *'esem* conveys all three senses of the term, *ousia*, namely existent thing, being and essence, it is proper to read all three interpretations as Gersonides' intention in this sentence.

[306] Cf. note 207 for the preference for the term, "being" in translation in this instance.

[307] I.e., God is self-caused which in turn is to say that He is a necessary being. Cf. notes 43 and 208.

[308] Ultimately they exist because of God. Cf. note 305. Because they do not

more properly called "entity" than what exists and persists from what is other than itself.

In this way[309] it should be clear that it is more proper to call God, may He be blessed, "existent" and "one" than anything ▶3c else. We already have explained in our commentary on/ the *Metaphysics* with respect to this the error of Ibn Sina's argument to deny that these attributes can be predicated of God, may He be blessed.[310] *(137)* And the Torah agrees (with the view that) both of these attributes more (properly) designate His being than anything else.[311] Therefore it[312] singles Him out by means of the Tetragrammaton which designates being and existence.[313] Concerning the (term) "one," (it also is the case, namely that the Torah singles out God by this term for unique

---

exist in virtue of their own natures they are contingent beings. Cf. notes 43 and 208.

[309] I.e., in the light of Gersonides' account of the two parts of the "aspect of plausibility" of Maimonides' argument.

[310] Cf. Ibn Sina, *Najat* III: Metaphysics (Avicenna, *Metaphysices Compendium*, ed. N. Carame (Rome, 1926)). Also note the following references to the dependency of Maimonides' doctrine of divine attributes on the thought of Ibn Sina: H. A. Wolfson, "The Aristotelian Predicables and Maimonides' Division of Attributes," *Essays and Studies in Memory of Linda R. Miller*, ed. Israel Davidson (N.Y., 1938), p. 213; Shlomo Pines, "Studies in Abu'l-Barakat's Poetics and Metaphysics," in *Studies in Philosophy*, ed. S. H. Bergmann (Scripta Hierosolymitana 6; Jerusalem, 1960), pp. 163-165; Shlomo Pines, translation of *The Guide*, Introduction, pp. xciii-ciii.

[311] I.e., the two terms "one" and "exist" refer primarily to God and derivatively to other things.

[312] I.e., the Torah.

[313] Cf. note 207. The tetragrammaton is both God's name and a term which designates being and existence. Thus the terms "being" and "existence" are God's name, i.e., they are terms which name and therefore uniquely refer to (in a primary sense) God.

reference) as is clear in the statement, "Hear O Israel *Yhwh* our God, *Yhwh* is one." This is also clear from the case where our master Moses, peace be unto him, asks, "And (if) they say to me, 'What is His name?' what shall I say to them?" and the reply came to him, " *'Eh^eyeh 'aser 'Eh^eyeh*"[314] for it is a term which designates being and existence.[315]

---

[314] *Exodus* 3:13.

[315] Cf. *The Guide* 1.63. The whole chapter is an interpretation of this Biblical passage. Specifically in relation to what Gersonides says here, Maimonides states the following:

> Accordingly God made known to (Moses) the knowledge that he was to convey to them and through which they would acquire a true notion of the existence of God, this knowledge being: I AM THAT I AM. This is a name deriving from the verb *to be*, which signifies existence, for *hayah* indicates the notion: he was. And in Hebrew, there is no difference between your saying: he was and he existed. The whole secret consists in the repetition in a predicative position of the very word indicative of existence. For the word THAT (in the phrase "I am that I am") requires the mention of an attribute immediately connected with it. For it is a deficient word requiring a connection with something else; it has the same meaning as *alladhi* and *allati*, the male and female relative pronouns in Arabic. Accordingly the first word is I AM considered as a term to which a predicate is attached; the second word that is predicated of the first is also I AM, that is identical with the first.
>
> Accordingly Scripture makes, as it were, a clear statement that the subject is identical with the predicate. This makes it clear that He is existent not through existence. This notion may be summarized and interpreted in the following way: the existent that is the existent, or the necessarily existent. This is what demonstration necessarily leads to: namely, to the view that there is a necessarily existent thing that has never been, or ever will be, nonexistent. I shall make clear the demonstration of this thesis.
>
> (Pines tr., pp. 154-155)

Note that Gersonides again is using Maimonides' argument as a proof for his doctrine of divine predication against Maimonides' theory.

In this (way) it should be clear that God necessarily must be described as being "intellect," "living," "comprehending," "benevolent," "powerful," "willing," and "doing," and that He is more deserving of these names than anything else. This is clear with little reflection by him who studies this book on what preceded this topic. Furthermore it will be clear completely, God willing, in Treatise Five of this book. However, these many terms only signify one perfectly simple thing, as we have explained.[316]

Now the distance[317] in meaning between these predicates[318] and those like them, when they are said of Him, may He be blessed, and (these predicates) when they are said of anything other than Him, is like the distance between His level of

[316] Cf. notes 297 and 298. It is worth noting that the term that Gersonides uses here for meaning is *kiwün*, which is meaning as sense or connotation, rather than his usual term, *mòreh*, which is meaning as reference or designation.

[317] I.e., the difference.

[318] Cf. note 279. Gersonides' use of the term, *tō'ar* confuses referent (attribute), meaning (predicate) and term (predicate term). However, what Gersonides intends to say in this passage is clear. With an equivocal term, the two meanings of that term vary as varies the kind of existence of the referents of the term. In other words, where a given term, "*a*" has two meanings, *a* and *b*, *a* referring exclusively to God and *b* referring exclusively to other entities, *a* and *b* differ in exactly the same degree that the two referents differ in their being. Again, the contents *a* and *b* have respectively referents a^1 and b^1. As a^1 and b^1 differ, so *a* and *b* differ.

However, the limitation of this explanation should be noted. The interpretation clearly distinguishes term, content (sense), and referent; Gersonides clearly distinguishes term and referent only. There are hints of a term-content distinction (cf. note 316), but the distinction is not as clear as this interpretation makes it out to be.

existence, may He be blessed, and their level of existence in terms of the perfection and excellence of being. I mean to say that they[319] are said in a more perfect way of God, may He be blessed, than the way in which they are said of what is other than Him.

After all of this is established, it is clear with respect to Philosophic Thought that the (term), "knowledge" can be said of God, may He be blessed, and of other things priorly and posteriorly, (and) not in absolute equivocation, and that Philosophic Thought rejects what the Master The Guide, may his memory be blessed, established as a fundamental principle concerning the knowledge of God, may He be blessed, in order to refute the arguments of the philosophers.

---

[319] I.e., these predicates.

CHAPTER FOUR

In Which We Shall Complete the Discussion of How God, May He be Blessed, Knows Things as Considered from the Speculative Point of View, and We Shall Make Clear that Nothing in the Arguments of our Predecessors Disproves What is Evident to Us Concerning This Knowledge.

After explaining[320] that Philosophic thought refutes what the Master The Guide, may his memory be blessed, posited in order to refute the arguments of the philosophers, and it being clear that properly there should be disagreement about the rejection of their arguments in terms of Philosophic Thought and not only in terms of the Torah,[321] it is proper that we should investigate the arguments of the philosophers which affirm that God, may He be blessed, does not know any of the contingent particulars. (We should investigate) whether or not (these arguments) are correct, and if they[322] are correct, whether or not what they claim to

[320] In chapter three.

[321] Cf. note 202. According to Gersonides, Maimonides believed that only on the basis of religion can the claim that God does not know particulars be refuted; at best all that Philosophic Thought can show is that the arguments affirming that God does not know particulars are not valid. Gersonides subsequently will argue that Maimonides was wrong in this claim. Below he will present three philosophic arguments, incorporating no appeal to religion, that God does know particulars. He will argue that these three arguments have "aspects of plausibility" to the same degree as the previously noted arguments of the philosophers that God does not know particulars.

[322] I.e., the arguments of the philosophers. Gersonides here intends the

follow necessarily from them[322] does (in fact) follow from them.[323] However, before we examine their arguments, we have seen fit to complete the investigation of the knowledge of God, may He be blessed, according to our limitations.[324] This is

---

premises and the mediate inferences of these arguments rather than their final conclusion, namely that God does not know particulars. This distinction between the premises of an argument and the conclusions entailed by an argument shed light on what Gersonides means by "aspects of plausibility" and "degree of truth" (cf. note 22). A given argument may be true in that all of its premises and mediate inferences are true but false in that the conclusions drawn from these mediate steps do not follow necessarily. Also, even where the conclusion drawn is true, it may be the case that the conclusion is ambiguous so that on one reading the conclusion is true whereas on another reading it is false. This in fact is what Gersonides argues to be the case with most of the arguments noted in chapter two of the philosophers. If the conclusion, "God does not know particulars" is read in a weak sense, viz. that in some respect God does not know particulars, then the conclusion is correct. If it is read in a strong sense, viz. in no respect does God know particulars, then this conclusion neither follows from the mediate steps in the argument nor is correct.

[323] Gersonides' investigation of the noted arguments involves two steps. In the first step he investigates whether or not the premises and the mediate inferences of the stated arguments are correct. The philosophers' arguments three, four and eight are noted not to be correct. These three arguments were noted already by him to be spurious. (Cf. notes 34, 36 and 94.) In the second step Gersonides investigates whether or not the inferred conclusion of the non-spurious arguments in fact necessarily follows. He concludes that these arguments do establish that in some respect God does not know particulars but they do not establish that in no respect does God know particulars. In chapters one and two Gersonides noted that these non-spurious arguments of the philosophers were intended to establish the former, weaker conclusion. (Cf. note 12.) Here in chapter four he gives the impression that these arguments were intended erroneously to demonstrate the latter, strong conclusion.

[324] The completion consists of presenting three philosophic arguments created by Gersonides which affirm that God knows particulars. These sub-

because in this way what I shall say about the arguments of the philosophers will be more complete and better understood to him who investigates our words.

We say that it seems that God, may He be blessed, knows these particulars from (the following) aspects.[325]

(The first) of these (aspects) is that since it is clear that God, may He be blessed, is the cause[326] of everything, substances and accidents, that is subject to generation and corruption in this lower[327] world, and (it also is clear) that the Active Intellect and the heavenly bodies are His instruments[328] — this is because all of these things emanate from the overflow which overflows upon them from God, may He be blessed (*138*) — it being clear in the case of an instrument *qua* instrument that it cannot move to do that for which it is an instrument except by means of the knowledge of the craftsman, it therefore clearly is apparent from this that God, may He be blessed, knows all of these particulars.[329]

---

sequently will be reconciled with the philosophic arguments which negate that God knows particulars and Maimonides' arguments in setting forth Gersonides' own position. Cf. notes 22 and 66.

[325] I.e., from aspects of plausibility. In other words, a number (namely three) of aspects of plausibility can be given for the claim that God knows particulars. Cf. note 22.

[326] Literally, the actuator or active agent. Although the term used here, *pô'el*, is Aristotelian, its sense in this context is clearly Platonic. God is a cause in this context in the way that the craftsman is the cause of what he makes.

[327] I.e., sublunar.

[328] Literally, "they are to Him in the level of the instrumental."

[329] This first argument may be structured as follows. (Premise 1) It is a necessary condition for the existence of anything created by a craftsman that the craftsman knows it. In other words, given anything which is an artifact, if

(The second) of these (aspects) is that since it is the case
necessarily that God, may He be blessed, knows His essence at a
level (which is equal to the level) of His existence,[330] and (since)
His essence is such that all existents emanate from Him by
degrees, it (therefore) necessarily follows that God, may He be
blessed, knows of all existents which emanate from Him. The
reason for this is that if He did not know them, His knowledge
of His own essence would be deficient.[331] This is because He
would not know what could possibly emanate from Him in accordance with that existence which He possesses. This being so,
and it (further) being clear that every substance and accident

---

it exists then its craftsman knows it. (Premise 2) God is the craftsman who
formed every substance and accident in the sublunar world. Therefore, since
there do exist substances and accidents in the sublunar world, God knows
them.

Premise 2 is based on the doctrine of emanation in terms of which the Active Intellect and the heavenly bodies are merely tools, i.e., instrumental
causes, by which God created the sublunar world.

[330] Assume two scales of perfection between which a one-to-one correlation
holds so that for every mark or grade on one scale there is a corresponding
mark or grade on the other scale. The one scale measures degrees of knowledge
and the other scale measures levels of existence. (Degrees or levels of existence
here must be understood in terms of a Platonic ontology of degrees of reality.)
Given these two scales what Gersonides is saying here is that the grade of
God's knowledge of His essence agrees with the grade of the existence of God's
essence, namely that both receive a perfect score.

[331] God knows His essence. From His essence certain things emanate.
Therefore, among the various things that can be known of God's essence is a
knowledge of the causal connection holding between God and these things. But
if God did not know the things He could not know these propositions which
express God's causal connections. Therefore there would be something about
God's essence that God did not know. Therefore God's knowledge of His
essence would be deficient.

which is subject to generation emanates from Him, (therefore) it is clear that He knows every substance and accident which is subject to generation which emanate (from Him). Therefore, it clearly follows necessarily from this that God, may He be blessed, knows all of these particulars.[332]

(The third) of these (aspects) is that it is clear from what was stated above that the Active Intellect in some way knows these things subject to generation in this lower[333] world. This being so, and it (further) being (the case) that God, may He be blessed, is the cause,[334] the form, and the end of all other separate intelligences, as is explained in the *Metaphysics*,[335] it necessarily follows that cognitions of all other intelligences are

[332] This second argument contains two distinct lines of reasoning. The first (A) contains the following steps. 1. (Premise 1) The level of perfection of God's knowledge is equal to the level of existence of God's essence (cf. note 330). 2. God's essence has perfect existence. 3. Therefore God's knowledge of His essence must be perfect. The second (B) contains the following steps. 1. (Premise 2) All of the existent substances and accidents of the sublunar world emanate from God's essence. 2. If God does not know these things, then there is something about God's essence that He does not know. (Cf. note 331.) 3. If there is something about God's essence that He does not know, then God's knowledge of His essence is not perfect. 4. But God's knowledge of His essence is perfect (from A). Therefore, God must know the substances and accidents which emanate from His essence. (This conclusion follows from B2, 3 and 4 by hypothetical syllogism and disjunctive syllogism.)

It should be noted that both this argument and the preceding argument rest on the Platonic doctrine of emanation. This second argument requires in addition the shaky support of the assumption (implied in the first premise stated above) that the degree of perfection of the knowledge of an object corresponds to the degree of perfection of the object itself.

[333] Cf. note 327.
[334] Cf. note 326.
[335] Cf. *Metaphysics* Λ .7-9.

found in God. This is because those cognitions proceed
materially from the cognition[336] of God, may He be blessed.[337]
Similarly it is necessarily the case that an architect of a house[338]
should know the form of the bricks and the beams which these
workmen know who are engaged in those arts which aid the art
of architecture.[339] But he who is engaged in the primary art[340]
will have more perfect knowlege of them with respect to their
being part of (the total plan of) the house, as was mentioned
above.[341] This being so, it is clear beyond any doubt that these

---

[336] Properly the term, $y^e di'\bar{a}h$ is translated as "knowledge." However the
term is used in this context as the counterpart of $hay^e di'\bar{o}t$, which are
cognitions. In order to preserve this relationship in English which is unpro-
blematic in Hebrew and since God's knowledge is His cognition, $y^e di'\bar{a}h$ is
rendered here as "cognition."

[337] I.e., on analogy with matter. The cognitions of the separate intelligences
which are the separate intelligences (since the separate intelligences are not
material, they and their cognitions are identical) are related to God's
knowledge as matter is related to form. This follows from the previous sentence in which Gersonides asserted that God is the form and the end of the
separate intelligences.

[338] Literally, he who knows the form (or plan) of the house.

[339] Literally, the art of house building.

[340] I.e., the architect.

[341] In the first argument. On why the architect's knowledge must be more
perfect, note *Metaphysics* Z.10. There Aristotle argues that those parts which
constitute the formula of a thing, the formula being that which expresses the
essence of a thing, are prior to it whereas its material parts are posterior to the
thing. On the architect-worker analogy, all that the workers need to know
are the material parts whereas the architect must know the formula or
blueprints. Thus the architect's knowledge is prior to the knowledge of the
workers. "Prior" and "posterior" in this context mean causally and logically
prior and posterior. A is prior to B means "B only if A, but it is not the case
that A only if B." The terms "prior" and "posterior" are conjoined in this

cognitions which the Active Intellect has of these things (are possessed) by God, may He be blessed, in a more perfect manner. This also shows that God, may He be blessed, knows particulars.[342]

3d   It now is established that these arguments affirm (the view) that God, may He be blessed, knows these particulars, while the above mentioned arguments of the philosophers refute (the affirmation of) His knowledge of them. Therefore there remains no alternative but (to posit) that in one way He knows them and in another way He does not know them. Would that I knew what these two ways are![343]

We[344] say that it already was made clear above[345] that these

---

context with the terms "more perfect" and "less perfect," i.e., if A is prior to B then the knowledge of A is more perfect than the knowledge of B.

[342] This third argument is closely related to the first argument. In both the case is presented that the Active Intellect in some way knows particulars, God's knowledge surpasses that of the Active Intellect, therefore God's knowledge also must include knowledge of particulars in some sense. In the first argument the reason why God's knowledge must surpass the knowledge of the Active Intellect is that the Active Intellect is merely a tool for the creative activity of God the craftsman. In this argument the reason given is that God is the cause, form and end of the Active Intellect.

[343] Cf. note 276.

[344] (MS) introduces this paragraph with דעת המחבר בידיעתו יתברך

[345] In chapter 1, pp. 120-121 of the Leipzig edition, Gersonides said the following:

The second group (of philosophers interpreting the words of Aristotle) think that the view of the Philosopher was that God, may He be blessed, knows those things which exist in this world insofar as they possess a universal nature, i.e., essences, (but He does) not (know) them insofar as they are particular, i.e., contingents.

Gersonides now states this position as his own.

contingents are defined and ordered in one respect and are contingents in another respect. This being so, it is clear that the respect in which He knows them is the respect in which they are ordered and defined.[346] Similarly, (this) is the case with the Active Intellect, according to what was explained,[347] because (only) in this respect[348] is it possible that they should be known.[349] The

---

In chapter 2, p. 127 of the Leipzig edition, Gersonides states the following:

> We have explained already in Treatise One of this book that our knowledge is dependent upon the intelligible ordering which these things have in the soul of the Active Intellect ... which is the aspect in which they are not particular.

Treatise Three presupposes this distinction between the respect in which particulars are ordered and the respect in which they are contingent particulars which was developed in Treatise One. On the reference to Treatise One, see note 127.

[346] I.e., God knows their essence. For an account of what this essence is see notes 12, 14, 16, 28, 38, 40, 67, 68, 101, 130, 204, 207, and 302. It is a single entity existing in the mind of the Active Intellect which is identical with the Active Intellect which can be expressed as the real definition of a thing, *ousia*, and the form, order and perfection of a thing.

[347] Cf. note 38. In fact all of the arguments given for how and what God knows apply directly to the Active Intellect. In each argument there is an implied or hidden inference of the form, "since such and such is true of the Active Intellect, how much the more so must it be the case that such and such is true of God." In the first and third arguments that Gersonides constructed for the claim that God knows particulars in chapter four this implicit inference is made explicit.

[348] Cf. notes 26, 105 and 138. Knowledge by definition is an ordering, defining, limiting process. To know particulars as non-ordered, incapable of definition, and numerically infinite, which is the aspect in which they properly are particular, is a contradiction in terms.

[349] Literally, "that knowledge should befall them."

respect in which He does not know them is the respect in which they are not ordered, which is the respect in which they are contingents. This is because in this respect it is impossible[350] that they should be known.[349] However, from this (latter) respect He knows that they are contingents which possibly will not be actualized with regard to the choice which God, may He be blessed, gave to man (*139*) in order to perfect what was lacking in the governance of the heavenly bodies,[351] as was explained in the preceding treatise.[352] But He does not know which of the two possible alternatives will be actualized from the point of view

[350] Cf. notes 40, 138 and 348.

[351] This sentence contains three distinct assertions. (1) With respect to particulars being contingent particulars, God only knows that they are contingent. He does not know them as particulars. This assertion is a consequence of Gersonides' implied solution to the problem of future contingents (cf. notes 20, 45-49, 159, 161 and 182) which he will make explicit in this chapter. (2) This limitation of God's knowledge (1) enables Gersonides to solve the classical problem of human choice and determinism. This solution will be presented in chapter six. (3) Gersonides also asserts here the nature of connection that holds between human choice and providence which was developed in the second treatise. Cf. note 352.

[352] Treatise Two on Dreaming, Fortune Telling and Prophecy. In chapter two of that treatise Gersonides raises the problem of God's omniscience and human choice, i.e., if God has foreknowledge of every particular event then there can be neither human choice nor contingent events. He proposes there as a solution to this problem the doctrine that is developed here, viz. that God has foreknowledge of particular events only insofar as these events are ordered, but insofar as they are not ordered, which is the respect in which they are material and not formal, these events are contingent.

In chapter five of Treatise Four Gersonides tells us how knowledge and human choice combine in the operation of divine providence with regard to man.

that they are contingents.[353] The reason for this is that if this were so,[354] there could be no contingency in this world at all.[355]

We say that with investigation it is clear that the Active Intellect governs what exists (in one of two ways). Either it sets bodily instruments in them (what exists) (which function as) capacities of the soul, which preserve the existence of the individuals possessing those instruments, by either removing the harmful object from them or by enabling them to remove themselves from it. I mean to say that some animals have horns or round hoofs, or jaws to preserve them from anything that comes to harm them and to protect the prey from the animals of prey. Also it (the Active Intellect) governs some of them (what exists) only by placing in them (certain) activities or aptitudes (*literally*, desires) of the soul. The imagination is an aptitude of the soul. I mean to say that it (the Active Intellect) places in the lamb a natural aptitude to flee from the wolf when it sees it, even if it (the lamb) does not feel that it (the wolf) is dangerous or it (the lamb) never saw one before. Also many birds are created to migrate in cold seasons to the south and in warm seasons to the north without their perceiving existent signs of the places to which they will move. The swallow places a certain kind of grass on the eyes of its offspring when it (the swallow) cleans it (the offspring) without knowing that this is medicine for its eyes. (So too with) the activities of the imagination. I mean to say that the bee possesses a skill / by which it can manufacture honey which sustains it at a time when it is lacking food, without having a practical intellect by which it could order (i.e., consciously plan) these crafts.

The way that Providence (operates) with man is much more perfect. It (the Active Intellect) has created in him (man) a practical intellect by which he can order (i.e., consciously plan) many crafts which serve to promote his preservation. Also it (the Active Intellect) has created for him (man) the intellect by which he can consciously plan to escape from many harmful things and to create (by himself) many profitable things. (Furthermore) this Providence extends to some men in a way (even) more perfect. I mean to say that it (the Active Intellect) makes known to them (these men) by means of prophecy evil and good things which are prepared to befall them so that they may guard against the evils and be

His lack of knowledge, may He be blessed, of which of two
possible alternatives *qua* possible will be actualized is not a

---

prepared for the goods, as was explained in Treatise Two of this book.
(pp. 165-166 of the Leipzig edition)

In all living creatures there are certain capacities graciously given to the
creatures to enable them to preserve themselves from extinction. Excluding
man these capacities are realized instinctually. Lambs run when they see
wolves, birds migrate when the seasons change, etc. All these activities take
place without intelligent planning even though they are manifestations of intelligence, i.e., the lamb flees *as if* it had the intellect to make the judgment,
"wolves are generally dangerous; this is a wolf; therefore this is dangerous. If
one can, one should flee from dangerous things; I can; therefore I will flee."
Also, the bird migrates *as if* it had the intellect to make the judgment, "when
the temperature is such and such a bird of a certain kind should depart; the
temperature is such and such; I am a bird of that kind; therefore I shall
depart."

It is in this way that Providence "watches over" all living creatures. The
agent of Providence, viz. the Active Intellect, does not know these things individually. Rather it knows them generally, which enables them to be given instinctual survival mechanisms. In the case of man this survival mechanism is
an intellect, while some men, called prophets, possess in addition a more perfect mechanism which enables them to receive prophesy.

What is to be noticed is that the proposition which expresses the imperative
asserted through these mechanisms is always universal. Lambs are told in effect to flee all wolves and not this or that wolf. Hence a lamb may flee from a
wolf which he need not fear at all. (For example when the wolf is lame, blind
and toothless.) Human providence, which comes through man's capacity to
reason, must be understood in the same terms. If he is a scientist Providence,
i.e., reason, tells him, "If such and such conditions prevail there will be a
storm." When those conditions prevail our scientist knows that this is not a
good time to take a sea voyage. He therefore may decide to stay home whereas
others, equally concerned with safety but less scientifically informed, may
choose to travel.

It is in these terms that Gersonides understands the foreknowledge of the

deficiency in Him. This is because perfect knowledge of a thing consists in knowing the nature of the thing.[356] Were (the thing)

---

prophet. For example, from the Active Intellect the prophet Jeremiah knows that when certain conditions prevail if a nation of F description goes to war against a nation of G description, then that first nation will be destroyed. Then through the use of his faculty of imagination and his senses Jeremiah is able to instantiate this general proposition in order to know that Judah had F description, Babylonia has G description, and the requisite conditions prevail. In this way Jeremiah prophesies to King Zedekiah that if Judah goes to war against Babylonia at this time, Judah will be destroyed.

Two further features of this situation of human providence need to be noted. What man knows from the Active Intellect, be it philosophy or prophesy, is expressed in the form "given any thing of such and such a kind, if such and such is true of it, then such and such will follow." It is propositions of this form that express the knowledge of the Active Intellect. Note that this knowledge includes no particular instantiated instance. The instantiations in the case of the things which occupy the sublunar world come through perception and imagination. Further note that even, though it be instantiated, what we have from Providence is expressed as a conditional and not as an assertive proposition. Through providence and sense experience (the latter instantiating the general formula provided by the former) we may know that if we sail in a boat today the boat will be destroyed. But that does not tell us that the boat will be destroyed. We may choose not to sail today, and if the boat is ours the boat will not be destroyed. Our foreknowledge can in no way impinge upon the contingency of the final event in question.

However a qualification to this picture is necessary. It is not completely accurate to say that what we know rationally and what the Active Intellect knows are universal conditional propositions. Gersonides still conceives of the knowing situation in terms of a strict reference theory of meaning. What is known is not a proposition but an object. In this case the object is an essence. However, as has been noted already, the essence of a thing is that by which it is ordered. It expresses the true nature of a thing which is the formal and final cause of that thing. As such it entails and therefore is expressible in terms of a set of essential properties of a thing which in turn entail and therefore are expressible in terms of a set of universal conditional propositions. Thus, for

to be conceived to be other than it is,[357] this would be error and
not knowledge.[358] This being so, (it is clear that) He knows all

---

example, to know the essence of a piece of steel is to know that it lacks the
dispositional property of flexibility which is to say that if this given object is
subject to such and such pressure it will break.

[353] Gersonides here is continuing to comment on what in note 351 was
noted as his first point in the previous sentence. God knows particulars insofar
as they are ordered but not insofar as they are contingent which is the respect
in which they are material, the form expressing the essence of the thing. This
position arises on Gersonides' terms as a consequence of his discussion of
ways four and five in Maimonides' five ways that God's knowledge differs
from ours.

[354] I.e., if God knows which alternative among a set of possible alternatives
will be actualized.

[355] The consequence of the sixth argument of the philosophers against God
knowing particulars and a mediate conclusion in the statement of the fourth
way in which, according to Maimonides, God's knowledge differs from ours.

[356] Literally, "knowing the thing according to what it is."

[357] "Other than it is" intentionally has two senses in this context: (1) to
conceive of a thing in terms other than knowing its essence or nature; (2) to
conceive falsely of a thing.

[358] In this statement we can extract another basis for Gersonides' asserting
a doctrine of different levels of truth and partial truths. In absolute terms the
only kind of knowledge which would qualify as knowing a thing is to know the
essence of a thing. But only God and the Active Intellect have such knowledge.
Since our knowledge necessarily arise as an effect of the thing having this
essence (cf. note 26), our knowledge can never be equal to the knowledge of
God and the Active Intellect. Knowledge must in this context be understood as
picturing. The object of knowledge which God and the Active Intellect possess
is the original. It is the blueprint or model of which the thing itself is only a
copy, an artifact. What we know then is only a picture of the picture. The truth
of our picture, called a universal, is measured in terms of its proximity to the
original in the mind of God. As pictures can vary in terms of being better or
worse copies, thus truth so conceived can vary in terms of being more or less
exact. Cf. notes 26, 68, 72, 73, 116, 171, and 204.

these things in the most perfect way possible.[359] This is because He knows them with respect to their being ordered[360] in a clear and definitive way. In addition He knows those respects in which they are contingent with regard to choice, according to their contingency.[361] Therefore, by means of His prophets God, may He be blessed, could command individuals upon whom evil was about to come that they should improve their ways so that they might be saved,[362] as (when) He commanded Zedekiah to make peace with the king of Babylonia.[363] This is one (of the Biblical texts) which shows that (concerning) the future events which God, may He be blessed, knows, He knows that they need not come about. However, He knows it[364] with respect to its being ordered in connection with His knowing that possibly it[364] will not be actualized with respect to its being contingent.

We shall (now) explain that the above-mentioned arguments

[359] I.e., the way that God knows these things is not perfect in every respect but it is the most perfect way possible. This serves as a reply to Maimonides' first argument to establish that God knows particulars. Cf. notes 76 through 85 in connection with Gersonides' discussion in chapter two of the validity of this first argument on page 125 of the Leipzig edition.

[360] Which is to know their real essence. Cf. notes 13, 26, 40, 130, and 352.

[361] Which is the respect in which they are not ordered. In other words, in this respect all that God knows of these particulars is that they are contingent. Insofar as the contingent particulars are contingent particulars, God knows that they are but not what they are.

[362] Cf. note 352. By means of providence and instantiation through his senses, the prophet Jeremiah was able to tell Zedekiah that if he leads Judah to war against Babylonia, Judah will be destroyed. But that did not mean that Judah would be destroyed. It was up to King Zedekiah to decide to go to war against Babylonia or not to go to war.

[363] Jeremiah, chapter 22.

[364] I.e., each single future event which He knows, considered individually.

to affirm that God, may He be blessed, knows these things,[365] do not demonstrate that He knows them in a greater degree than this.[366] And (we also shall explain) that the above-mentioned arguments of the philosophers to deny the knowledge of God, may He be blessed, of (these) things[365] does not truly deny the kind of knowledge which we have affirmed of God, may He be blessed.[367]

It is clear that it does not follow necessarily from the above-mentioned arguments that God, may He be blessed, knows (particulars) in a greater degree than this.[366] This is because the first argument[368] demonstrated that God, may He be blessed, knows these things since the Active Intellect and the heavenly bodies are His instruments in performing these acts.[369] It is clear that this argument only necessitates the consequence that He knows the orderings[370] from which theses acts[371] emanate. This is

[365] I.e., contingent particulars.

[366] I.e., that God knows the contingent particulars with respect to their ordering but with respect to them as unordered all that God knows of them is that they are contingent.

[367] Gersonides will show now that all of the previous arguments for and against God knowing particulars support Gersonides' own position which he had just stated. He begins by considering the philosophic arguments that he constructed in the beginning of this fourth chapter to demonstrate that God knows particulars.

[368] Namely that it is necessarily the case that a craftsman knows what he creates by his instruments; every particular was created by God by means of His tools, the Active Intellect and the heavenly bodies; therefore, it is necessarily the case that God knows every particular.

[369] I.e., in making particulars.

[370] Cf. notes 13, 26, 40, and 130.

[371] I.e., the acts of actually making or creating particulars. On the architect-worker analogy what the architect knows are the blueprints of the house that

because a separate (intelligence),[372] insofar as it is separate, moves[373] all that which is prepared to receive its moving[374] without being aware of each particular instance (which is moved) of this class.[375] (It is) in this way (that) the Active In-

---

he is making whereas the workers have a detailed acquaintance with the specific tools which the architect only knows generally. The blueprints on this analogy are the essences.

[372] I.e., anyone of the ten intelligences which move their respective spheres, the lowest of which is the Active Intellect which is the mover of the sublunar world.

[373] Literally, "acts upon."

[374] Literally, "its action."

[375] Literally, "of each part of the parts in what belongs to this part." In other words, the separate intelligences are aware of the appropriate general class of all things capable of receiving a given action appropriate to the separate intellect in question. But they are not aware of all of the members of the respective classes of which they are aware. Each separate intelligence acts generally, i.e., the proposition which expresses the motion of each is expressed in universal and not particular terms. For example, consider a train moving along railway tracks which traverse a cow pasture. Some cows crossing the tracks are killed by the train. Other cows not crossing the tracks or crossing the tracks at a different time are not killed. Now it happens to be the case that the cows that the train kills are individuals. But the train and its engineers are not aware of them. The train simply is moving along its tracks. We may say of the engineer that given any cow, if it traverses the tracks while the train is passing then the engineer by his train will kill it. But we may not say that the train moves in such a way as to kill the cows Mary and Jane even though in fact the train does kill them. In this sense we can say that the engineer by his train generally but not individually kills cows. The engineer knows that if any cow will cross the tracks at the wrong time then that cow will be killed. But he need not be aware of any individual cow that his train kills. (For example, he may be looking out the side and not see any objects directly in front of the train.)

Similarly in the case of the Active Intellect's action upon contingent par-

tellect moves all of these things,[376] as is clear from what was said above.

However, with regard to the action of a corporeal being *qua* corporeal being, it is correct that it[377] does not act upon something in a craftsmanlike way[378] if it[377] has no awareness of this particular upon which it acts. Thus craftsmanlike actions[378] are (brought about) by the mediation of the intellect and the imagination, as is explained in the *De Anima*.[379] This is so since (a given thing) must necessarily be proximate to what made it. This is because what is moved cannot receive (the mover's) intention unless it meets[380] (its mover), and (only) then can (the mover) place upon (the moved) the desired form. However, matter receives the intention of the incorporeal cause with great ease, and therefore it is not necessary that the incorporeal cause be aware of the particular which it makes as this particular.[381]

---

ticulars, there is a certain motion in which the Active Intellect constantly is involved. If a given particular possesses the appropriate disposition, then it is affected by the Active Intellect's action. If that particular lacks the appropriate disposition, then it will not be affected. What the Active Intellect knows is that given any particular that has the required disposition, that particular will be affected by it. But the Active Intellect is not acquainted with the individuals which either are or are not so disposed.

[376] I.e., the particulars in the sublunar world.

[377] I.e., the corporeal being.

[378] I.e., with that kind of causation that is involved in a craftsman creating his artifact. Such causal actions involve skill and intention on the part of the causal agent. In other words, these are consciously planned causal actions. Cf. note 326.

[379] See *De Anima* 3.8, 432a3-8.

[380] Literally, "touches."

[381] Cf. note 375. In the case of a material agent acting on a material receptor to produce a given effect, the agent must be in direct contact with the

We can understand the ease with which matter receives the intention of the form by understanding (*140*) the motions which a man determines[382] by his conception. For example, when a man desires to sing some song which he has conceived in his mind, (his) voice organ is moved immediately on the basis of that conception with such wonderful movements that no activity

---

receptor. However, where the agent is not material, where it is an intellect or a mind, this requirement could not hold since mental entities properly do not have spatial position. The problem then is how can a mental agent affect a material receptor if this kind of causation is to be understood on the model of causation when both the agent and the receptor are material. The most obvious answer would be that a different model is needed. However for Gersonides as for his Moslem-Jewish predecessors and contemporaries such a solution would be granted only after every other way of explanation would be tried first which would preserve a unified causal schema for both the sublunar and translunar worlds. The consequence of a different causal model in this case would only further deepen the wedge separating these two spheres, a wedge whose dimensions already were considered to be problematic. (Cf. Wolfson, *Crescas's Critique* pp. 114-127.) Gersonides' explanation in terms of "ease" is an attempt to solve this problem. The point seems to be that it is easier for a mental agent to affect a material receptor than it is for a material agent to affect a material receptor. Hence the agent in the former case is free of at least one of the barriers present in the latter case, viz. the requirement of physical contact. But the problem still remains, why is it easier in the former case than the latter? If the answer is because in the former case no physical contact is necessary whereas in the latter case it is, then nothing has been said. Gersonides attempts to present some examples that show this to be the case, but he offers no account.

It also should be pointed out that the claim that physical contact as a precondition for a physical agent acting upon a physical receptor was itself problematic at this time given the difficulty that the physicists of this time encountered in accounting for the behavior of magnets. (Cf. Wolfson, ibid., pp. 90-92, 255, 257, 563-568.)

[382] Literally, "calculates."

with any musical instrument could bring about such movements as these.[383] Similarly, the fingers of the musician, as a result of his mind's conception, move back and forth on the musical instrument with great ease without his contemplating the motion itself as to how it should be executed properly. Similarly when a man speaks, he does so by using the intended letters[384] with ease without contemplating in his speech each letter[385] (as to) how the voice box should be used so that each letter[385] would be spoken properly.[386] This being so, it clearly is established that

[383] In this example the voice organ itself is conceived of as a musical instrument, namely that instrument through which singing is produced. This instrument is moved directly by the mind whereas other instruments are moved through the mediation of material limbs, e.g. fingers with guitars. To play even the simplest tune on any other musical instrument requires work and practice, but with the voice organ this is not the case. Any child can do it.

[384] Better, syllables. Letters are written and read but not spoken.

[385] Better, syllable.

[386] As noted in note 381 Gersonides offers what are supposed to be illustrations of how a mental agent more freely acts causally than does a material agent. However, the examples are not clear. In each of his examples the instrument is manipulated freely or "with ease" only after the form of manipulation has become habitual. At first in none of the cases was the movement in question easy. A baby cannot sing songs. Fingers must be trained to play an instrument. Speaking does not come easily.

Two arguments arise immediately against the effectiveness of Gersonides' examples to make their point. (1) Just as in cases such as this repetition of the causal activity makes the action of the causal agent easier, so there are similar cases where the causal agent is material and not mental. For example automobiles operate better once they have been "broken in." (2) Many cases of instinctual behavior can be found where the affective agent acts with far greater ease than does the mind in bringing out any of its directly intended physical effects. For example, to keep a heart beating is at least as complicated

God, may He be blessed, can move these (particular) things without comprehending them with respect to their particularity, although He does comprehend them in a more perfect way.

24a   The second argument[387] established that God, may He be blessed, has knowledge of these/things with respect to His own essence. It also is clear (in this case) that this argument only necessitates that God knows the intelligible ordering[388] of these things from which their existence emanates.

---

as singing a song. Yet the body is able to carry out the former activity without any conscious behavior, without any training whatsoever.

As hinted at in note 381, part of the problem here is just what does "ease" mean without begging the question. There is one answer that immediately presents itself which is consistent with what Gersonides is arguing in this chapter, provided we exclude these illustrations as simply weak illustrations. In the cases of material causation wher *A* is the cause of *B*, *A happens* to be the cause of *B*. *B* could have just as well been produced in some other way by some other agent. In the cases involving a mental agent, viz. the Active Intellect and the other intelligences considered here, the situation is different. *A* happens to be but is not necessarily the cause of *B* since *A*, being a material entity, has accidental movements. But the intelligences being free of matter only act necessarily. Thus it might be argued that where *x* is necessarily the cause of *y* rather than just happening to be the cause of *y*, the action of *x* can be seen to be "easier." While this is sometimes the case with material agents, it is always the case with the actions of the separate intelligences. This explanation has the consequence that neither the separate intelligences nor God are subject to choice. However, this is a consequence that Gersonides must accept anyway for independent reasons since Gersonides already has indicated that he will accredit man's choice to the fact that he is a material entity. In other words only that which is material and only insofar as it is material can be considered free of compulsion.

[387] Of the three arguments that Gersonides constructed to show that God knows particulars. For the steps involved in this second argument see note 330.

[388] I.e., the essences. Cf. notes 13, 21, 40, and 130.

The third argument[389] establishes that God, may He be blessed, knows these things since the Active Intellect has knowledge of them. It also is clear that this argument only necessitates that God knows the intelligible ordering[388] which these things possess. This is because this is the way in which the Active Intellect has knowledge of them, as was explained above.[390] However, God's knowledge, may He be blessed, of this ordering is different from the Active Intellect's knowledge of it in that God's knowledge, may He be blessed, of this ordering is more perfect, as was explained above.[391] This explanation will be made clear completely, God willing, in the fifth treatise of this book.

Similarly we say that it does not follow necessarily that God, may He be blessed, knows these things to a greater degree than this[392] from what we mentioned[393] that the Master The Guide, may his memory be blessed, argued in order to establish that

[389] Of the arguments that Gersonides constructed to show that God knows particulars. For the steps involved in this third argument see note 342.

[390] In Gersonides' analysis of the first argument above. Cf. footnotes 368, 371, and 375.

[392] I.e., that God only knows the essences or intelligible orderings of particulars and that the particulars are contingent.

[393] In chapter two. Gersonides will examine here Maimonides' two major arguments presented in that chapter, viz.: (1) to attribute ignorance of particulars is to attribute an imperfection to God, but God is subject to no imperfections, and (2) all of the arguments concerning God's knowledge assume some analogy between our knowledge and God's knowledge when in fact no such analogy can be drawn. In chapter five and not here Gersonides will examine the five ways that God's knowledge differs from ours according to Maimonides. These five ways formally are not distinct arguments. Rather they are illustrations of the major premise of Maimonides' second argument, viz. that there is no analogy between our knowledge and God's knowledge.

God, may He be blessed, knows all of these things. The reason
for this is that the first argument (of Maimonides) establishes
that God, may He be blessed, knows all of these things by
denying of Him the imperfection of ignorance, but it is clear that
when He knows things[394] in the way that we have explained,
there remains no ignorance in His knowledge of them. Rather,
He knows them perfectly as what they are.[395]

(Furthermore) we already have mentioned when we stated the
second argument (of Maimonides)[396] that it (only) seems to
necessitate (the conclusion) that God, may He be blessed, knows
the intelligible ordering of these things from which the existence
of these things emanates, and no greater degree (of knowledge)

[394] I.e., particulars.

[395] What He knows is their essence and the essence of a thing is what a
thing is. Cf. notes 357 and 358.

[396] The subject matter of chapter three. In outline, what Gersonides argued
there is the following. (1) It is true that there is no proper analogy between
our knowledge and God's knowledge. The predicate, "knowledge," like all
predicates applied both to God and to us, must be understood as equivocal.
(2) But equivocation itself can be understood in several senses. (Cf. notes 89
and 91.) Maimonides claims that in the case of terms predicable of God and
man the equivocation is absolute, but this is not so. In the first part of chapter
three Gersonides gives three arguments for why it is not so. (3) Maimonides'
second argument shows legitimately that there is no relation between God and
us and that no plurality can be predicated of God. From these two facts it
follows that terms predicated of God and man are *pros hen* equivocals. (4) *Pros
hen* equivocals (cf. notes 91, 210, and 301) are such that the predicate term is
applied primarily without qualification of one subject and of all other subjects
derivatively with qualification. In the case of terms predicated of God and man
the terms are applied primarily to God and derivatively to man. In the case of
the predicate, knowledge, this understanding of equivocal predication entails
the kind of interpretation of divine knowledge as opposed to human knowledge
that Gersonides presented at the beginning of chapter four.

than this. But this is what we posit here concerning the knowledge of God, may He be blessed.

This being clear,[397] we shall explain that none of the arguments of the philosophers which we mentioned[398] necessitates (the conclusion) that God, may He be blessed, does not know these things in the way that we have posited (that He knows them).

The reasons for this are (the following). The first of these arguments which we ascribed to the philosophers — which states that God, may He be blessed, cannot perceive particulars since He has no hylic faculty — does not necessitate (the view) that God, may He be blessed, does not know the intelligible ordering (141) which these things possess with respect to their being ordered and defined. Rather, all that (this argument) necessitates is (the conclusion) that God, may He be blessed, cannot know them with respect to their particularity and concreteness.[399] This is self-evident.

The second argument states that God, may He be blessed, cannot possibly perceive these particulars since they are temporal. It also is clear that (this argument) does not necessitate the denial of what we postulated concerning God's knowledge, may He be blessed, of these things. This is because we did not

---

[397] I.e., that all of the arguments that God knows particulars stated by Gersonides and by Maimonides only establish that God knows particulars to the extent that Gersonides claims that He knows them, viz. that God knows their essences and that they are contingent.

[398] In chapter two.

[399] Matter is the necessary and sufficient condition for a thing being concrete or particular. But matter is not intelligible. (Cf. notes 105 and 348.) We can have sense acquaintance with particulars but no intelligible knowledge of them. (Cf. note 26.)

postulate that He knows them with respect to their being temporal. Rather we postulated that He knows their intelligible ordering with respect to their being ordered by it,[400] and in this respect they are not temporal.

The third argument states that God, may He be blessed, cannot possibly perceive these things, neither in their universality nor in their particularity, since if this were possible, the excellent would be perfected by the deficient, and this clearly is absurd. When we examine it[401] we find that what is inferred from the premise of this conditional syllogism does not follow necessarily.[402] This is because from our postulating that God, may He be blessed, knows the intelligible ordering of substances and accidents which inhere in things that exist in this world, it does not follow necessarily that God, may He be blessed, is perfected by these things. This is because God, may He be blessed, does not acquire this knowledge from these things which exist in this world. Rather His knowledge of them is dependent upon their intelligible ordering within Him.[403] Therefore, it is clear

[400] I.e., by the intelligible ordering or essence of the thing.

[401] I.e., this third argument of the philosophers against God knowing particulars.

[402] Gersonides here conceives this argument to have the following form: given any x, if something knows x, then that thing *qua* knower is perfected by x. If God knows anything other than Himself, then that thing perfects God. Everything other than God is less perfect than God. Therefore, if God knows anything other than Himself, then what is less perfect than God perfects God. The first sentence above is the major premise of the argument. The second sentence is an instantiation of that premise. Gersonides will argue that the second sentence is false. While the major premise is generally true (cf. note 404), it is not true when the knower is God. For the reasons why Gersonides would claim that this premise is generally true see notes 28 and 35.

[403] On how God's knowledge differs from ours see notes 26, 67, 68, 72,

that God, may He be blessed, is not perfected in this knowledge by anything other than Himself. Rather, this intelligible ordering which is within God, may He be blessed, Himself is that which caused these things to acquire their existence. This being so, it is clear that this argument is not correct.[404]

The fourth argument states that if God, may He be blessed, perceives[405] these things His essence would be complex, and

---

73, 171, 204, and 358. In God are the essences which serve as the models by which particulars are created. These essences as they truly exist are a single entity, i.e., they exist in God in a unified way. (Cf. notes 26, 130, 138, and 171.) As such they are God, since God is one, which in this case means that God, His intellectual activity and His knowledge are numerically one. (Cf. footnotes 37, 101, 102, 104, 130, and 153.) Thus in knowing these essences God knows Himself. Hence God is not perfected by anything less than Himself.

[404] To be correct the major premise of the argument (cf. note 402) must be qualified in its range. It would be acceptable in the following form: given any x, if something knows x — where x is not identical with the something that knows it and x is the cause of the knowledge of the something that knows it — then that thing *qua* knower is perfected by x. Stated with this restriction in range, Gersonides could accept the premise without qualification. But this restriction eliminates the major inference of the argument, viz. that if God knows anything other than Himself, then that thing perfects God. This inference is valid only if God knows particulars as particulars, but it does not apply to God's indirect knowledge of particulars through His direct knowledge of their essence. Hence Gersonides can claim that this third argument of the philosophers, once it is stated properly, supports his position.

[405] As used in the fourth argument proper, "perception" means sense perception. As Gersonides uses the term here, however, it has a broader meaning. It includes conceptually grasping what a thing is as well as sensibly knowing the thing. Generally in English the term, "perception" is limited to sense perception. However, the term, "seeing" is used often in these two senses. For example, after struggling with the solution to a problem in mathematics, the student might exclaim, "Now I *see* it," i.e. he understands how the answer is

therefore it necessarily follows that God, may He be blessed, does not know these things which are in this world, neither what is common to these things, which are their essences, nor that through which they are particulars, which are contingencies. Indeed, with investigation it becomes clear that what is inferred does not follow necessarily from the premise.[406] The reason for this is that from our positing that God, may He be blessed, knows these things which are in this world it does not follow necessarily that His essence is complex. The reason for this is that the orderings which all these things possess are unified. In other words, there is a respect in which they are one, as we have mentioned many times before,[407] and it is from this respect that God, may He be blessed, perceives them, not from the respect in which they are not unified, which is the respect in which they possess particularity and concreteness. This is because from this (latter) respect[408] they could be perceived only by a hylic faculty.

---

deduced. If the narrower sense of "perception" were preserved, Gersonides would have no objection to this argument. While God can perceive particulars conceptually, from Gersonides' point of view, He cannot perceive them sensibly. To do the latter requires, as the first argument asserts, a hylic faculty. Furthermore, to do the latter also would require, as this fourth argument asserts, that God's essence is complex.

[406] The premise is that if God perceives things His essence would be complex. The inference is that God can in no way know particulars. If "perceives" is understood in the strict sense of the term (see note 405) the premise is true but the influence is invalid. If "perceives" is understood in the broad sense of the term (see note 405) the inference is valid but the premise is false. It is in terms of this second reading of the argument that Gersonides judged the argument to be spurious. Cf. notes 36 and 38.

[407] Cf. notes 26, 130, 138, 150, and 171.

[408] I.e., the respect in which they are disunified or discrete particulars.

But perception in this way[409] also would be a deficient perception. This is because it is not (perception of a thing) as it (truly) is.[410] Rather it is (perception of a thing) in terms of its being an accident. Therefore, (such perception) cannot possibly be attributed to God, may He be blessed.

4b   What is said in it,[411] (namely) that if God, may He be blessed, perceives these things, His essence would be divisible into what is most deficient and into what is most perfect,[412] is not correct.[413] This is because the Active Intellect is one (and) simple, as is the Acquired Intellect, (even) with this kind of plurality in their perception.[414] (142) This matter is explained fully, God willing, in the fifth treatise of this book.

The fifth argument states that particulars are infinite, and (that) therefore knowledge cannot encompass them. It is clear that the negation of what we posited concerning God's knowledge, may He be blessed, of these things does not necessarily follow from it.[415] The reason for this is that the intelligible orderings which these things possess are not infinite but necessarily are finite, and it is from this respect that

---

[409] I.e., sense rather than conceptual perception.

[410] What a thing is is its essence, which cannot be perceived sensibly. See note 357.

[411] I.e., in this fourth argument.

[412] The statement of this fourth argument in this form occurs in chapter one rather than in chapter two. There the argument is presented as the major argument for those who interpret Aristotle's position with respect to divine knowledge of particulars to be that God does not know particulars in any respect, neither their orderings or essences nor as particulars.

[413] Cf. note 10.

[414] Cf. note 38.

[415] I.e., from this fifth argument.

knowledge of them is possible. What does necessarily follow from this argument is that there can be no knowledge of them from the respect in which they are particulars, which is the respect in which they are infinite.[416]

The sixth argument states that God, may He be blessed, cannot possibly know these things subject to generation. The reason for this is that if this were possible, either He would know them before they come to be or He would know them only with their coming to be. If He knew them before they came to be His knowledge would be related to what does not exist.[417] Furthermore, it would follow necessarily, if this were so,[418] either that He knows them according to their nature as contingent beings,[419] so that the contradictory[420] of what He knows will be actualized remains a possibility,[421] or that He knows perfectly which one of these contradictory alternatives would be actualized, and its contradictory does not remain possible.[422] If we assume that He knows them according to their nature as contingent beings, it necessarily follows that His knowledge of these entities before they come to be changes with their coming to be. This is because they were possibilities which either could be actualized or could not be actualized before their generation, but after their generation the possibility is eliminated.[423] Since the intellect is actualized by what it knows, it necessarily follows

[416] Cf. note 41.
[417] Cf. note 42.
[418] I.e., that God knows particulars before they come to be.
[419] Cf. note 43.
[420] Cf. note 44.
[421] Cf. note 45.
[422] Cf. note 46.
[423] Cf. note 47.

that the essence of God, may He be blessed, is in continuous flux. But this is absolutely absurd.

It we assume that God, may He be blessed, knows perfectly which one of the pair of possibilities will be actualized, then the nature of the contingent would be eliminated.[424] If it is assumed that God, may He be blessed, knows these things only with their coming to be, then His knowledge is in continuous flux, and (thus) His essence is in continuous flux.[425] Since all of this is absurd, (the philosophers) necessarily concluded from it[426] that God, may He be blessed, does not know these things at all.[427] [428]

[424] I.e., nothing would be contingent and everything would be necessary. Cf. note 48.

[425] In the original presentation of this argument in chapter two Gersonides says the following:

> Since the intellect is actualized by what it knows, it would follow necessarily from this that the essence of God, may He be blessed, is in continuous flux.

This argument presupposes the identity of the knower and the known (cf. notes 38 and 291) and the identity of God's essence with His intellect.

[426] I.e., from this sixth argument.

[427] By "at all" Gersonides means that the Aristotelian philosophers used this argument to deny that God knows even the essence or intelligible ordering of particulars in addition to God not knowing particulars as particulars. In the presentation of these eight arguments of the philosophers in chapter two Gersonides indicated that arguments three and four were to be so interpreted, but not this sixth argument.

[428] Gersonides has repeated this sixth argument from chapter two rather than summarizing it. The presentation here is almost identical with the presentation in chapter two. As was noted in note 49 the form of the argument presented here in the name of the philosophers is weaker than the form that the argument takes as the fourth way according to Maimonides that God's knowledge and man's knowledge differ.

We say that clearly the denial of what we posited concerning God's knowledge, may He be blessed, of these things does not follow necessarily from this argument. The reason for this is that when we posited that God, may He be blessed, knows these things in this world with respect to their being ordered, and (that) He also knows their contingent nature with respect to human choice,[429] none of the absurdities stated in this argument necessarily follow.[430] The reason for this is that it does not follow necessarily from this that His knowledge is related to what does not exist.[431] This is because we posit (that) His knowledge of these things is related to the intelligible ordering[432] in His intellect,[433] (and is) not (related to) these things subject to generation (themselves). Furthermore, it does not follow

[429] Cf. notes 351 and 352.

[430] The sixth argument can be summarized as follows. (Step 1) God knows particulars either (A) before they come to be, or (B) when they come to be. (Step 2) If (A) is the case, then (step 2a) God's knowledge is related to non-existence. (The first absurd consequence noted.) Also if (A) is the case, then (step 2b) God knows these particulars either (a) as possibilities which need not come to be, or (b) as what will in fact come to be without any doubt. If (a) is the case then God's knowledge would be perpetually subject to change. (The second absurd consequence noted.) (Cf. note 47.) If (b) is the case then everything is necessary and nothing is contingent. (The third absurd consequence noted.) (Step 3) If (B) is the case then God's knowledge would be perpetually subject to change. (The second absurd consequence noted.)

Gersonides now will show in defense of his position that on his interpretation none of the three indicated absurdities follow. God's knowledge is not related to non-existence; God's knowledge is not in perpetual flux; God's knowledge does not entail the denial of the nature of the contingent.

[431] The first absurd consequence noted in note 430.

[432] Which also exists eternally.

[433] Literally, "in His soul" or idiomatically "in Himself." God and His intellect are one and the same thing.

necessarily from this (argument) that God's knowledge, may He be blessed, changes with the generation of these things.[434] This is because we did not posit that His knowledge is related to these particulars. Rather (we posited that it is related to) their intelligible ordering which is in His intellect,[433] and this ordering is eternally in His intellect[433] as a single unchanging thing. Furthermore, one need not deny the nature of the contingent[435] by our positing that He knows which one of the set of possible alternatives (*143*) will be actualized. This is because we postulated (that) He (only) knows (concerning) this alternative that it is proper that it should be actualized with respect to these things being ordered, (but) not absolutely. This is because He reckons that it is possible that it will not be actualized with respect to choice, which is the respect in which these things are contingents.[436]

[434] The second absurd consequence noted in note 430.

[435] The third absurd consequence noted in note 430, viz. that everything is determined and nothing is contingent.

[436] See note 352. God knows that if such and such is the case then a given contingent, known through its general description, will be actualized. But these conditions need not hold. Whether or not they do depends on choice. For example, God would know that given any liquid whose chemical composition is that of hemlock and given some specific man, if that man drinks the hemlock the man will die. Suppose that the specific man in this case is Socrates. From what God knows is true without any doubt it follows that if Socrates drinks the hemlock he will die. It is necessarily the case that once the hemlock was taken by Socrates he would die. But it is not necessarily the case that Socrates would die. He did not have to take the hemlock. He had a choice of going into exile or taking the hemlock: his decision to do the former and thus to die was a real choice.

There is an additional feature of this example that should be noted. In the example, while God does not know the individual, Socrates, He does know the

The seventh argument states that if God, may He be blessed, knows these particulars, it is proper that He should give them a

---

individual poison, hemlock. However He knows this poison not as a particular but as individually designated. While Gersonides insists that God cannot know particulars he does not deny that God knows individuals. (Cf. notes 135, 177, and 178.) A particular is an embodied form. The principle of embodiment is matter, which God cannot know. (Cf. notes 105, 348, and 399.) But God knows the form.

It is important to note that this form is not the universal that we know. It is a single entity, namely an essence. Thus in knowing this form God knows the individual. How such knowledge is possible can be illustrated as follows. Consider a general description such that it applies to one and only one individual, e.g., a man who is an ancient Greek philosopher who had a snubbed nose who drank hemlock whose student founded a major school in Athens, etc. Consider this description as designating a class with one member, namely Socrates. Now God cannot know the particular Socrates, but He can know the class of Socrates and in knowing this class He knows the individual Socrates. "To know" in this context does not mean to be acquainted with Socrates through the senses. God can neither see nor hear nor smell nor touch nor taste Socrates. But God knows who and what Socrates is and God can know truths about Socrates, e.g., if Socrates drinks this hemlock then he will die. (Cf. notes 253, 286 and 288.)

However it should be noted that we are not claiming that Gersonides posits that particulars possess unique, individual forms or essences. It is clear that Gersonides has a concern with identification through individuation which is not found among his Moslem-Jewish predecessors. (Cf. note 288.) But this is not to say that he posits any explicit doctrine of individual forms. Clearly he does not.

Furthermore it can be inferred from Gersonides' system that he would have to deny the doctrine of individual forms. Because God is simple, what God knows must be a single essence which is identical with Himself. In knowing this essence He knows the essence of each individual thing. But if these things had unique essences then either God could not know them, so that it would not be true that God knows individuals through their essence, or God's good and perfect ordering, but this is the opposite of what our senses find (to be the case) concerning these particulars. I mean to say that we find much evil and disorder in them. However, since it is clear that this ordering which these contingents possess and the contingency which was posited concerning them is just ultimately and a good ordering, (then the validity of) this argument is negated.[437] We have explained this fully in our com-

---

knowledge would be complex. Consequently it is not possible for Gersonides to maintain consistently that individuals have unique essences.

Nonetheless, although Gersonides tells us that God cannot know particulars, he does not say that God only knows essences. What he does say is that God knows particulars through their essence, i.e., Gersonides thought that in some way individuals can be known by knowing essences. What we have presented here is an explanation of in what way this knowing situation is conceivable. God knows a single form which, from a human point-of-view, is expressible in terms of a series of universal judgments. These judgments in turn can be characterized as class judgments.

Again note that what God knows are essences or forms and not classes. The class expressions are only expressions of but not identical with what God knows. (Essences exist; classes do not.) What it thus means to say that God knows the form of an individual is that the form that God knows is expressible through a complex class expression which designates a class which happens to have only a single member. It is important that this class "happens to" but does not "necessarily" have one member. The given class expression uniquely refers to a single entity, but it does not individuate that entity. (Cf. notes 177 and 178.) The given entity is a single, unique individual because of its matter and not because of its form.

[437] The seventh argument states the following. Either God knows particulars or He does not. If God does know particulars then He would give to them the best possible ordering. If God would give to them the best possible ordering then they would have the best possible ordering. But our experience of disorder and evil in the world tells us that they do not have the best possible

mentary on the Book of Job, and it also is explained, God willing, in Treatise Four of this book.

The eighth argument states that if God, may He be blessed, knows all of these things in this world, it necessarily follows from this that the impossible is possible.[438] This is because it is clear concerning the nature of continuous quantity[439] that everything divisible remains capable of (further) division *qua* quantity.[440] If it is assumed that God, may He be blessed, knows all these things, it would follow necessarily that He knows all the parts into which this continuous magnitude could be divided.
24c   If this were so,[441] continuous magnitude must possess/ parts

---

ordering. Therefore, by *hypothetical syllogism* and *modus tollens*, God does not know particulars.

Gersonides denies the minor premise of this argument, namely that experience teaches us that these particulars lack the best possible ordering. There is no doubt that they are not perfectly ordered. But this is very different from claiming that they lack the best *possible* order. Cf. notes 50 and 53.

The picture that Gersonides draws here is reminiscent of the picture in Plato's *Timaeus* where the demiurge is limited in its ability to impose order and good on the world because of the nature of the materials with which it has to work. In both cases God (or, the Demiurge) is limited by matter (or, the Receptacle). The central difference between the two views is that Plato's Receptacle limits intelligible ordering through passive, natural necessity (see *Plato's Cosmology*, transl. F. M. Cornford (London and New York, 1937), pp. 361-364) whereas Gersonides' matter limits intelligible ordering through the active choice of what is embodied in the matter. Plato's conception makes a clear-cut dichotomy between active and passive as well as will and necessity. This dichotomy is no longer so clear in Gersonides' picture of the world.

[438] In other words, this argument is a *reductio ad absurdum* argument.

[439] Literally, "it is clear from its meaning."

[440] In other words, magnitude is divisible into what is capable of further division, or magnitude *qua* magnitude is divisible. Cf. note 60.

[441] Namely that God knows all of the parts into which magnitude is divisible.

which cannot possibly receive division, which are the parts to
which the knowledge of God, may He be blessed, is limited.[442]
The reason for this is that if the case were not so posited,[443]
God's knowledge, may He be blessed, of this part would be
deficient.[444]

We say that (this argument) is not correct.[445] This is because
if we grant that God, may He be blessed, knows, for example,
the nature of each part of every material body, it does not follow
necessarily from this that the division (itself) is limited.[446]
Rather, He knows this division according to its nature. I mean

[442] What are the ultimate parts of the thing that God knows in knowing the
given magnitude.

[443] Namely, if continuous magnitude does not consist ultimately in indivisible or atomic parts.

[444] If magnitude is not composed ultimately of indivisible parts then it is
composed of an infinite number of parts. If this is the case then either God
does not know all of the parts of the magnitude in question, in which case His
knowledge is deficient, or He knows what He thinks are the ultimate parts but
He is mistaken since these proposed ultimate parts also must be magnitude and
as such they are capable of further division, in which case again His knowledge
is deficient. On the first alternative His knowledge is deficient because it is incomplete. On the second alternative His knowledge is not correct.

The point of the argument is not that there are atomic magnitudes. The conclusion of the argument is that since there are not atomic magnitudes by
hypothetical syllogism and *modus tollens* it follows that God does not know
particulars. However, as Gersonides will say subsequently, some of his contemporaries defended God's knowledge of particulars against this argument by
admitting atomic magnitudes.

[445] Cf. note 58.

[446] It is claimed that God knows their nature and not them. There need not
be an agreement between the number of things and the number of their
natures. For example, many coins are produced from a single mold. On Gersonides' understanding of what a nature or essence is, viz. the model from
which a thing is created, this mold-coin analogy is appropriate.

to say that He knows that everything which is divisible can be divided (further) in that it is continuous magnitude, (but) He does not know the limit of the divisibility which by nature is limitless. (He does not know this) because such knowledge would be called error rather than knowledge.

Furthermore, we say, according to what we have explained concerning the nature[447] of the knowledge of God, may He be blessed, that He knows the universal nature of quantity *qua* quantity, (namely that it) is divisible infinitely into what is divisible (itself), (but) He does not know this concerning each instance of quantity.[448] The reason for this is that if this were the case,[449] His knowledge in this matter would be deficient. This is because (that knowledge) would not be about the nature of the thing.[450] I mean to say that this division into each particular is only insofar as it[451] is quantity, and not, for example, insofar as it is made of wood or copper.[452]

---

[447] Literally, "the meaning of."

[448] God knows the essence of magnitude which is expressed in the proposition, "given anything, if it is magnitude then it is capable of division." But He does not know an infinite set of particulars that are magnitude and divisible.

[449] Namely that God knows that *a* is magnitude and divisible, *b* is magnitude and divisible, *c* is magnitude and divisible, etc. *ad infinitum*.

[450] Literally, "from the way of what is." To know the essence of a thing is to know what it is. To know a thing otherwise is to know accidents of a thing. Knowing a thing in this latter way is deficient because it is knowing a thing not as it really or truly is. An essence is what a thing is and accidents are not essences. Cf. note 357.

[451] The magnitude that is divisible.

[452] Consider for example a wooden or copper plate. To be sure, because it is wooden or copper necessarily it is a magnitude and divisible. Part of what it means to be wooden or copper is to be a magnitude. But wooden and copper

Some contemporaries[453] have explained concerning this argument that magnitude is composed of indivisible parts, since they grant that God, may He be blessed, knows perfectly this possible division of magnitude.[454] The reason for this is that if those possible parts were divided (actually),[455] God's knowledge, may He be blessed, would not encompass all of the parts into which it is possible that the magnitude be divisible.[456]

(144) (This argument) also is clearly absurd. The reason for this is that it does not follow necessarily from our granting that God, may He be blessed, knows all of these things that He knows every part into which this (given) magnitude could

---

are not identical with magnitude. They both belong to the genus magnitude but further contain specific differences which designate them as species of magnitude. To accredit the divisibility of the plate to the plate being wooden or copper fails to isolate the true cause, for it attributes the cause to the conjunction of the genus magnitude and the appropriate specific difference. But this specific difference has nothing to do in itself with the divisibility of the plate. Hence the plate is divisible not insofar as it is wooden or copper but insofar as it is magnitude.

[453] See note 57.

[454] Aristotle said that "magnitude is not actually infinite. But by division it is infinite" (*Physics* 3.6, 206a16). In other words while a magnitude is capable of division at an infinite number of points, no such division actually occurs. The number of actual parts of a magnitude always is finite. These contemporaries of Gersonides maintain that God must know each of the possible parts of magnitude as well as its actual parts.

[455] I.e., if the division of which magnitude is capable were actually carried out so that magnitude was divided actually at every point where it is capable of division.

[456] Knowledge is a process of encompassing or limiting, but the infinite is unlimited and unencompassable. Thus by definition there can be no knowledge of the infinite (cf. note 40). The number of parts in this case is infinite. Hence, God cannot know them.

possibly be divided. This is because this statement is clearly absurd. In other words, we (may) say (that God knows) "all parts," (only) because by this statement we render (in thought) universal what is not (in actuality) universal, because what is infinite is not universal.[457] It necessarily follows from this[458] that

[457] In saying "all parts" we speak of an intelligible but not of an actual collection, because there can be no actual infinite collection.

The term, $k^e lal$ in its basic sense means "to include." From this basic sense the term takes on the additional senses of "principle," "generalization," and "universal" in its derived noun forms, $k^e lal$, $k^e lalim$, and $k^e lalôt$. These noun forms in turn are the source from which the verb, $kālal$ also derives the senses of "to generalize," "to compile," and "to make perfect." The is the identification of the referent of a term that expresses a universal with the essence and perfection of that to which the universal refers. Cf. notes 40, 101, 130, 204, 207, and 304.

Gersonides, like his Moslem-Jewish predecessors, makes no clear distinction between general terms and terms which designate universals. (Cf. note 178.) A term which designates a universal at the same time designates a class. Thus, for example, the term, "cat" both designates the universal, cat, and the class of all cats.

What is of particular importance in this context is that universals are what is known and that universals function as general terms, i.e., they designate a class of things. Gersonides' point here is that this reference to a class must be understood collectively rather than distributively. In speaking of the possible parts of a given magnitude we refer to the class of these parts but not to the parts themselves. To do the latter is not possible. For Gersonides a term is intelligible only if it refers to a known entity. Thus, a term which refers to an infinite number of entities cannot be intelligible, because in principle an infinite number of anything cannot be known. However, an infinite number of things may share something in common. That which they share in common can be known, since it is a single thing. This thing in this case is the essence. This knowable essence is the principle by which this infinite number of things is collected into a single class, i.e., all of these things belong to a single class because they all share this one feature in common. Some classes are actual. Others are only intelligible. Where the members of the class are infinite in

He knows that every part into which a magnitude is divided remains (itself) capable of division into what is magnitude.[459] This possibility is known in this way according to its nature as what is infinite,[460] (but this is) not (to say) that He knows the limit of what is limitless by nature. This is because anything like this would be error and not knowledge.

This problem[461] is similar to the problem[461] mentioned by the Philosopher[462] in (his) book, *De Generatione et Corruptione*,[463] which states (the following) in order to explain (the doctrine) that body is not infinitely divisible.[464] Assume that body is divisible completely[465] into all that into which it possibly can be

---

number the classification can be intelligible only and not actual since it is a contradiction in terms to say that what is "beyond limit," i.e., is infinite, is "limited," i.e., contained in a class. (Cf. notes 40 and 457.)

The basis of this and the subsequent discussions in this chapter is the intimate link of Gersonides' doctrine of universals or essences, his reference theory of meaning, and the doctrine that an infinite number of anything is in itself unintelligible.

[458] I.e., from the claim that God knows all of the parts of a given magnitude.

[459] I.e., God knows that magnitude *qua* magnitude is infinitely divisible. In other words, God knows that given any magnitude, it is divisible and that into which it is divisible is itself a magnitude.

[460] I.e., it follows from the nature of magnitude that there are an infinite number of magnitudes. What is known is the nature (or, essence) of magnitude, and not the magnitudes.

[461] Literally, "doubt."

[462] Aristotle.

[463] 1.2, 316a15ff.

[464] Literally, "that body is divisible into what does not receive division".

[465] At one and the same time, even though the division had not been brought about simultaneously. For example, A is divided into parts a and b, a is divided into a^1 and b^1 while b is divided into c^1 and d^1, etc., until all of the possible division is carried out.

divided. This (division) might not (in actuality) be able to occur, but its occurrence is not a logical impossibility. However, when this is assumed, the body (must) be divided into divisible parts, since, if they were divisible, the body would not be divided into every possible part according to what was assumed.[466] This being so, it would seem[467] that it necessarily follows from this (argument) that body is divisible into what is indivisible.

It is not proper that we should solve[468] this problem in the way that the scholar Ibn Rushd understood the Philosopher's[469] solution[470] in this place.[471] This is because that solution is not correct. Furthermore,[472] the problem remains with it,[473] as we

---

[466] Our hypothesis is that every possible division has been carried out in actuality. Thus what remains after this division itself must be indivisible. According to Aristotle (*De Generatione et Corruptione* 1.2, 316a24ff) what remains cannot be a magnitude since magnitude is by definition divisible. (Cf. notes 60, 61, and 152.) What remains must either be points or nothing. The latter alternative is impossible since something cannot be constituted of nothing. But the former alternative also is impossible, since it has the consequence that magnitude ultimately is constituted of what is not itself magnitude.

[467] In this way Gersonides indicates that the argument is spurious.

[468] Literally, "release."

[469] Aristotle's.

[470] Literally, "the release of the philosopher."

[471] See Ibn Rushd/Averroës, *Corpus Commentariorum Averrois in Aristotelem*, Versio Anglica 4:1-2, *On Aristotle's De Generatione et corruptione: Middle Commentary and Epitome*, ed. and transl. Samuel Kurland (Cambridge, Mass.: Mediaeval Academy of America, 1958), pp. 12ff (Bk. 1, Pt. 3, Chap. 2, 316a23ff).

[472] Literally, "with (the fact) that."

[473] I.e., the proposed solution would be false even if it solved the above stated problem, but it does not even do that.

shall explain. This is because it is said there[474] in (Ibn Rushd's) solution to this problem that the material element is not divided completely and infinitely in all respects. Rather, in one respect it is possible while in another respect it is not possible. What is possible for us is the potential division, but not the actual division which would occur simultaneously at each of the points which it[475] contains.[476] The reason for this is that if this were so, it would follow necessarily that body would be dissolved into indivisible components.[477] But it does not follow necessarily that if

[474] By Ibn Rushd in his Middle Commentary on *De Generatione et Corruptione*. See note 471.

[475] The magnitude in question.

[476] Aristotle says that a complete division of magnitude could not occur in actuality but we can conceive of its actually occurring. Ibn Rushd further qualifies this statement and says it is conceivable that such an occurrence is possible, but it is not conceivable that such an occurrence is actual, because it is impossible to conceive of something as actually possible which we know to be impossible in actuality. It might be objected that if it is not possible to conceive of a given occurrence as being actual then it is equally impossible to conceive of that occurrence as being possible. What does it mean, the objector would claim, for something to have a possibility that could not possibly happen. The answer that Ibn Rushd can give to this particular objection follows from a distinction between two different senses of the terms "possible" and "necessary." Let us speak of "logical possibility" or "logical necessity" as opposed to "natural possibility" or "natural necessity." We might say, for example, that while it is logically possible for a body to be red and green all over, it is naturally impossible for this to occur. In other words, the definitions of body, red, and green in themselves do not exclude the possibility in question, but nonetheless in fact this state of affairs could never obtain. In Ibn Rushd's terms, we can conceive of this fact as a possibility but we cannot conceive of it as an actuality. Cf. notes 3, 43, 49, 161, and 208.

[477] Literally, "things." Gersonides varies here from Ibn Rushd's statement of the argument. What Gersonides wants to say here is that Ibn Rushd makes

it is divided completely in potentiality at each of (its) points which are infinite (in number) that in actuality it would be so divided. The reason for this is that when each point in a body would be divided into equal dimensions,[478] it does not follow necessarily that all of them would be divided simultaneously. Nor (does it follow) that the body would be divided at (all of) them simultaneously.[479] Even if it[480] were divided at each of them[481] in equal dimensions,[478] (it does not follow necessarily that this would happen simultaneously). Similarly it does not follow necessarily that because we say that man can acquire all

---

this distinction solely to escape the *reductio ad absurdum* mentioned above whose consequence is that magnitude ultimately consists in indivisible elements. This is Gersonides' interpretation but not what Ibn Rushd explicitly says. However, Gersonides' argument is almost a word for word reproduction of Ibn Rushd's words. At this place in the statement of the argument by Ibn Rushd, following Aristotle's statement of the argument, Ibn Rushd says that if this were possible, then body could be divided into either points or into nothing. The latter alternative is omitted from Gersonides' statement.

[478] I.e., every part of a body which is divisible would undergo the same kind of division.

[479] In his original statement of this dilemma, Aristotle says the following:

then it (the magnitude or body) might *be*, at one and the same moment, *divided* through and through, even though the dividings had not been affected simultaneously and the actual occurrence of this result would involve no impossibility.

(1.2, 316a16-18)

In other words, while Aristotle denies the possibility of actual simultaneous division, he grants the possibility of all possible parts being divided actually at the same time. Ibn Rushd here denies this latter possibility as well as the former.

[480] I.e., the given magnitude or body.

[481] I.e., the points.

of the sciences,[482] he can acquire them simultaneously. This is because what is true of a thing separately need not be true of that thing in composition,[483] according to what is stated in the book, *De Sophisticis Elenchis*.[484] This is the sophistic argument which is (found) in this place.

It would be possible for (a body) to be divided at all of its points simultaneously only if the points meet each other.[485] However, it has been explained already in Book 6 of the *Physics*[486] that one point cannot be (immediately) next to another point. Therefore, it would seem that when we divided magnitude at a (particular) point it is not possible for division to occur at a point next to it. Before the division had occurred at the other point[487] this division was just as possible (at this point) as it was at the point at which the division (in fact) occurred. But when *(145)* the original division occurred the

[482] I.e., to an equivalent degree, i.e., in equal dimensions.

[483] E.g., a man can walk and a man can sit, but a man cannot walk while sitting.

[484] 2.4, 165b23-26; 166a21-33.

[485] I.e., if the points were immediately next to or adjoining each other.

[486] 6.1, 231a21-231b18. In this passage Aristotle demonstrates that in terms of both time and space, two points can be neither continuous nor contiguous (231a21-29) and that one point cannot be next in succession to another (231b6-18).

[487] This reading of the Hebrew text, found in the (MS) but not in the Leipzig edition, agrees with the Hebrew translation of Kalonymos Ben Kalonymos of Ibn Rushd's commentary. In the light of the close identity of terminology and sentence structure in the whole of this argument between the Hebrew translation of Ibn Rushd's argument and Gersonides' presentation of that argument, it is reasonable to assume that Gersonides used the Kalonymos Ben Kalonymos Hebrew translation rather than the Arabic original.

possibility of the division at what is next to it is negated.[488]
Thus, when we take any point, it is possible to divide the
magnitude (at that point) at any place we want, but[489] when we
divide the magnitude (at that point) in that place, it is no
(longer) possible for us to divide it (at) a second point at any
24d place/ we want, since it is impossible for us to divide it at a
point (immediately) next to that (first) point.

It is clear that this solution is not correct. This is because
with respect to the nature of magnitude, divisibility at each of its
points is possible. I mean to say that division at a point is
possible with respect to division occurring at the point immediately next to it.[490] If this were impossible in body, it would
be so with respect to it being a natural body. This is because it is
from this respect that the division would be concluded after a
definite amount[491] less than which the form of that body could
not receive,[492] as is explained in the *Physics*.[493]

---

[488] In other words, since the parts of magnitude are continuous the relation
between any two points in a magnitude is such that while division is possible
at any point, some points are so related that division at one of them is possible
only if no division occurs at the other. Two points are so related when they are
immediately adjacent to each other.

[489] The (MS) recommends that although the text reads הנבה it should read
אבמנן .

[490] In other words, at the initial point at which the division occurred. Given
two points, one adjacent to the other, actual division at one of these points
remains possible even if actual division took place at the other point.

[491] Literally, "at a definite measure," i.e., if division were limited, the
limitation would be a consequence of the nature of body itself.

[492] In other words, given that it follows from the nature of a body that it is
capable of receiving n divisions at n points, whether n is an infinite or a finite
number, in no sense can it be said that the form of that body is susceptible to
only $n-y$ divisions, at $n-y$ points, where y is any determinate number less
than n.

Furthermore, it is clear that the problem remains with him.[494] This is because between (any) two of these points is an infinite number (of points) potentially in the body which, according to what was postulated (by Ibn Rushd), cannot receive division.[495]

[493] In *Physics* 6.10, 241a26-241b10, Aristotle argues that no process of change is infinite because every change is from something, i.e., a definite nature, to something else, i.e., another definite nature. Aristotle notes this general point specifically with respect to the increase and decrease of magnitude, i.e., both processes of change are limited by the particular nature of the magnitude in question with respect to either increase or decrease (241a35-241b1). However, this passage establishes the first part of Gersonides' claim, viz. that the amount of division in a body is limited by the nature of that body, but it does not support the second part of Gersonides' claim, viz. that a body is not capable of receiving less than the amount of division which is a consequence of the nature of the body in question. However, this point is not problematic. Gersonides' contention is that it does not make sense to say that although a given thing is capable of such and such it is not really capable of such and such. It may be true that that of which it is capable is never actualized, but it makes no sense to say that it is not capable of that of which it is capable. Concerning this second point Gersonides may have in mind specifically Aristotle's general argument in refutation of the doctrine that magnitude is divisible into indivisible parts presented in *Physics* 6.1, 231b15-232a23.

[494] With Ibn Rushd. In other words, grant that Ibn Rushd's position was correct, namely that it is true that given two points *a* and *b*, division is possible at *a* only if division is not actual at *b* when *a* and *b* are immediately next to each other. Even then this position does not solve the above stated problem.

[495] Since magnitude is by nature infinitely divisible, between any two points there is an infinite number of additional points. Thus, if it is the case that division is not possible at a given point because it is immediately next to a point at which division already has occurred, there are in effect an infinite number of points at which division no longer is possible. The force of the argument comes from the term, "immediate." In Ibn Rushd's view all

Therefore body will (have to) be composed of things which cannot receive division, and these things are in it[496] potentially.[497] (Therefore) we cannot escape from this problem by saying that (body) cannot possibly be divided (only) in actuality, as is stated (by Ibn Rushd) in (his proposed) solution (to) his problem.

We say in solution to this problem that no absurdity occurs in our positing that a possibility exists when the existence of what is possible is posited.[498] But when the existence of what is not possible is posited an absurdity occurs.[499] But is is clear that this statement[500] posits the existence of what is not possible.[501] This is clear because from our positing that when a continuum is divided it is divided into what is (itself) divisible, as was explained (above) in various places, it necessarily follows that it is impossible that it[502] can be divided into what is not capable of

---

division ceases to be possible only at an immediately adjacent point. But if magnitude is infinitely divisible the notion of an immediately adjacent point is unintelligible. Since at each point there is an infinite number of further possible points, no point can be said to be immediately adjacent to any other point. Such a statement could be made only if there were parts which themselves are not divisible.

[496] I.e., in the body.

[497] In other words, there are things in the body which potentially and not only actually are not subject to division. Such things would by their nature be indivisible; it does not merely happen to be the case that they are indivisible.

[498] I.e., it is intelligible to say that what is possible is a possibility.

[499] I.e., it is not intelligible to say that what is not possible is a possibility.

[500] Viz., assume that a body is completely divided into all that into which it is divisible. In Aristotle's presentation of the *reductio ad absurdum* argument for magnitude ultimately consisting of indivisible parts it is assumed initially that a complete division of magnitude is carried out. Gersonides here claims that if magnitude is infinitely divisible, this assumption cannot be made.

[501] Namely that a magnitude can be divided infinitely.

[502] I.e., a continuum.

division.[503] When we posit that body in actuality is divisible into all that into which it is capable of division, we posit the existence of what is not possible, because it can only be divided into divisible parts.[504] The reason that error occurs at this point[505] is with respect to their[506] positing the existence in unity and completeness of the possible which essentially is neither unified nor complete.[507]

---

[503] Gersonides distinguishes between the claim that magnitude is divisible into what is itself divisible and the claim that magnitude is infinitely divisible. The former is correct but the latter is not. Nor is the latter logically entailed by the former since it is impossible to carry out infinite division.

[504] In other words, the aforementioned argument stated by Aristotle and repeated by Ibn Rushd and Gersonides proves that if magnitude can be divided into all that into which it is capable of division then magnitude necessarily consists in indivisible elements. But this does not prove that magnitude consists in indivisible elements. Rather it proves that such a division is not possible. Hence, while magnitude is divisible into what is itself divisible, magnitude is not *infinitely* divisible. Rather it is *endlessly* divisible, i.e., if you begin to divide a magnitude you never will arrive at a point where further division is not possible. The problem arises from taking the term, "infinite," in a positive sense. "Infinite" here is understood literally as this term is rendered in Hebrew, namely, "without end."

[505] Literally, "is caused to enter in this place."

[506] I.e., those philosophers who used the aforementioned argument to establish the existence of indivisible material elements.

[507] In other words, predicates which assert potentialities in a thing have very different logical features from predicates which assert actualities in a thing. To say that "a is F" asserts a fulfilled unity between a and F, i.e., there is a relation that in fact holds between a and F. But this is not the case with "a is F-ible." Gersonides does not tell us what is involved in saying "a is F-ible" as opposed to saying "a is F." He is only asserting that the logical analysis of these two kinds of statements is very different and that the error involved in

This is also the more (adequate) solution for the aforementioned problem of the contemporaries concerning the

---

the above *reductio ad absurdum* argument for indivisible magnitudes is that
this difference is overlooked.

The distinction that Gersonides is making here results from Aristotle's
analysis of what is involved in judgments about the infinite, specifically with
respect to the infinite divisibility of magnitude. Aristotle comments,

> The infinite exhibits itself in different ways — in time, in the generations
> of man, and in the division of magnitudes. For generally the infinite has
> this mode of existence: one thing is always being taken after another, and
> each thing that is taken is always finite, but always different. Again,
> 'being' has more than one sense, so that we must not regard the infinite
> as a 'this,' such as a man or a horse, but must suppose it to exist in the
> sense in which we speak of the day or the games as existing — things
> whose being has not come to them like that of a substance, but consists
> in a process of coming to be or passing away; definite if you like at each
> stage, yet always different.
>
> (*Physics* 206a25-31)

To say that something is infinite is not to say that there is a thing which
resides in that which is infinite. Rather it is to note a process to which what is
infinite may be subject. Gersonides in this passage makes the same judgment
about propositions of the form, "*a* is *F*-ible."

This discussion contains a suggestion of how Gersonides conceives the difference and the relation of essences and universals. Universals are the instrument by which we know essences. Yet essences and universals are not the
same thing. Essences are the cause of things whereas universals are effects by
abstraction from the appearance of things. Also, essences exist whereas universals do not. (Cf. notes 12, 14, 15, 26, 38, 40, 67, 68, 101, 130, 204, 207,
305, and 346.) At the same time it cannot be said that universals and essences
are totally dissimilar. For Gersonides what we know are essences by way of
universals; it is not exactly true to say that we know universals. (Cf. notes
356, 371, and 458.) How all of these judgments are to be reconciled is not an
easy matter. Yet there may be a way.

When we say that "*a* is *F*" and *F* is understood as an essential rather than

divisibility of the continuum with respect to God's knowledge, may He be blessed. This is because it does not follow necessarily from our positing that God, may He be blessed, knows perfectly this division of a continuum that God's knowledge, may He be blessed, completes this division into what is indivisible.[508]

---

an accidental property, we are asserting that a certain essence, the-F, is the cause of a. In other words what a is, although it is it in an imperfect way, is the-F. At the same time in saying that "a is F" we also are asserting that "a is F-ible." In other words, any statement about the essence of a thing, which is a reference statement, at the same time asserts that a certain process holds with respect to that thing, which is not a reference statement in the sense that the predicate names something. More precisely a sentence of the form, "a is F," where F is an essential property of a, at one and the same time refers to the essence which is the proper cause of a and asserts a process applicable to a by which a was known to us. The former expression concerns essences whereas the latter expression concerns universals. Thus, for example, after experiencing a number of times rubber bending rather than breaking under tension I form the judgment that rubber is essentially flexible. By this judgment I am expressing the essence or nature of rubber, i.e., I am referring to "the-rubber," while at the same time I am expressing that given anything, if it is rubber then it is flexible. In this latter context the initial statement expresses a universal which is reducible to a universal conditional proposition. That universals do not themselves exist is noted by the feature of the proposition expressing that universal, that it is a universal conditional proposition rather than an existential proposition.

However, it must be noted that this discussion is purely conjectural. None of this is made explicit by Gersonides. If in fact Gerssonides had a clear conception of the relation and difference between essences and universals, he never explicitly stated it.

[508] I.e., it does not follow that because God knows perfectly the division of a continuum that He knows every possible division individually into which that continuum is divisible. If this were a legitimate entailment it would be the case necessarily that God knows ultimate divisions of the continuum into parts which themselves are not divisible.

Rather, what does follow necessarily is that He knows this division according to its nature, (namely) that everything into which a continuum is divisible is (itself) something which is capable of division.[509] It is not (the case) that He knows the limit of the division of what by nature has no limit.[510]

In exactly the same way that a problem arises concerning the divisibility of the continuum it is possible to raise a problem concerning number.[511] One might say that there might possibly exist a non-augmentable number[512] and that this number is known to God, may He be blessed. The reason for this is (*146*) that number is augmentable by what can possibly be augmented. But if we assume that God, may He be blessed, knows perfectly all of these additions,[513] or (if) we assume (that) the possible exists in actuality,[514] there would exist there a non-augmentable

---

[509] In other words, God knows the essence of magnitude and this knowledge is expressible in the judgment that magnitude is divisible into what itself is divisible, i.e., given anything if it is magnitude then it is divisible and that into which it is divisible is itself divisible.

[510] I.e., God does not know the ultimate constituents of magnitude since magnitude does not have ultimate constituents. In saying that magnitude is infinitely divisible we are not saying that magnitude has *n* parts, where *n* is an infinite number. Rather we are making a judgment about the effects of the process of division on magnitude, viz. that if a magnitude is divided that into which it is divided is itself divisible. Cf. notes 504 and 507.

[511] "In a way the infinite by addition is the same thing as the infinite by division." *Physics* 2.6, 206b4.

[512] Literally, "a number upon which addition is not possible."

[513] I.e., that which is added rather than the various addition processes. For example, after the number 1 God knows the numbers 2, 3, 4, etc. rather than simply knowing the formula, $(n)(n \supset (\exists y)(y = n + 1))$, where *n* stands for any natural number.

[514] I.e., that anything that is possible must in some way actually exist. For

number. But this is absurd.[515] The cause of this error is our assumption of the existence of what cannot possibly be assumed.[516] But it is only proper that what is in accordance with the nature of the thing known should be called knowledge, (and) not that which is other than the nature of the thing known.[517] This is because this (latter case) is more appropriately called ignorance and error than knowledge.[518]

It is proper that it should not be hidden from us that error befell the aforementioned solution which Ibn Rushd inferred[519] from the words of the Philosopher from a different respect from the respect we have mentioned.[520] This is because his supposition that in a body an infinite number of aggregated points exist potentially at each of which division is possible[521] is clearly absurd. The reason for this is that if a body contains finite dimensions which are potentially infinite, then, since these dimensions would not be in contact, according to what is ex-

---

example, a possible number which no one has ever reckoned might be said to have, on this assumption, real existence as a potentiality and that after that number is reckoned by someone it has real existence as an actuality. Gersonides will judge this assumption to be absurd.

[515] Because "in the direction of largeness it is always possible to think of a larger number." *Physics* 3.7, 207b10-11.

[516] Viz., that the possible in some way exists. Cf. note 514.

[517] True knowledge exclusively consists in knowing the nature or essence of a thing.

[518] Cf. notes 357 and 449.

[519] Literally, "understood."

[520] Gersonides argued above that it is false that division at one point precludes division at a second point and that even if this were true the dilemma that this supposition was meant to solve would not be solved.

[521] Literally, "it is possible that it (the body) is divided at each one of them."

plained in Book 6 of the *Physics*,[522] there would be some
measurement between each pair of dimensions. Since they[523] are
posited as being infinite, the measurements between each pair of
these dimensions would be infinite in number. But since it is
clear that with regard to some particular chance measurement,
when multiples which are infinite in number are multiplied, then
infinite measure changes as a result of the multiplying, clearly it
necessarily follows from this that a finite body would be infinite,[524] which is utterly absurd. This being so, it is clear that

[522] 6.1, 231a20-231b15. What is infinitely divisible is continuous and not
in contact. Things are in contact if their extremities are together. But since between any two points on a given magnitude there is an infinite number of other
points at which the magnitude may be divided, no two points can be said to be
together. Since they are not together and they are not the same, i.e., they are
not identical, there is a distance between them which at least theoretically is
measurable.

[523] I.e., the number of possible points between any two given points on a
magnitude.

[524] The finite body contains an infinite number of points each infinitely
distant from each other, i.e., each separated by an infinite number of points. If
all of these distances within the finite body were totalled the result would be an
infinite number, with the consequence that a finite body, i.e., a body whose
dimensions are determinate, is infinite, i.e., a body whose dimensions are indeterminate.

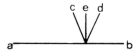

Consider, for example, a determinate line, *ab* whose total measurement is a
finite number, *n*. Let this line be divided at points *c* and *d*. Further assume that
the distances between *ac* and *db* are finite. Still the distance between *c* and *d*
would be infinite since between *c* and *d* is an infinite number of points where
further division is possible. Let us assume that the line fragments *ac* and *db*

the continuum does not contain dimensions which are infinite in number, neither potentially nor actually.

However, the lack of limit which is found in the division of the continuum lies in the act of division, (and) not in the number of divisions. This is because the number of divisions into which it can be divided always is finite, except that this number may be continuously augmented. For example, when we imagine it[525] divided into two parts, each of them is divisible[526] into two

25a (more) parts so that there would be four parts, and each one/ of these parts (in turn) is divisible[526] into two more parts so that there would be eight parts. Thus the number of parts is continually augmented, while (that number) always (remains) a

---

are of the same length, m, where $n > m$, and that the distance between points c and d is the infinite number, i. The result would be that $2m + i = n$. But n is a finite number, whereas the sum of $2m + i$ would have to be an infinite number. Furthermore, assume an actual division of the line fragment cd at point e. The distance between c and e as well as the distance between e and d again would be infinite since each line segment contains an infinite number of points at which further division is possible. However, again this total of $2m + 2i$ would be equal to n, with the further consequence that $2i = i$. There is no difficulty in saying that $2i = i$ since i is an infinite number. But it is strange to say that any infinite number is equal to a finite number. Namely that number which expresses the distance between a and b.

What is crucial to Gersonides' argument is that these divisions need only be potential to make possible an actual measurement since in order for an infinite number of divisions to be possible the line must contain in actuality an infinite number of points. Gersonides' solution to this riddle is that the line does not contain an infinite number of points and infinite division is not possible. Given any amount of division the number of divisions carried out will always be some determinate number. All that can be said otherwise is that no amount of division will exhaust the possible division of the line.

[525] I.e., the given continuum.

[526] Literally, "it is possible that each will be divided ...."

finite number. In this way it would seem that the lack of limitation in divisibility is a lack of limitation in terms of numerical increase.

Just as number is not augmentable, neither actually nor potentially to what is infinite in number, so is this the case with the division of a continuum. That number cannot be augmented potentially to what is numerically infinite is clear from (the following) two premises. The first is that every number is finite, since every number is either an even or an odd, and each of these is finite.[527] The second is that no number has the power to be augmented by what is not number, but (147) (only) by what is a number greater than it.[528] This being so, it is clear that no number has the power with respect to this unceasing augmentation to be an infinite number.[529] From this it is clear that no continuum can contain[530] parts which are infinite in number. Therefore it (also) is clear that it cannot contain[530] dimensions which are infinite in number.

We have explained this matter at length in our commentary on the *Physics*. However, we needed to explain here (the reason for) denying what Ibn Rushd posited in solving this problem, namely that in a body an infinite number of aggregated points exist potentially at each of which division is possible, since, if

---

[527] The odd is limited in not being even and the even is limited in not being odd.

[528] Any number may be increased by any other number to form a number greater than it, but it cannot be increased by what is not a number. Gersonides' use of the term, "number" is limited to rational numbers.

[529] Any number may endlessly be augmented, but it cannot be increased to a sum which is an infinite number. Again, Gersonides' arithemetic excludes irrational numbers.

[530] Literally, "no continuum has power over."

(this supposition) were correct, the problem which they[531] had with respect to knowledge and with respect to the assumption of the existence of the contingent would remain as it is. This is clear with (only) a little thought.

It is now clear that there is nothing in the aforementioned arguments of the philosophers that necessitates the view that God, may He be blessed, does not know these things in this world in the way in which we posited God's knowledge, may He be blessed, of these things.[532]

[531] I.e., the contemporaries.

[532] Gersonides has not yet considered the five ways noted by Maimonides that God's knowledge differs from our knowledge. This is the topic of chapter five. However, he still can claim that his consideration of the arguments of the philosophers, including Maimonides, is complete since these five ways are an illustration of what Maimonides claimed in his second argument which Gersonides discussed in the first part of chapter four.

CHAPTER FIVE

In Which It Will be Made Clear Completely that What is Evident to Us Concerning This Knowledge is Very Adequate in Every Respect.

What will add complete clarity[533] to what we have mentioned concerning God's knowledge, may He be blessed, of these things is that none of the negations which necessarily follow from what the Master The Guide, may his memory be blessed, posited[534] concerning God's knowledge, may He be blessed, — these being the five aforementioned cases[535] which, according to that postulate,[536] are characteristic of the knowledge of God, may He be blessed, each of which is inconceivable (as characteristic) of our knowledge — necessarily follows for this postulate.[537]

The first of them[538] is that a single (act of) knowledge is equal to and agrees with many different species of things. It[538] also necessarily follows in the case of our knowledge.[539] (This also is

---

[533] Literally, "from that which adds clarity and completeness."

[534] In chapter two.

[535] Literally, "things."

[536] Namely, that God knows particulars as particulars.

[537] Namely, that God knows particulars insofar as they are ordered but not insofar as they are particulars.

[538] I.e., the first of the five cases.

[539] As the subsequent discussion will show, Gersonides has altered slightly Maimonides' first case. Maimonides claims that God knows many different things, particulars and essences, in a single act of knowledge. Gersonides limits the range of the term, "things" to essences excluding particulars. Only with this change in the meaning of Maimonides' terminology can Gersonides

the case for us) when we know a plurality of things with respect to their being one,[540] which is when we intelligibly comprehend[541] their intelligible orderings and we conceive concerning them that some of them are the form and perfection of others of them.[542] Since we posited that God, may He be blessed, knows this plurality of things in this way — i.e., He knows their intelligible orderings with respect to their being ordered, and He knows them with respect to their being one[543] — clearly it does not follow necessarily from this respect that we should posit the distinction between the knowledge of God, may He be blessed,

---

claim that what Maimonides said in this case about God also applies to us. More properly Gersonides' case would have to be stated as follows. According to Maimonides, God knows many different particulars as particulars in a single act of knowledge and God knows many different essences of particulars in a single act of knowledge. The former claim is not true of us, but neither is it true of God, since God does not know particulars as particulars. The second claim is true of God, but it also is true of us.

[540] What is crucial in this case as it was stated originally in chapter two was that God knows in a single act of knowledge a diversity of things which are not naturally unified. That these things lacked natural unity, which is true of particulars *qua* particulars but is not true of essences of particulars, is what made God's knowledge in this instance radically different from our knowledge.

[541] *Hiśkil* is a causative (*hiphil*) form of the root, *śkl*, whose noun form means intellect. The verb designates the activity of the intellect in doing what is the proper function of the intellect, viz. actualizing concepts (cf. note 26) as opposed to the natural activities of the senses and the imagination.

[542] Essences can be conceived as belonging to a hierarchy of essences such that some essences are the form and perfection of other essences. For Gersonides, genus-species relation expresses such a hierarchy. (Cf. notes 103 and 104.) But particulars cannot be conceived in such a hierarchy, as Gersonides argued at length in chapter two. (Cf. notes 105-115.)

[543] Concerning the sense in which they are one see notes 101, 102, and 104.

and our knowledge that the Master The Guide, may his memory be blessed, posited. The distinction between these two (instances of) knowledge consists for us in the fact that these intelligible things[544] are one in Him.[545] This is because the difference between the unity of what is actualized from this[546] in our intellects and the unity which is in the intellect of God, may He be blessed, is very great,[547] so that there is utterly no relation between them,[548] which is clear from what was said above in the

[544] I.e., essences.

[545] Whereas they are many in us. In other words, as we in knowing a single essence know many things, so God in knowing His own essence knows our many essences. God's essence, in this sense, is the essence of essences. However, more exactly it is not that the essence that God knows is different from the essences that we know. Rather it is the case that we know that essence as essences.

[546] I.e., from knowing multiple particulars and their essences.

[547] Cf. notes 26, 68, 72, 73, 116, 130, 138, 150, 171, 204, and 358. Whereas God knows things as their cause, so that the things are an effect of God's knowledge, our knowledge is gained by abstraction from what we sensibly experience of the things, so that our knowledge is an effect of the things. Hence God knows essences whereas what we know are universals. Essences and universals indeed are different, but the difference is not so great as to constitute absolute equivocation between our knowledge and God's knowledge. Universals and essences are in some sense related. (Cf. note 507.) The equivocation involved is rather *pros hen* equivocation. (Cf. notes 89, 91, 210, and 301.)

[548] That there is no relation between them is an overstatement. Cf. note 302. Literally, there is a relation. What we know ultimately is dependent upon what God knows since our knowledge is an effect (through abstraction from phantasms) of what is an effect (namely, sense particulars) of God's knowledge (the essence of the essences which are the model for the sense particulars). Rather the point is that these two kinds of knowledge are entirely different kinds of things. Hence they share no common species, i.e., there is no *thing* that they share in common.

first treatise of this book.[549]

The second of them[550] is that His knowledge is connected with non-existence.[551] It[550] is something that does not follow necessarily from what we posited concerning God's knowledge, may He be blessed, of these things which exist in this world. The reason for this is that we say that God's knowledge, (*148*) may He be blessed, of these things with respect to their being ordered in Him is dependent upon the intelligible ordering which they have in God,[552] which exists eternally. (It is) not (dependent) upon these things (themselves) subject to generation. This is because He does not acquire knowledge of them. Rather, they acquire (their) existence from His knowledge of them, i.e., because their existence is caused by the intelligible ordering which they have in God,[552] may He be blessed. This being so,[553] it does not follow necessarily from this[553] that His knowledge is connected with non-existence. Rather it is connected with something that exists eternally in unchanging unity.[554]

---

[549] Treatise One deals with the question of the immortality of the soul. The first six chapters of that treatise discuss the nature of human intellect in order to provide the premises that Gersonides needs to establish his view on human immortality. It is in these six chapters, particularly in chapters five and six, that Gersonides presents the theory of human knowledge outlined in note 26 which is the basis for Gersonides' comparison between God's knowledge and our knowledge.

[550] I.e., the second of the five cases.

[551] Cf. note 117.

[552] Literally, "in His soul." God, His soul and His intellect are one and the same thing.

[553] I.e., that God knows the intelligible ordering of particulars but He does not know particulars as particulars.

[554] Since the object of God's knowledge is one and unchanging, His knowledge of this object raises no difficulty about His knowledge and (consequently) His essence being one and unchanging.

The third of them[555] is that God's knowledge, may He be blessed, encompasses what is infinite with respect to its being infinite. It[555] also is something which does not follow necessarily from what we posited concerning the knowledge of God, may He be blessed. The reason for this is that we say that He knows them[556] with respect to their being one. (But He does) not 25b /(know them) with respect to their being infinite and non-unified, which is the respect in which they are particulars.

The fourth of them[557] is that His knowledge, may He be blessed, of things which will come to be in the future does not necessitate that the known will be actuated; rather its contradictory[558] remains possible. This[558] is also the case with our knowledge when we gain knowledge[559] of such things by a dream or by a vision or by prophecy.[560] This is because we know

---

[555] I.e., the third of the five cases.

[556] I.e., the particulars.

[557] I.e., the fourth of the five cases.

[558] Cf. note 157.

[559] Literally, "when knowledge is actualized for us."

[560] For Gersonides dreaming, having visions and receiving prophecy are closely related. The nature of each and their interrelationship is the subject matter of the second treatise of the *The Wars of the Lord*. It is specifically in chapter two of that treatise that Gersonides raises the problem concerning the compatibility of the doctrine of indeterminism, i.e., some events are contingent and not necessary, with the doctrine that there can be knowledge of future contingents. What follows below in the text is a summary of Gersonides' solution to this problem as it was developed in Treatise Two, chapter 2.

Dreaming and receiving visions are characterized in the same way that prophecy is characterized. (Cf. notes 352 and 362.) In all three cases the knower in question acquires from the Active Intellect conceptual knowledge which is expressible in a universal conditional proposition, which is immediately instantiated through the activity of the imagination. The emphasis

them[561] with respect to their being ordered, but they remain contingent with respect to choice.[562] It is from this respect[563]

---

here is on the term "immediately," since in the cases of dreaming and having visions, as opposed to the case of prophecy, no conscious inferences are made by the knower. The reason for this is the following.

Gersonides notes (*The Wars of the Lord* 2.6, p. 105 of the Leipzig edition) that although dreaming and having visions result from the activity of the Active Intellect upon the intellect of the knower, fools and children are capable of dreams and visions. (They are not capable of prophecy.) He accounts for this presumed fact in the following way. (Ibid. 2.6, pp. 111-115 of the Leipzig edition.) In all three cases the prerequisite for this kind of knowledge is that the intellect have dominion over the senses. Everyone who achieves this state receives the causal influence of the Active Intellect with respect to knowledge. Now this dominance can come about in one of two ways, either by strengthening the intellect, which happens in the case of prophecy, or by weakening the senses, which happens in the cases of dreaming and having visions. The person who receives visions is a person whose sense ability is weak. (This is why seers often are blind.) The dreamer has normal sense ability, but while he is asleep the strength and activity of his senses are greatly diminished.

The situation as Gersonides describes it can be pictured in the following terms. Consider a radio station which is transmitting from a very great distance. Its transmissions themselves are strong, but because they come from such a great distance they are difficult to receive. Anyone who can receive the signals does so. (The radio station transmits to all and not to some. Only some receive the signal, but these individuals are unknown to the radio station.) But not everyone can receive them. Some receive the signals because they have excellent radios with high antennas which are capable of picking up signals that people with inferior radios and lower antennas are incapable of receiving. Some live in areas where there are no local competing stations. Hence there is no interference with the strong, distant station. Others cannot receive the station during the day because of the competition of the weaker, but closer stations, but at night, when most of the closer stations have ceased to broadcast, these individuals can tune in on the stronger, more distant station. On this analogy, the distant, strong station is the Active Intellect, the weaker

that we have this information[564] in order that we may reckon with the evil that is ready to come upon us and that we may beware (in order) that (the evil) would not be realized,[565] as all of this was explained in the preceding treatise.[566]

We can confirm[567] this (view) by investigating[568] what the prophets, peace be unto them, said when they predicated a certain evil, (namely) that it is found (written) that they gave advice in order to beware of that (particular) evil (in order) that it would not be realized. Similarly, in the case of what Joseph interpreted for Pharoah[569] you find that he gave him advice in order that the famine would not be realized in the way that it was ready to be realized on the basis of what was revealed[570] in his dream.[571] Similarly, in the case of what Daniel, peace be unto

---

but closer stations are the senses, and the individual listeners are respectively prophets, seers and dreamers. Their radios are their intellects.

[561] I.e., the future contingents.

[562] As is the case with divine knowledge and prophecy. Cf. notes 352 and 362. In all three human cases what is known of the future is that if *a* does *b* then *c* will happen to *a*, but *a* need not do *b*. Gersonides develops this point in Treatise Two, chapter 2, pp. 95-98 of the Leipzig edition.

[563] I.e., the respect in which the future contingents are ordered.

[564] About the future.

[565] Cf. note 352.

[566] Treatise Two, chapter 5.

[567] Literally, "we can stand upon." An alternate translation could be "we can defend." However the sense of "defense" here, as the context makes clear, is that the biblical account of prophecy conforms with the above stated schema of divine and human knowledge of particulars.

[568] Literally, "when we investigate."

[569] From Pharoah's dreams.

[570] Literally, "the knowledge which was caused to be actualized by him in the dream."

[571] *Genesis* 41:1-48.

him, interpreted for Nebuchadnezzar from what he[572] dreamed concerning the troubling of his mind and his being like the beasts for seven years, you find that (Daniel) gave him advice in order to beware of that evil[573] so that it would not be realized.[574]

Since we posited that God, may He be blessed, knows these things with respect to their being ordered, it is not strange that they should remain contingent with respect to choice. In this way the problem is solved,[575] (a problem) which men have never been able to solve,[576] namely, how it is possible for God, may

[572] Nebuchadnezzar.

[573] I.e., the evil of Nebuchadnezzar becoming like a beast, living with animals in the field and eating grass for seven years. Actually the biblical passage says 'idanin, which means z'ᵉmanim, "times", and not śânim, which means "years."

[574] *Daniel*, chapter 4.

[575] Literally, "the doubt is removed."

[576] Literally, "remove."

The argument that Gersonides has presented here is only a supplementary proof of his thesis that God knows particulars with respect to their intelligible ordering but not with respect to their being particulars. It is for this reason that Gersonides identifies this argument as a confirmation or a defense (cf. note 567) rather than as a demonstration. In other words, his thesis already has been demonstrated. Now that he has demonstrated it he adds factors which further confirm the thesis. Nonetheless, even in these limited terms the structure of Gersonides' argument is interesting. It closely resembles what Kant would call later a "transcendental deduction."

In this case we are given certain data, namely biblical accounts of prophecy. These data themselves are not subject to question. We are not to ask, "Are these data true?" but it is legitimate to ask, "How is it possible for these data to be true?" The answer to this second admissible question consists in giving a schema which "accounts for" the data, i.e., in enumerating a schema with which the total data are compatible.

All that Gersonides has claimed is that if his posited schema is true then all

He be blessed, to know things which are subject to generation
while they remain contingent. (A solution is possible) because
this is from two respects, (and) not from one respect.[577]

The fifth of them[578] is that God's knowledge, may He be
blessed, of things subject to generation does not change with the

---

of the given biblical data are intelligible. From this it does not follow that the
posited schema is true. However, by implication, Gersonides' claim is stronger.
What he is arguing here is that *only if* this schema is true are all of the given
biblical data intelligible. Grant that Gersonides has demonstrated this stronger
claim and assume, as Gersonides and his contemporaries would have assumed,
that there is no question of the truth of the biblical accounts (once they are
adequately understood), it follows that Gersonides has presented here an absolute transcendental deduction of his schema concerning divine knowledge.
That Gersonides is making this stronger "only if" claim rather than only the
weaker "if" claim is what I would read to be the force of his observation that
he has solved here a problem "which men have never been able to solve." In
other words, given this schema a given area of religious data (namely, the conjunction of the religious dogma that not all events are determined, the religious
dogma that God has foreknowledge, and the phenomena of prophecy) is accounted for, which could not be accounted for by any other schema.

However, while this clause indicates that Gersonides would claim that only
this schema is adequate to account for the data in question, he has only argued
that if this schema is true then the data in question are accounted for. For this
reason also Gersonides identifies this arguments as a "confirmation" rather
than as a "demonstration."

[577] I.e., once it is recognized that contingent particulars can be known from
two respects rather than one, a solution can be given. In other words, to say
that God knows particulars is to say either that God knows their essence or
that God knows them as particulars. Once this ambiguity is recognized in the
sentence, "God knows particulars," we can reconcile the apparent in-
compatibility of the doctrine of God's foreknowledge and the phenomena of
prophecy, dreaming and having visions with the doctrine of indeterminism,
i.e., there are future contingents. This reconciliation is achieved by affirming
God's knowledge in the former sense while denying it in the latter sense.

[578] I.e., the fifth of the five cases.

generation of these things of which He has knowledge prior to their coming to be even though the object with which that knowledge is connected changes. (The reason for this is) that at first it[579] was a possibility and afterwards it actually existed.[580]

This[578] also must be the case with our knowledge when we attain knowledge of things with respect to their ordering. The reason for this is that even though the contrary of what (we) have knowledge is actualized, that knowledge remains as it is[581] (*149*) with respect to the ordering of these things. I mean to say that from this respect what was known that it would be actualized would have been actualized were it not for the human choice which caused what is fitting to be actualized not to be actualized.[582]

[579] I.e., any given thing subject to generation.

[580] Cf. note 182.

[581] I.e., the occurrence of a contrary of what we know will happen does not change the truth value of what we originally knew where what we knew was the essence or ordering of the original thing known. In other words we know that such and such will happen even if it does not happen. The statement is paradoxical, but Gersonides' point is not. See note 582. A less paradoxical statement of his point would be that in knowing the essence of something we claim that something will happen in such a way (viz. as the consequence of a universal conditional proposition) that the occurrence of a contrary of that event does not affect the truth value of what is known.

[582] In knowing an essence what we know is that if *a* does *b* then *c* will happen to *a*. This remains true when both the antecedent and the consequent in this conditional proposition are false. Whether or not the antecedent will be true depends on the choice of *a*. If the antecedent is true then the consequent must be true.

It is not clear what Gersonides would say in a case where the antecedent is false and the consequent is true. The asserted relationship between the antecedent and the consequent in such propositions is stronger than material implication. It does not just happen to be the case that if *a* does *b* then *c* will

Since God, may He be blessed, has this knowledge with respect to the intelligible ordering which is in Him[583] and this ordering is always in Him in unity,[584] it is clear that His

---

happen to *a*. Because this proposition is an expression of the essence of *a*, it is necessarily the case that if *a* does *b* then *c* will happen to *a*. For example, in knowing the essence of number as that which is augmentable, it is necessarily the case and it does not merely happen to be the case that if something is a number then there exists a number greater than it. The same thing can be said about knowing magnitude as divisible, i.e., if anything is a body then it is divisible and that into which it is divisible is itself divisible.

In both of these examples it is clear that the respectively asserted conditional propositions are false when the antecedent is false and the consequent is true. In other words necessarily something is a number if and only if it is augmentable and something is a body if and only if it is divisible. But once the example is changed to one of the main cases that Gersonides has in mind, namely cases involving human decision, the situation is not so clear. It would be true according to Gersonides' account of the content of prophecy that if Zedekiah goes to war with Babylonia then Israel will be destroyed, and this does not merely happen to be the case. This is no mere statement of coincidence. If Judah goes to war with Babylonia that war will be the cause of the destruction of Israel. But can it be said that only if Judah goes to war with Babylonia Judah will be destroyed? Certainly not, for times can change and Judah can be destroyed in any number of other ways all of which will follow as necessarily as would the destruction from this cause.

There is no way to account for what Gersonides is claiming within the framework of material implication. What we know when we know the essence of *a* is a proposition of the form if *A* then *B* where *a* is a constituent of *A* and/or *B*. The implication that is asserted is stronger than material implication but weaker than the claim *A* if and only if *B*. The connection between the antecedent and the consequent is causal and not coincidental, and such claims lie outside the framework of material implication.

[583] Literally, "in his soul." Cf. notes 433 and 552.

[584] I.e., the multiple orderings or essences of things in the world exist in God as a single essence or ordering which is identical with God Himself. Cf.

knowledge does not change with the generation of these things. This is because His knowledge, may He be blessed, is not connected with them.[585] Rather it is connected with the intelligible ordering which they have in Him,[583] may He be blessed.

One may not reply that by God, may He be blessed, knowing that these things are contingent with respect to choice (His knowledge) changes with the generation of what is subject to generation.[586] (One may not say this) because we do not maintain that God, may He be blessed, acquires knowledge from things subject to generation.[587] Similarly, He does not know them with respect to the specification which these things possess.[588] Rather, (He knows them) by way of (their) genus and

---

notes 26, 130, 138, 150, and 171. This is a major way that God's knowledge differs from ours, but this difference is accounted for in terms of the *pros hen* equivocation rather than the absolute equivocation of the term, "knowledge" with respect to God and man.

[585] I.e., with the particulars which are or are not generated.

[586] Given two contrary events a and b where a happens and b does not, the following would be claimed by the objector to be the case: first God knows that a may happen if such and such is the case and that b may happen if such and such is the case; then God learns that a happened and b did not.

[587] The consequence of this defense by Gersonides is that God can have no existential knowledge. God knows that given anything, if it has the property F then it will have the property G. But He does not know that that thing is F or that that thing is G. Such knowledge would be connected with the thing itself, with the consequence that God's knowledge would be subject to change. (The one exception to this is that God knows that God exists.)

[588] God cannot know that any given particular is anything for the reasons noted above in note 587. To know that any particular has a given property, i.e., specification, is to know an existential proposition (viz. there is something such that it is F) and that knowledge is connected with the subject of the proposition.

universality,[589] and from this respect the contingency in His knowledge, may He be blessed, of them is not removed.[590] This is very clear to him who investigates this book.

[589] God knows the class of F things, but He does not know any member of that class. Only insofar as the particular a is F can it be said that God knows a.

It might be objected that in claiming that God in some way knows a when He knows F confuses the "is" of identity with the "is" of predication. "a is F" asserts that a exemplifies F, but it in no way asserts that a is identical with F. However, as has been noted already in notes 177, 178, 253, 286 and 288, once a distinction is noted between individuals and particulars, Gersonides can be acquitted from this accusation of confusion. It is possible for God to know classes with only one member. In knowing such a class He is not acquainted with the particular but He has individuated that particular. In other words He knows that particular not as a particular but as an individual. In the same way we can say that while we are not acquainted with Socrates we know Socrates, i.e., although we would not recognize Socrates if we met him we have a general description of him which applies to him and him alone. Thus in saying the name, "Socrates" we express a class with only one member through which we refer to that member as an individual, i.e., a unique entity.

[590] Since what God knows is expressible always as a universal conditional proposition, what is contingent are the things known but not the knowledge of them. What God knows about any particular is necessarily the case. But this knowledge in no way entails that the thing known is necessary. For example, that it is necessarily the case that if A then B is perfectly compatible with the claim that A is only possible and B is only possible.

CHAPTER SIX

IN WHICH IT WILL BE EXPLAINED THAT OUR CONCLUSION
FROM PHILOSOPHIC THOUGHT CONCERNING HIS KNOWLEDGE IS
THE VIEW OF OUR TORAH.

It is proper that we should explain that this view which was
concluded from Philosophic Thought is also the view of our
Torah.[591] We say that the basic tenet of the Torah and the axis
upon which it revolves is that in this world there exist contingents. Therefore the Torah can command (us) to do certain
actions and to refrain from doing certain (other) actions.[592] (At
the same time) the basic tenet of the words of the prophets in
general, peace be unto them, is that God, may He be blessed,
made known to the prophets, peace be unto them, these contingents prior to their coming to be. As (Scripture) says, "Surely
the Lord God does nothing without revealing His secret to His
servants the prophets."[593] But it does not follow necessarily
from their testifying to a certain evil[594] that it will be actualized.
As (Joel) said, peace be unto him, "For the Lord is gracious ...
and repents of evil."[595] Thus a combination of these two tenets

[591] Cf. note 2.

[592] The main concern of the Torah is to set forth positive and negative
commandments, but commandments are possible only if man has choice, and
choice is possible only with respect to what is possible.

[593] *Amos* 3:7.

[594] I.e., from their prophesying that some event will take place which will be
evil for the people to whom the event will occur. For example, prophesying to
Zedekiah that Judah will be destroyed by Babylonia.

[595] *Joel* 2:13.

is possible only if it is posited that these contingents are ordered in one respect, namely the respect in which knowledge of them occurs, and that they are not ordered in another respect, namely the respect in which they are contingent.[596] (Furthermore) since God, may He be blessed, knows all of these things with respect to their being ordered, and He knows that they are contingent,[597] it is clear that the view of our Torah is (in agreement with) what was concluded from Philosophic Thought concerning the knowledge of God, may He be blessed.

Furthermore, it clearly is the view of the Torah that God, may He be blessed, knows these things universally (and) not particularly. (This view) is clear from what (Scripture) says, (viz.)
25c   "He who fashions/ the hearts of them as one,[598] and comprehends all[599] of their deeds,"[600] i.e., He fashions the heart[601] and thoughts of mankind as one by making these orderings which the heavenly bodies possess from which generally they are ordered.[602] In this way,[603] (God) comprehends all of their

---

[596] I.e., given that what the tradition claims is true, viz. that some events are contingent and God has foreknowledge of them, the schematic distinction between particulars as ordered and conceptually known and particulars as not ordered and not conceptually known is necessarily the case. This schema is of necessity a precondition for the possibility of the conjunction of these two religious claims. Cf. note 576.

[597] I.e., that they are but not what they are as contingent. Only what they are as ordered and essential is known to God.

[598] I.e., in the way that they are one, i.e., in terms of their general nature. Cf. notes 37, 101, 102, 104, 130, and 153.

[599] I.e., universally.

[600] *Psalm* 33:15.

[601] I.e., the soul, which is the form of man.

[602] The heavenly bodies are the tools of God by which men's lives are regulated insofar as man is ordered. In knowing astrology man knows approximately how God knows man and the heavenly bodies. I say "ap-

deeds,[604] i.e., in unity.[605] (But it is) not (the case) that His knowledge is connected with the particularity of a particular.

---

proximately" because God has this knowledge as the cause of these things in a single act whereas we have this knowledge as an effect of these things in multiple acts.

In Treatise Two, chapter 2, pp. 96-98 of the Leipzig edition Gersonides explains the relationship between divine providence, human intelligence and choice, and astrology, the purported science of the effects of the heavenly bodies upon the lives of man.

We say that it is clear beyond any doubt that these things are defined and ordered, from which respect there is foreknowledge of their generation and from which respect the senses reveal to us that they (the particulars) are defined from the heavenly bodies.[a] However, the respect in which they are contingent, undefined, and not ordered is the intellect and the choice found in us.[b] (This is) because our intellect and choice move us to what is different from what was defined (to happen to us) by the heavenly bodies. Indeed this is the case because human events are ordered from the heavenly bodies, and the heavenly bodies govern the generation of what is below the sphere of the moon when one opposite[c] dominates[d] at one time and another at another time. This[e] (may happen) because of the

---

[a] I.e., through the senses we discover that the formal and efficient cause of all particulars is the heavenly bodies.

[b] I.e., insofar as we have intellect we have choice, and insofar as we have choice what happens to us is indeterminate.

[c] I.e., any one of a set of different states of affairs all of which have the same subject, and all of which are so related that if one of them is the case the others cannot be the case.

[d] I.e., is the case. The image is of all of these states of affairs (see footnote c) competing with each other to come to be. To say that at a certain time a state of affairs A is the case is to say in this imagery that state of affairs A prevailed over or dominates the others in the given set (see footnote c).

[e] I.e., that one state of affairs prevails at one time and another state of affairs from the same set (see footnote c) prevails at another time.

Thus it is clear that He understands all of their deeds[604]
generally.[605]

---

changing situation of the stars.[f] For example when the sun is in the north
the natural (elements) air and fire dominate simple and complex bodies
but when (the sun) is in the south the natural (elements) water and earth
dominate simple and complex bodies in the north. Or (it may happen)
because the stars undergo change. For example, (because of) Mars the
natural element fire dominates and (because of) the moon the natural
element water dominates. From the mixture of these opposites[c] which are
subject to generation, individual human beings are marked by them (i.e.,
by the heavenly bodies' determination of the elements in either of the two
ways noted above) with virtue and prudence.[g] (Thus) the heavenly bodies
necessitate that in a certain situation man is ordered with respect to a
given attribute, whereas in the opposite situation he is ordered[h] with
respect to an opposite (attribute). Similarly (this is the case with all of the
events which are ordered by (the heavenly bodies).

Also it necessarily follows that differences are necessitated by the different stars in that some men are ordered with respect to a given attribute
and others of them (are ordered) with respect to its opposite, so that some
of them (are ordered) with respect to a certain event while others (are ordered) with respect to its opposite. Consequently it happens as a result of
this that when wicked men perceive evils, God, may He be blessed,
governs this,[i] because He set in us a finite intellect to enable us to bring
about what is different from what has been determined[j] by the heavenly

---

[f] I.e., changes in their relative
positions.

[g] I.e., the degree of practical
wisdom and moral character that an
individual possesses varies depending
upon his particular relationship at
specific times to the positions and in-
fluences of the heavenly bodies on

the elements from which man is constituted.

[h] Literally, "is set right." See note
13 of the main text. Gersonides uses
seder and yòṡer as synonymns.

[i] I.e., it happens because of divine
providence.

[j] Literally, "defined."

Furthermore,[606] it is the view of our Torah that the will of God, may He be blessed, does not change. As (Scripture) says,

---

bodies (to take place), to prepare for something else to happen insofar as (this is) possible.[k]

In this way the heavenly bodies govern man preserving men from many evils intended to befall them so that (some) men encounter evils[l] in all of their attempts to kill or harm others. They (the murderers) hardly ever succeed, because they are directed in these acts by proper reasons.[m]

(2.2, pp. 96-97 of the Leipzig edition)

The passage continues with an account of how the combination of the determinations of the heavenly bodies with the modifications of intelligence and choice make life possible in the political state. Otherwise all men might choose

---

[k] Cf. note 352 of the main text. Assume for example that it is determined that if Clyde robs a bank today he will be caught. Now Clyde will be caught ultimately because of the position of the stars. but perhaps Clyde learns through his study of astrology that today is not a good day for robbing banks. On the basis of this knowledge Clyde may decide not to rob a bank today and therefore not to be captured.

In fact Clyde might have decided not to be a bank robber at all. Clyde possesses in his physical-chemical composition a natural tendency to rob banks. But through his studies he may have learned that all banks robbers eventually either are caught and go to jail or are killed. Clyde does not care for either consequence, so he decides that in spite of his inclination or natural tendency toward bank robbing he will not rob them. Thus there are two ways in which a man may not have the vice of bank robbing: either through efficient, natural causation by means of the influence of the heavenly bodies or through choice.

Choice and knowledge are not the same thing for Gersonides. Rather knowledge makes choice possible. Without intellect we would be totally subject to the tendencies within us determined by the heavenly bodies.

[l] I.e., what is evil to these men but not what is in itself evil.

[m] See footnote k. If Clyde had robbed a bank that day he would have killed a bank guard. In this way not only Clyde but the bank guard was saved.

"I the Lord do not change."[607] (*150*) (Similarly,) Balaam said at the time that he was a prophet, "God is not man that He should lie, or a son of man that He should repent."[608] However, it is found in the words of the prophets, peace be unto them, that God, may He be blessed, does repent of some things. As (Scripture) says, "And the Lord repented of the evil which He thought to do to His people,"[609] (and) "For the Lord is gracious ... and repents of evil."[610]

If it is impossible that this problem[611] be solved by our

---

the same occupations. Thus both choice through intelligence and the determination of the heavenly bodies are consequences of divine providence. Intellect and choice make it possible to avoid determined evils and chosen evils are prevented through the determination of the heavenly bodies. Life at a human level, in Gersonides' view, is the best possible result of the positive tension of these two factors through which divine grace is rationally administered.

[603] I.e., in knowing a single essence which is identical with Himself.

[604] I.e., all man's deeds.

[605] I.e., God knows a series of universal conditional propositions about human actions and their consequences through a single act of knowledge, viz. His knowledge of His own essence. He does not know that a will do b and c will happen to him; a^1 will do b^1 and c^1 will happen to him; a^2 will do b^2 and c^2 will happen to him; etc.

[606] Gersonides begins here a second transcendental deduction (cf. notes 572 and 592) from the assumed claims of Scripture. Here what is assumed is that God's knowledge and will is not subject to change although in fact God does alter His decrees.

[607] *Mal.* 3:6.

[608] *Numbers* 23:19.

[609] *Exodus* 2:13.

[610] *Joel* 2:13.

[611] I.e., the problem of God not being subject to change although He repents of some things.

positing that God, may He be blessed, knows particulars with respect to their being particulars while it can easily be solved by our positing that He, may He be blessed, knows them in the way that we posited (that He knows them), then clearly it is proper with respect to the Torah that one should posit that God, may He be blessed, knows these things which exist in this world in the way that we posited (that He knows them).[612] It is evident that this problem is solved easily according to what we posited[613] concerning the knowledge of God, may He be blessed. The reason for this is that He, may He be blessed, as knower does not judge that[614] a particular event will be actualized for this (particular) man. Rather He judges[615] everything which is ordered by this ordering from the respect in which these events are ordered.[616] In addition, He, may He be blessed, knows that this thing is a contingent which need not be realized with

[612] In other words, Gersonides is offering what amounts to a transcendental deduction of his schema concerning God's knowledge from Scripture. Cf. notes 576 and 596.

[613] I.e., by using the posited schema the stated problem (see note 612) is easily solved.

[614] Literally, "His knowledge, may He be blessed, does not judge that." Gersonides may speak this way because God and His knowledge are the same thing. However, more properly it is God the knower and not the knowledge that makes judgments.

[615] Literally, "it (His knowledge) judges." Cf. note 614.

[616] I.e., God knows the essence of things but not the things that exhibit that essence. Thus, for example, God knows that any human being who drinks poison will die, but He does not know that Socrates will die by drinking hemlock. However, this judgment needs qualification. Cf. note 436. While it is true that God cannot know, for example, the particular Socrates, He may know what is expressed as a class, 'Socrates' which uniquely identifies the individual, Socrates as its only member.

respect to human choice.[617] However, when we posit that He has such knowledge about this particular man *qua* particular, then it must follow that His will, may He be blessed, is subject to change.

In general there is nothing in the words of the prophets, peace be unto them, which would necessitate (the view) that the knowledge of God, may He be blessed, differs from what we posit according to the conclusion of Philosophic Thought. / This being so, clearly it is proper that we should follow Philosophic Thought in this matter. The reason for this is that whenever the Torah, according to what appears from the external meaning of its words,[618] disagrees with some things which are clear from the

25d

[617] For example, God knows that if a human being drinks poison he will die, but he need not drink poison. In this way Gersonides explains how God's knowledge does not change although God repents. Through the laws by which ultimately God regulates the universe, if a man drinks hemlock he will die. In this sense it can be said that God has ordained that Socrates, drinking hemlock, will die. But should Socrates not drink the hemlock, then he will not die. In this sense it can be said that God repented of killing Socrates. But these are mainly "ways of speaking." (What Maimonides calls "the language of the sons of man" [*The Guide* 1.46, p. 100 of the Pines transl.; cf. note 621].) What God knows, expressible in a universal conditional proposition, does not change.

[618] I.e., according to the literal meaning of the text as opposed to the internal or interpreted meaning (*hatôk*). In his introduction to *The Guide*, Maimonides tells us that the first purpose of *The Guide* is to explain the meaning of certain terms in Scripture. In this connection he notes the following:

Some of these terms are equivocal; hence the ignorant attribute to them only one or some of the meanings in which the term in question is used. Others are derivative terms; hence they attribute to them only the original meaning from which the other meaning is derived. Others are am-point of view of Philosophic Thought, it is proper that we should interpret them[619] in a manner which is in agreement with Philosophic Thought. In this (way) none of the tenets of (our) revealed religion will be destroyed.[620] (In following such a

---

phibolous terms, so that at times they are believed to be univocal and at other times equivocal.

(The Guide, 1. Intro. p. 5 of the Pines tr.)

Interpreting a text largely is showing how terms within a given context are properly to be understood not as univocal terms but as equivocal (*miš'tatēp*) or derivative (*môšel*) or amphibolous (*m'sùpak*). However, there are also circumstances in which it is not the individual terms which are not univocal in one of these three ways, but the passage as a whole which is equivocal, derivative or amphibolous in its meaning. Most of the interpretations that Maimonides gives are cases where the terms or passages are either equivocal or derivative.

[619] I.e., the words of Scripture.

[620] In other words, Gersonides lays down the following general rule to guide the reconciliation of apparent conflicts between doctrines of philosophy (philosophic thought) and religion (Torah): whenever there is a conflict between the two, the religious doctrine is to be reinterpreted to agree with the philosophic doctrine by interpreting the Scriptural passages which support the given religious doctrine to agree with the philosophic doctrine.

The source of this formulation is Ibn Rushd's *Kitāb Faṣl al-Maqāl*. In this treatise on the relationship of philosophy and religion, Ibn Rushd states the following:

> Since Islamic Religious Law[a] is true and it brings to Philosophic Thought[b] what is true knowledge, it follows that we the congregation of Moslems know with certainty that Demonstrative Philosophic Thought[b]

[a] *Shir'a* is equivalent for Islam, as the term is used by Ibn Rushd, to *Torah* for Judaism, as the term is used by Gersonides.

[b] *Al-burhān* and *al-naẓar, al-naẓar al-burhāni* are each equivalent, as they are used by Ibn Rushd, to *ha'iyùn* as it is used by Gersonides.

procedure we act) as did the Master The Guide, may his memory
be blessed, with many things in his honorable book *The Guide*

(i.e., reasoning by means of syllogistic proofs) cannot (*literally*, cannot
come) contradict what Islamic Religious Law[a] sets down, for truth cannot
contrast with truth; rather it (i.e., Philosophic Thought) concurs with it
(i.e., Islamic Religious Law) and it (i.e. Philosophic Thought) gives evidence for it (i.e., Islamic Religious Law). Since this is so, Demonstrative
Philosophic Thought[b] leads to a particular aspect of knowledge about
some existent with the consequence that (*literally*, "thus it is necessary
that") it (i.e., Philosophic Thought) is silent concerning what is in
Islamic Religious Law[a] or it knows it. If it (Philosophic Thought) is
silent about it (Islamic Religious Law) then there is no contradiction
there, and it (i.e., the particular topic in question) belongs to the category
of that concerning which no religious judgment is applicable (*literally*,
"that about which one is silent from the [religious] judgments"), and the
judge (i.e., he who makes judgment) judges it (i.e., this question) by a
religious syllogism.[c,d] And if Islamic Religious Law[a] speaks about it (i.e.,
the particular topic in question) then necessarily (either) the meaning
(i.e., the external or literal meaning) of the statement corresponds (i.e.,
agrees) with what is concluded from Demonstration (*literally*, "what
demonstration brings to it") or it (i.e., the meaning of the statement from
Islamic Religious Law) contradicts (the conclusions of Demonstration). If
it corresponds, then there is nothing to say here (i.e., there is no
problem). But if it contradicts, its (i.e., the statement from Islamic
Religious Law) interpretation (as apposed to its external or literal
meaning) is to be sought. The (inner or interpreted) meaning (i.e., "the
interpretation") brings out the referential meaning of the term from the

[c] I.e., by an argument based on
reference to religious tradition and
texts as opposed to an argument
based on the premises or fundamental principles of the sciences.
[d] In other words, there are
propositions which do not enter into
the scope of Philosophic Thought. In
such cases Philosophic Thought is
neutral. Decisions in these cases are
made solely with reference to the
religious tradition.

of the Perplexed.[621] How much more proper is it that we should

literal meaning to the metaphorical meaning — without doing violence in this way to the customary usage of the Arabic language by (determining) the metaphor — either by giving a synonymn (*literally*, "from calling [or naming] a thing by what is like it") or by (giving) its cause or (by giving) its effects (*literally*, "by what is adjoined to it") or (by giving) its concomitant or (by giving) something else from the things which belong to (*literally*, "are counted among") the branch of knowledge (whose subject matter) is the classes of metaphorical speech.

> (Ibn Rushd, *Kitāb Faṣl Al-Maqāl*, 7:7-18
> Arabic text edited by George F. Hourani
> (Leiden: E. J. Brill, 1959), pp. 13-14)

Ibn Rushd, as does Gersonides, presupposes the validity and truth of the following syllogism: the true doctrines derived from true philosophy (i.e. Aristotle) and true religion (i.e., Islam for Ibn Rushd and Judaism for Gersonides) are true; there can be only one truth; therefore it necessarily follows that the doctrines of true philosophy and true religion are in agreement. Either the same conclusions are reached independently through each or a conclusion is reached through one which does not enter into the range of discourse of the other. (Actually what Ibn Rushd says is that there will be doctrines concerning which religion can pass judgment that lie outside of the scope of philosophy. Ibn Rushd does not raise cases in which philosophy surpasses the scope of religion. However it could not be concluded from this alone that Ibn Rushd considers religion to be superior to philosophy. All that follows is that the range of judgments in religion are not identical with the range of judgments in philosophy, but to the extent that the ranges of both coincide, the judgments of both are the same.) If it should happen that there is an apparent conflict ("apparent" since in principle there cannot be a "real" conflict), that conflict should be resolved through interpreting the religious doctrine to conform with the philosophic doctrine. (Ibn Rushd notes five ways in which terms in Religious Law can be interpreted. In what way these five procedures agree with and differ from the three procedures listed by Maimonides [note 618] need not concern us here. For both the terms to be reinterpreted are to be regarded as ambiguous rather than univocal terms.)

[621] In the introduction to *The Guide*, Maimonides states that the second

not disagree with Philosophic Thought when we do not find the
Torah disagreeing with it.[622]

---

purpose of his book (for the first purpose see note 618) is the following:

> the explanation of very obscure parables occurring in the books of the
> prophets, but not explicitly identified there as such. Hence an ignorant or
> heedless individual might think that they possess only an external sense
> (*pàsùt*) but no internal one (*tôk*). However, even when one who truly
> possesses knowledge considers these parables and interprets them ac-
> cording to their external meaning, he too is overtaken by great perplexity.
> But if we explain these parables to him or if we draw his attention to their
> being parables, he will take the right road and be delivered from this per-
> plexity. That is why I have called this Treatise "The Guide of the Per-
> plexed".
>
>   (*The Guide* I. Intro., p. 6 of the Pines tr.)

In effect Maimonides lays down the same rule of procedure stated by Gersonides and discussed by Ibn Rushd (note 620). Cases of confusion are settled
by interpreting the scriptural passage that is the source of the confusion. But
when does such confusion arise? If a person holds both Jewish teaching and
Aristotelian philosophy to be true, and he finds a scriptural passage whose
literal meaning contradicts the teachings of Aristotelian philosophy, then he is
confused.

Multiple instances can be found of Maimonides employing this his stated
method. The most numerous and for Maimonides the most important cases are
cases where a literal understanding of the biblical passage results in attributing
corporeality to God. The major part of Book 1 of *The Guide* consists in
showing how references to corporeality in God are to be understood either
metaphorically or as equivocal expressions. He summarizes his main points in
this discussion as follows:

> God, may He be exalted above every deficiency, has had bodily organs
> figuratively ascribed to Him in order that His acts should be indicated by
> this means. And those particular acts are figuratively ascribed to Him in
> order to indicate a certain perfection, which is not identical with the par-
> ticular act mentioned. For instance, an eye, an ear, a hand, a mouth, a

In Part 3, chapter twenty of his honorable book *The Guide of the Perplexed*, the Master The Guide, may his memory be

---

tongue have been figuratively ascribed to Him so that by this means, sight, hearing, action and speech should be indicated. But sight and hearing have been figuratively ascribed to Him with a view to indicating apprehension in general. For this reason you will find that the Hebrew language substitutes the apprehension made by one sense for that made by another. Thus Scripture says, "See the word of the Lord" (Jer. 2:31); which is like "hear," for the intended meaning of His speech. Similarly, "See the smell of my son" (Gen. 17:27); which is like saying, "smell the smell of my son," for the intended meaning refers to the apprehension/ of his smell. In conformity with this it said, "And all the people saw the sounds" (Ex. 20:15) although this station also constituted "a vision of prophecy," as well known and universally admitted in our community. Action and speech are ascribed to God so that an overflow proceeding from Him should thereby be indicated, as shall be made clear further on [2.12]. All bodily organs that you can find mentioned in all of the books of prophecy are either organs of local motion mentioned with a view to indicating life, or organs of sensation mentioned with a view to apprehension, or organs of speech mentioned with a view to indicating the overflow of the intellects towards prophecy, as will be made clear. The guidance contained in all these figurative senses is intended to establish in us the belief that there is an existent who is living, is the agent who produces everything other than He, and in addition apprehends His own act. ... The purpose of the present chapter is solely to make clear the meaning of the bodily organs ascribed to God, may He be exalted above every deficiency, and to explain that all of them are mentioned with a view to indicating the actions proper to these organs, which actions — according to us — constitute a perfection. In this way we indicate that He is perfect in various manners of perfection, a circumstance to which the Sages draw our attention by saying: "The Torah speaketh in the language of the sons of man" (B.T. Yebamoth, 71a; B.T. Baba Metsia, 31b).

(The Guide 1.46, pp. 99-100 of the Pines tr.)

All of the references to bodily organs are in fact references to forms of actions which are generally associated with these organs as their agents. Thus referen-

blessed, says that some philosophers were inclined to say that
knowledge is connected with species and at the same time
extends to all individual members of that species.[623] (Maimoni-

---

ces to the sense organs indicate apprehension, and references to speech organs
indicate communication as in the divine overflow or emanation to prophets in
their reception of prophecy. Yet even these actions are not to be taken literally.
They too have an inner meaning, which is that God is in every way perfect.
Such expressions as these are used only because such is "the language of the
sons of man." By such language all men can understand at whatever their level
of comprehension that God is in every way a perfect being.

It should be noted further in this connection that Gersonides is saying more
than simply that he in this instance is following the method prescribed by
Maimonides. He also is accusing Maimonides of failure to follow his own
principles. (Cf. notes 6, 161, 202 and 592.) Maimonides in fact does not
always follow this principle. In certain cases he maintains the literal meaning
of Scripture against the generally accepted conclusions of Philosophic
Thought. A notable instance of this is Maimonides' rejection of the doctrine
that the universe is eternal. In *The Guide* 2.25, Maimonides justifies this exception to the rule. He argues that this question cannot be settled by Reason,
contrary to popular belief, and in such cases where Philosophic Thought cannot pass judgment the literal meaning of Scripture should be followed. Hence
this apparent exception is not an exception at all. As we have noted already,
and as Gersonides will note below, Maimonides treats the question of divine
attributes in the same way as he does the doctrine of the eternity of the world.
In both cases Gersonides is asserting that Maimonides' argument that
Philosophic Thought cannot pass judgments on these matters is false, and that
Maimonides attempted to argue this way only because, in contradiction of his
own methods of procedure, he believed that these two doctrines of the
philosophers contradicted the teachings of the Torah. That Maimonides is in
this respect "intellectually dishonest" has been argued here with respect to the
doctrines of divine attributes and divine knowledge. The same accusation is
raised again in Treatise Six with respect to the eternity of the universe. Cf.
notes 6, 143, 161, and 202.

[622] As Gersonides has argued here in this chapter.

[623] This is the second and weaker interpretation of Aristotle's doctrine of

des) says that this is the view of every master of the Torah, according to what they of necessity concluded from Philosophic Thought.[624] So it is clear that (Maimonides) was of the opinion that this view also agrees with the view of our Torah.[625]

(Furthermore) it seems that the sage Rabbi Abraham Ibn Ezra, may his memory be blessed, is in the same class. This is because he stated in his commentary on the words of the Torah[626] that the truth is that He knows every individual generally but not individually.[627]

The demonstration that the view of our Torah concerning the knowledge of God, may He be blessed, agrees with the conclusion of Philosophic Thought will be presented more completely in the following treatise on Providence, according to the view of our Torah.[628]

---

divine knowledge. As we already have seen, it is also Gersonides' position. Gersonides' wording here is practically identical with the wording in the Ibn Tibbon translation of *The Guide* 3.20.

[624] This is given in the sentence immediately following the sentence noted in note 623. Again the wording of Gersonides is practically identical with the wording in the Ibn Tibbon translation of *The Guide*, 3.20.

[625] Maimonides would not say that this is the view of the Torah, but he would admit, on the basis of the above noted passage in *The Guide* 3.20, that this doctrine of divine knowledge proposed by Gersonides is not in conflict with the teachings of Jewish tradition. For the purposes of this chapter that is enough. At least at a surface level Maimonides has rejected this doctrine on philosophic and not religious grounds. (Cf. note 621.) But Gersonides already has replied to the philosophic objections in chapters 3, 4 and 5.

[626] Ibn Ezra's commentary on *Genesis* 18:21.

[627] Literally, "that He knows every part by way of (the) general but not by way of (the) part."

[628] The (MS) adds the following comment:

The explanation of the words of Rabbi Abraham Ibn Ezra is that God knows every part generally but (he does) not (know every part by means

Treatise Three of this book is hereby concluded. May praise
be to God, may He be blessed, Who has helped us in the writing
of it. By His loving kindness He will aid us to have knowledge
of Him, to love Him, to observe His Torah, and to arrive at the
truth in which no doubt can occur. Amen.

---

of each) part (i.e., He knows them collectively but not distributively). The
explanation of Rabbi Abraham Ibn Ezra (is given) in the Book of Psalms,
Psalm 1 (in his explanation of) "For God knows."

In his commentary on "For God knows" (*Psalm* 1:6) Ibn Ezra says the
following:

Without doubt God the Glorious One knows universals and particulars.
The universals are "the soul of every living thing," (i.e.,) of every
creature. The particulars are each species in its essential aspect, or even
each creature in its essential aspect.

"In its essential aspect," *bip^e nè 'aṣ^e māh*, means, on Gersonides' rendering of
the passage, in terms of its intelligible ordering, which is its essence.

SELECTED BIBLIOGRAPHY

Abraham ben David, ha-Levi (Ibn Daud). *Hā-Ĕmùnāh hā-rāmāh* (האמונה הרמה), with a German translation by Simeon Weil (*Das Buch Emunah Ramah oder der erhabene Glaube*). Frankfurt a. M., 1852; photoreprint (Hebrew only), n. p., [1966 or 1967].

Aristotle. *The Works of Aristotle Translated into English*, ed. W. D. Ross. Oxford; The Clarendon Press, 1908-1952.

—— *The Basic Works of Aristotle*, ed. Richard McKeon. New York: Random House, 1941.

—— *The Metaphysics*, transl. Hugh Tredennick. London: Heine-mann, 1933-1935.

—— *Physica*, transl. Robt. P. Hardie and Russell K. Gaye. (Separate issue of part of vol. 2 of *The Works*, ed. W. D. Ross.) Oxford: Clarendon Press, 1930.

Averroes. See Ibn Rushd.

Avicenna. See Ibn Sina.

Bleich, J. David. *Providence in the Philosophy of Gersonides*. New York: Yeshivah University Press, 1973.

Blumenkranz, Bernhard. *Auteurs juifs en France médiévale*. Toulouse, 1974.

Broyde, Isaac. "Levi ben Gershon." *Jewish Encyclopedia* 8: 26-32. New York and London, 1904.

Diesendruck, Zevi. "Samuel and Moses Ibn Tibbon on Maimonides' Theory of Providence." *Hebrew Union College Annual* 11 (1936) 341-366.

Gersonides. See Levi ben Gerson.

Goldstein, Bernard R. "Preliminary Remarks on Levi Ben Gerson's Contribution to Astronomy." *The Israel Academy of Sciences and Humanities Proceedings* 3 (1969) 239-254.

Guttmann, Julius. "Levi ben Gersons Theorie des Begriffs." In *Fest-schrift zum 75 Jahrigen Bestehung des Jud. Theol. Seminars.* Breslau, 1929, 2: 131-149; reprinted as "Torat Hamûṡag Ṡel Ralbag," in Guttmann, *Dat Umada.* Jerusalem, 1966.

Husik, Isaac. *A History of Mediaeval Jewish Philosophy,* New York: The Jewish Publication Society of America, 1940.

—— "Studies in Gersonides." *Jewish Quarterly Review,* N.S. 7 (1916-1917) 553-594.

Ibn Daud. See Abraham ben David.

Ibn Rushd. *Corpus Commentariorum Averrois in Aristotelem.* Ver-sionum Hebraicarum 7. *Compendia librorum qui Parva naturalia vocantur,* ed. Harry Blumberg. (Hebrew Title: קצור ספר החוש והמוחש ל'אבן רשד) Cambridge, Mass.: Mediaeval Academy of America, 1954.

—— *Corpus Commentariorum Averrois in Aristotelem.* Versio Anglica 4: 1-2. *On Aristotle's De generatione et corruptione: middle com-mentary and epitome.* Ed. and transl. Samuel Kurland. Cam-bridge, Mass.: Mediaeval Academy of America, 1958.

—— *Kitab Fasl al-Maqal* (On the Harmony of Religion and Philo-sophy). Arabic text ed. by Georges F. Hourani. Leiden: Brill, 1959.

—— *Tahafut al-Tahafut* (The Incoherence of the Incoherence), ed. Simon van den Bergh. "E. J. W. Gibb Memorial" Series, N.S. 19. 2 vols. London: M. Juzac, 1954.

Ibn Sina. *Avicenna's De anima,* ed. by Fazlur Rahman. New York: Ox-ford, 1959.

—— *Metaphysices compendium,* ed. Nematallah Carame. Rome: Pont. Institutum Orientalium Studiorum, 1926.

Joël, Manuel. *Lewi ben Gerson (Gersonides) als Religionsphilosoph; ein Beitrag zur Geschichte der Philosophie und der philosophische Exegese des Mittelalters.* Breslau: Schletter, 1862.

Kellner, Menachem M. "Gersonides, Providence, and the Rabbinic Tradition." *Journal of the American Academy of Religion* 42 (1974) 673-685.

Levi ben Gerson (Gershom, Gersonides). מלחמות השם (*The Wars of the Lord*). Riva di Trento, 1560.

—— מלחמות השם (*The Wars of the Lord*). Leipzig, 1866.

—— *Les guerres du seigneur, livres 3 et 4*, transl. Charles Touati. Paris: La Haye, Mouton, 1968.

—— *Die Kämpfe Gottes von Lewi ben Gerson*, transl. with notes by Benzion Kellermann. Berlin: Mayer and Müller, 1914.

Moses ben Maimon (Maimonides). *The Guide for the Perplexed*, transl. Michael Friedländer. New York: Hebrew Publishing Co., 1910.

—— *The Guide of the Perplexed*, transl. Shlomo Pines. Chicago: University of Chicago Press, 1963.

—— סֵפֶר מורה נבובים להרב משה בן מימון (*The Guide of the Perplexed*), transl. Judah ben Saul Ibn Tibbon. Berlin, 1925; reprint Jerusalem, 1960.

Owens, Joseph. *The Doctrine of Being in the Aristotelian Metaphysics: A Study in the Greek Background of Medieval Thought*. Toronto: Pontifical Institute of Mediaeval Studies, 1951.

Pines, Shlomo. "Scholasticism after Thomas Aquinas and the Teachings of Hasdai Crescas and his Predecessors." *The Israel Academy of Sciences and Humanities, Proceedings* 1 (1967) no. 10, 101 pp.

—— "Studies in Abu'l-Barakat's Poetics and Metaphysics." In *Studies in Philosophy*, ed. S. H. Bergman. Scripta Hierosolymitana 6: 120-198. Jerusalem, 1960.

Plato. *Plato's Cosmology; the Timaeus of Plato*, trans. by Francis M. Cornford. London and New York, 1937.

Samuelson, Norbert. "Gersonides' Account of God's Knowledge of Particulars." *Journal of the History of Philosophy* 10 (1972) 399-416.

Smith, Gerard. "Avicenna and the Possibles." *New Scholasticism* 17 (1943) 340-353.

Steinschneider, Moritz. *Die hebräische Ubersetzungen des Mittelalters und die Juden als Dolmetscher.* 2 vols. in 1. Berlin, 1893; photoreprint Graz, 1956.

Touati, Charles. *La pensée philosophique et théologique de Gersonide.* Paris: Les Editions de Minuit, 1973.

Vajda, Georges. *Introduction à la pensée juive du moyen âge.* Paris: J. Vrin, 1947.

Wolfson, Harry Austryn. "The Amphibolous Terms in Aristotle, Arabic Philosophy, and Maimonides." *Harvard Theological Review* 31 (1938) 151-173.

—— "The Aristotelian Predicables and Maimonides' Division of Attributes." In *Essays and Studies in Memory of Linda R. Miller,* ed. Israel Davidson, pp. 201-234. New York, 1938.

—— "Avicenna, Algazali and Averroes on Divine Attributes." In *Homenaje a Millàs-Vallicrosa* 2: 545-571. Barcelona, 1956.

—— "The Classification of Sciences in Mediaeval Jewish Philosophy." *Hebrew Union College Jubilee Volume,* pp. 263-313. Cincinnati, 1925.

—— *Crescas' Critique of Aristotle.* Harvard Semitic Series 6. Cambridge: Harvard University Press, 1929.

—— "Maimonides and Gersonides on Divine Attributes as Ambiguous Terms." *Mordecai M. Kaplan Jubilee Volume,* ed. Moshe David, pp. 515-530. New York, 1953.

—— "Maimonides on the Internal Senses." *Jewish Quarterly Review* N.S. 25 (1934-1935) 441-468.

Zedler, Beatrice Hope. "St. Thomas and Avicenna." *Traditio* 6 (1948) 105-160.

INDEX OF TEXTUAL REFERENCES

INDEX OF PHILOSOPHERS

See also the Index of Textual References

INDEX OF TECHNICAL TERMS

INDEX OF TOPICS